AFTER POSTMODERNISM

INQUIRIES IN SOCIAL CONSTRUCTION

Series editors
Kenneth J. Gergen and John Shotter

This series is designed to facilitate, across discipline and national boundaries, an emergent dialogue within the social sciences which many believe presages a major shift in the western intellectual tradition.

Including among its participants sociologists of science, psychologists, management and communications theorists, cyberneticists, ethnomethodologists, literary theorists, feminists and social historians, it is a dialogue which involves profound challenges to many existing ideas about, for example, the person, selfhood, scientific method and the nature of scientific and everyday knowledge.

It has also given voice to a range of new topics, such as the social construction of personal identities; the role of power in the social making of meanings; rhetoric and narrative in establishing sciences; the centrality of everyday activities; remembering and forgetting as socially constituted activities; reflexivity in method and theorizing. The common thread underlying all these topics is a concern with the processes by which human abilities, experiences, commonsense and scientific knowledge are both produced in, and reproduce, human communities.

Inquiries in Social Construction affords a vehicle for exploring this new consciousness, the problems raised and the implications for society.

AFTER POSTMODERNISM

Reconstructing Ideology Critique

EDITED BY

HERBERT W. SIMONS
and MICHAEL BILLIG

SAGE Publications
London • Thousand Oaks • New Delhi

Introduction and editorial arrangement
© Herbert W. Simons and Michael Billig 1994
Chapter 1 © Richard Harvey Brown 1994
Chapter 2 © Steven E. Cole 1994
Chapter 3 © Kenneth J. Gergen 1994
Chapter 4 © Ian Angus 1994
Chapter 5 © Patti Lather 1994
Chapter 6 © Herbert W. Simons 1994
Chapter 7 © Michael Billig 1994
Chapter 8 © Stanley Deetz 1994
Chapter 9 © Dwight Conquergood 1994
Chapter 10 © Dana L. Cloud 1994

First published 1994

SAGE Publications Ltd
6 Bonhill Street
London EC2A 4PU

SAGE Publications Inc
2455 Teller Road
Thousand Oaks, California 91320

SAGE Publications India Pvt Ltd
32, M-Block Market
Greater Kailash – I
New Delhi 110 048

British Library Cataloguing in Publication Data

After Postmodernism:Reconstructing
Ideology Critique. – (Inquiries in Social
Construction Series)
   I. Simons, Herbert W.   II. Billig,
   Michael   III. Series
   306

   ISBN 0–8039–8877–X
   ISBN 0–8039–8878–8 (pbk)

Library of Congress catalog card number 94–066195

Typeset by The Word Shop, Bury, Lancashire
Printed in Great Britain by Biddles Ltd, Guildford, Surrey

Contents

To our families

Acknowledgements

This book was born of a conference on 'Ideology Critique and Beyond', Temple University's Twelfth Annual Conference on Discourse Analysis, sponsored by the Department of Rhetoric and Communication. That conference spawned not only this book, but also a special issue of the journal *Argumentation* entitled 'In Search of a Postmodern Rhetoric of Criticism'. Mick Billig, on leave for a semester from Loughborough University, was visiting coordinator of the conference. Herb Simons, old-timer at Temple, was inside coordinator. We wish to thank Temple's Lectures and Forums Committee and its School of Communications and Theater for their generous support of the conference. Thanks also to the Department's secretarial staff for their help with both the conference and the book project. Thanks especially to the conferees, both for those essays which have been included in the book, and for commentaries on included essays, which led to subsequent revisions.

Notes on Contributors

Ian Angus is Associate Professor in the Department of Sociology and Anthropology at Simon Fraser University. He is the author of *Technique and Enlightenment: Limits of Instrumental Reason* and *George Grant's Platonic Rejoinder to Heidegger*, editor of *Ethnicity in a Technological Age*, co-editor (with Sut Jhally) of *Cultural Politics in Contemporary America*, and co-editor (with Lenore Langsdorf) of *The Critical Turn: Rhetoric and Philosophy in Postmodern Discourse*.

Michael Billig is Professor of Social Sciences at Loughborough University. His recent books include *Talking of the Royal Family*, *Arguing and Thinking*, and *Ideology and Opinions*, as well as *Ideological Dilemmas*, which was co-authored by members of the Loughborough Discourse and Rhetoric Group.

Richard Harvey Brown is Professor of Sociology and Affiliate Professor of Comparative Literature at the University of Maryland. His books include *A Poetic for Sociology*, *Society as Text*, and *Social Science as Civic Discourse*. Brown is currently working on *Science as Narration*.

Dana L. Cloud is Assistant Professor of Speech Communication at the University of Texas in Austin. Her work includes analyses of racial tokenism and stereotyping on television, the rhetoric of the women's movement, gender and the Gulf War, the rhetoric of therapy in popular culture, and the 'materiality of discourse' hypothesis in rhetorical theory. Cloud has also written a series of essays critiquing postmodernist discourse theories and asserting the continuing relevance of the project of ideology critique.

Steven E. Cole is Assistant Professor of English at Temple University. He has published essays on critical theory and romanticism in *Criticism*, *Modern Philology*, and *Studies in Romanticism*, and is presently completing a book, *Romanticism and Social Agency*.

Dwight Conquergood is Chair of the Department of Performance Studies and Faculty Fellow at the Center of Urban Affairs and

Policy Research, Northwestern University. His teaching and research interests are in critical ethnography, cultural studies, and performance perspectives in the human sciences. He has conducted ethnographic fieldwork in refugee camps in Thailand and the Gaza Strip, as well as with street gangs and other marginal groups in Chicago. In addition to several publications in journals and edited volumes he has co-produced two award-winning documentaries based on his field research: *Beyond Two Worlds: The Hmong Shaman in America* (1985), and *The Heart Broken in Half.*

Stanley Deetz is Professor of Communication at Rutgers University, New Brunswick where he teaches organizational theory, interpersonal relations, and communication theory. He is author of *Democracy in an Age of Corporate Colonization*, *Managing Interpersonal Communication*, and editor or author of five other books. He has published numerous essays in scholarly journals and books regarding decision making, human relations, and communications in corporate organizations, and has lectured widely in the US and Europe. He is an Associate of the World Business Academy and has served as a consultant for several major corporations.

Kenneth J. Gergen is the Mustin Professor of Psychology at Swarthmore College. He is the author of, among other works, *The Saturated Self*, *Toward Transformation in Social Knowledge* and *Realities and Relationships*.

Patti Lather is Associate Professor, Educational Policy and Leadership, at Ohio State University where she teaches qualitative research in education and feminist pedagogy. Her work includes *Getting Smart: Feminist Research and Pedagogy With/in the Postmodern* and *Within/Against: Feminist Research in Education*. Her most recent article is 'Fertile Obsession: Validity after Poststructuralism' (*Sociology Quarterly*, 34(4), 1993) and her current work is researching the lives of women with HIV/AIDS.

Herbert W. Simons is Professor of Rhetoric and Communication and founder of the Discourse Analysis conference series at Temple University. Among his conference-related books are *The Legacy of Kenneth Burke* (with T. Melia), *The Rhetorical Turn*, and *Rhetoric in the Human Sciences*. Simons is currently preparing *The Persuasion Society* with B. Gronbeck and J. Morreale.

Introduction

Michael Billig and Herbert W. Simons

The central concern of this book is with the possibilities for ideological criticism in a postmodern age. This issue cuts across disciplines in the humanities and the social sciences. It raises the question whether it is possible to criticize fundamentally the society in which we live. Or are academics, as salaried employees of private or state universities, marked by the very habits of thinking which need to be criticized? And, thus, are academic attempts at criticism compromised from the very outset? This is not merely a dilemma for critical academics, but it encompasses something much wider. The general tenor of the times – the so-called postmodern age – seems to undermine the possibility of confident criticism. Every claim to truth is immediately placed under suspicion. In these circumstances, one must ask whether it is possible for ideology critique to perform its task of exposing ideological illusions, in the hope of emancipating those who are enslaved by those illusions. Or is this hope yet another illusion?

The notion of ideology critique, with its twin aspirations of emancipation and exposure, is to be traced back to Marx and Engels. The very first sentence of *The German Ideology*, which introduced the term 'ideology' in its modern social scientific sense, is filled with optimism: 'Hitherto men have constantly made up for themselves false conceptions about themselves, about what they are and what they ought to be' (Marx and Engels, 1970: 37). But now, so Marx and Engels claimed, rational, scientific inquiry would expose the truths which lay behind those false conceptions of the past. Above all, *The German Ideology* announced that ideas themselves served the interests of power: 'the ideas of the ruling class are in every epoch the ruling ideas' (p. 64). It was in the interests of domination that this idea itself – the idea about the origins of ideas – had been concealed. Thus, the exposure of ideology was a mission of enlightenment and liberation. The old order, scooped out from its protecting carapace of lies, would be exposed, like a vulnerable, shell-less snail on a garden path.

The famous phrase about the ideas of the ruling class bursts with confidence, as the writers claimed to have discovered the facts about 'every epoch'. Today, in an epoch when postmodern ideas are fast becoming the ruling fashion, such unqualified statements appear dated. They resemble the brass compasses and pith-helmeted uniforms which the European explorers of the last century took on their expeditions. Those explorers had few doubts about their mission to throw light into dark continents; nor about the suitability of their equipment to do so. Today, the mood is changed. The difference between light and dark – between truth and illusion, enlightened continents and dark spaces – is itself shaded. There are no more Africas for European explorers to 'discover'. Does this also mean that social criticism on the grand, confident scale envisaged by Marx and Engels is no longer possible?

Most particularly, the suspicion is raised that Marx and Engels's project of 'enlightenment' was itself in the grip of an ideology, one which put an innocent trust in the power of reason and an optimistic faith in modernity. Perhaps the age of modernism has passed, so that the confidence, to be found in the preface of *The German Ideology*, now seems naïve to us. If so, does this mean that our age of scepticism is impelled to undermine the emancipatory hopes of modernism? Is there, in consequence, a de-politicizing of the academy at precisely the time when a critical stance is most needed?

These are among the questions addressed by contributors to this book. Their responses indicate a variety of positions. Some are concerned to restore the ideas and aspirations of ideology critique. Others explore possibilities for moving beyond ideology critique, in order to combine postmodernist insights with liberatory ambitions. In the remainder of this Introduction, we attempt to provide a clearer sense of the tensions between ideology critique and postmodernism, and, then, to preview the individual contributions to the book.

The Contemporary Appeal of Ideology Critique

In its origins, ideology critique claimed to reveal a hidden truth about the nature of ideas. The ruling ideas of any given society might be displaced by new ideologies, which reflect changes in political and economic arrangements. However, the general inter-connections between economic and political conditions, ruling-class power and mass consciousness, persist. There is a methodological implication in this insight. The critic should not merely be content with assessing the conceptual coherence or logical elegance of philosophical systems. Philosophy, and other intellectual ideas, have to be situated in relation to ruling-class interests. Therefore, to explain the rise and fall of philosophies, the power of logic was less adequate than the logic of power.

This insight has had an enormous impact on twentieth-century thinking. This is to be seen not only in Marxist thinkers, who have sought to understand how capitalist society has survived well beyond its predicted collapse. Liberal thinkers, too, have taken up the project of ideology critique. Most notably, Karl Mannheim, in *Ideology and Utopia* (1960), argued that Marx's critical insight was too important to be left to the Marxists. It should be broadened into a general sociology of knowledge, which would explain the structuring of knowledge in all forms of society. Most importantly, this broadening of ideology critique cuts back on itself. Not only does it encompass a critique of Marxism as an ideology with its own ideological illusions, but also the sociology of knowledge needs to explain its own ideological origins and biases. And this explanation itself is open to further ideological examination. In arguing thus, Mannheim was prefiguring the sort of self-reflexivity which marks postmodernist analyses.

Originally, Marx and Engels were referring to formal philosophies when they discussed 'the ruling ideas'. In the present century, ideology critique has been extended to cover mass popular culture. The outlines for this extension are to be found in the *Prison Notebooks* (1971) of Antonio Gramsci. A ruling class, argued Gramsci, cannot maintain its power on its own. It must consolidate its control through creating a hegemonic bloc which involves alliances with different factions and which widely diffuses common ideological assumptions. In Gramsci'; hands, the model of ideological processes becomes more complex. The dominant ideas of a culture are not simply the inevitable end-product of what Marx saw as the material base of ideas. Rather, they are themselves causal entities, operating interactively with material conditions as part of the base. Just as ruling-class ideas are not fully determined, so also they are not fully determinative. In place of a single ruling class within any given society, there are multiple and competing factions. Moreover, ruling-class hegemony is never complete; there is always the opportunity for oppositional readings. Yet, as Gramsci emphasized, critical insights need to be incorporated into the construction of a counter-hegemonic culture if they are to be more than merely intellectual ideas.

The Gramscian position has deeply influenced contemporary cultural studies, and in particular the projects of Raymond Williams and Stuart Hall. Their work examines the construction of hegemony in the mass cultural products of capitalist society (i.e. Hall, 1988; Williams, 1974; see also Eagleton, 1991). As much importance is attached to 'low' culture as to 'high' culture – to Rambo as to Rimbaud, as Barbara Herrnstein Smith (1992) has put it. In fact, as attention is paid to the 'culture industry', the intrinsic distinctions between 'high' and 'low' become less easily made. Whether in pop music, fashion or Hollywood films, the ruling trends – now iconic images as much as ideas – are assumed to reflect and reinforce dominant interests. The makers of situation comedies or afternoon soaps may not intend to offer political statements, but their programming inevitably reproduces ruling ideas as it is readied for mass consumption (e.g. Fiske, 1990).

The growth of cultural studies also expresses, often indirectly, an increasing political pessimism, at least as compared with the bright optimism of the early pages of *The German Ideology*. No longer do cultural critics believe that a sudden ray of illumination will, like a laser beam, remove the cancer of ideological illusion. Each work of cultural analysis emphasizes the depth and breadth of the ideological processes in the age of the mass media. In so doing, each reveals the enormity of the task of emancipation. Nowhere has the pessimism been more deeply felt than in the works of the Frankfurt School, and particularly in what Rose (1978) has called Theodor Adorno's 'melancholy science'.

For Adorno and Horkheimer, science itself is central to the ideology of the modern age. Modernity has constructed a new sense of rationality – a so-called scientific rationality – and this has destroyed the earlier rationality of the Enlightenment. In these conditions, scientific rationality could no longer be, in any simple sense, the means to reveal the illusions of ideology, for it was compromised by becoming a dominant and dominating component of contemporary ideology. Thus, scientistic philosophy, in its modernist guise, becomes a force which suppresses rather than emancipates. Such themes reappear with an added political force in those contemporary feminist writings which have developed ideology critique by seeking to explain how Western philosophy and science have been constructed around phallocentric assumptions. For example, thinkers, such as Luce Irigaray and Hélène Cixous claim that the scientific voice, confident of its own rationality, suppresses the voices of intuition, magic and enchantment, which are voices alleged to be female in tone and feminist in spirit. Such insights can be turned back against the history of ideology critique. The scientific rationalism of its original forms can stand accused as an ideology of power itself, reifying rationality and science and thereby continuing the patriarchy which underwrites those ideas.

In a further respect, the writings of the Frankfurt School foreshadow the dilemmas of postmodernism. Works such as

Adorno and Horkheimer's *Dialectic of Enlightenment* (1973) express the difficulty of making a total critique of contemporary mass society. What is to be criticized has reached deeply into the general culture of society. In consequence, the critic cannot unreflectively use the traditional language of philosophy, argumentation or science, for these have become ideological. New forms of rhetoric – oblique, allusive and self-consciously marginal – must be employed to enable critical themes to escape from the increasing totality of mass ideology. There is a political dilemma: the more that oblique expression is employed, the more the critic's language appears obscure, and the further it is removed from the arena of direct action. This represents a central dilemma of ideology critique in the postmodern period. Does the self-reflexivity and the distrust of an unreflexive use of language itself cripple the potential for emancipation?

The Postmodernist Threat to Ideology Critique

There seems to be an unwritten agreement among postmodernists that postmodernism should forever elude a consensus as to its definition. Certainly the corpus of postmodern theorizing, read as a single discourse, is definitionally incoherent and even contradictory (Kontopoulos, forthcoming). Given this book's interest in postmodernism's relation to ideology critique, it is not necessary to take on the task of conceptual re-mapping. Instead, it is possible to endorse Patti Lather's (this volume) conception of postmodernism as the 'code-name for the crisis of confidence in Western conceptual systems'. The postmodern times are those which follow, and criticize, the certainties of modernistic belief. As Lyotard (1984) argued, the postmodern age is characterized by a loss of faith in the grand meta-narratives. Chief among these meta-narratives is Enlightenment rationality, which includes Marx and Engels's own 'science' of ideology.

If there is no faith in the grand meta-narrative, then the question is raised whether optimism in a future emancipation can be retained. The tensions between ideology critique and postmodernism are nicely revealed in Henri Giroux's (1988: 60–2) analysis. Giroux, a 'critical pedagogue', claims that postmodernism has 'declared war on all the categories of transcendence, certainty, and foundationalism'. In consequence, 'all attempts at defining a notion of the truth capable of sustaining a political project that engages rather than simply dismisses history and meaning have become suspect.' Thus, the flight from foundationalism, and the suspicion against claims of truth, is at the same time a flight from politics. But

Giroux is unable to dismiss postmodernism completely, for post-modernism is still rooted in criticism: 'there are a number of oppositional elements in postmodern philosophy that constitute important critical interventions against the dominant cultural ideologies of late capitalism' (p. 61).

The problem is not that the postmodernist spirit lacks a critical impulse, but that critique is running rampant without political direction. Zygmunt Bauman, in *Intimations of Postmodernity*, describes how the new mood can appear to be one of 'all-eroding, all dissolving *destructiveness*' (1992: viii; emphasis in original). He goes on: 'the postmodern mind seems to condemn everything, propose nothing', as if 'demolition is the only job the postmodern mind seems to be good at' (p. ix). The genie of critique has escaped its bottle, and now, unstoppably, it darts hither and thither in random flights of mischief. It does not merely attack the ruling ideas, or the mass-produced ideas of economically organized popular culture. What Paul Ricoeur (1986) calls 'the hermeneutics of suspicion' has become the prevailing mood. Every assertion of truth is to be a target of critique, for every such assertion, so it is alleged, makes claims which cannot be securely substantiated. Moreover, it is an exercise of power, for each claim about 'the true', or 'the real', asserts its own voice, and thereby suppresses alternative voices.

No voice is secure in this mood of promiscuous critique. No claim is to be privileged – not even the claim to be exposing the claims of privilege. The voice of ideology critique, confident in the powers to expose 'the real' behind 'the appearance' of ideas, is suspected of suppressing the voices of others and of making unwarranted, foundationalist claims about the 'real'. Thus, the radical urge to re-assert the suppressed voices of others (or, more generally, the voice of the Other) and to expose the illusions of the powerful is turned against itself. Radicalism is radically suspect if it claims to know the 'the truth'. Nothing is to remain securely in its place: pith helmet and brass compass, stripped of their earlier functions, are put in the dressing-up box for make-believe games of pastiche.

If this is the case, then can critique still be critique? Does not criticism rely on a boldness – even blindness – of moral purpose? If ideology critique is criticized for believing in 'true' political principles, will this result in a conservative acceptance of ideological forces? Should not radical politics put a firm fence around the critical impulse in order to limit its anarchic impulses? And does not feminism have a crucial part to play in the reconstruction of a postmodernist ideology critique? These are the dilemmas with which the contributors to this volume are struggling. In so doing, they are also struggling for the forms of language to express such dilemmas, for today the dilemmas of critique are very much dilemmas of language.

About the Essays

The essays in this volume are broadly divided into two parts. Richard Harvey Brown leads off the first section with an essay that explores the problems of postmodernist critique. Brown seeks an escape from the destructive pessimism of some forms of postmodernism. He suggests that the emancipatory postmodernist can reject judgemental relativism while championing epistemological relativism. The latter, he says, in no way precludes principled political action. Alongside the postmodernist's habitual 'hermeneutics of suspicion', a 'hermeneutics of affirmation' is required. Rather than a view of 'truth' as an outmoded relic of modernism, one may develop a sense of truth in language. The entire reconstruction, he suggests, can be intellectually playful but must be politically serious.

Steven Cole illustrates how postmodernism can be turned upon itself with critical effect. He examines recent writings of three leading American postmodernists: Stanley Fish, Barbara Herrnstein Smith and Richard Rorty. Their contingency theories claim that oppression begins with epistemological certitude, particularly of the universalizing sort that purports to know what is true for all time and for all possible modes of experience. Cole turns the insights of contingency theory against itself by suggesting that its claim to knowledge about the contingency of our own subjectivity 'is both logically deluded and pragmatically disastrous'. What is required, he suggests, is a theory of communication which can make possible the public articulation of an intersubjective world.

Kenneth Gergen problematizes criticism itself, or, more pointedly, those omnipresent tendencies in contemporary criticism (including ideology critique) which conceive issues and alternatives in binary terms. Binarism narrows the range of relevant discussants and discussables, and treats assertion and critique as verbal warfare. The result, he suggests, is alienation, rivalry and hostility, especially in academic debate. By contrast, Gergen recommends the potential of self-irony and, like Brown, he emphasizes the search for agreement rather than disagreement. Thus, he advocates experiments in communication designed to encourage mutual exploration and avoid unnecessary contentiousness. Gergen's own text exemplifies his recommended rhetoric. He avoids direct confrontation with fellow writers, whose views he might wish to criticize. If he attacked them directly, with the conventional rhetorical tools of academic debate, then he would find himself being dragged into the very rhetorical binarism from which he seeks to escape.

Ian Angus, in the final contribution to Part I, puts forward a proposal for recovering an ethico-political standpoint for criticism in the face of postmodern cultural theory's seeming endorsement of a cultural pluralism that is tantamount to cultural relativism. He confronts the argument that any critical or evaluative stance is internal to cultural forms, and is therefore hostage to the very discourses and practices it purports to scrutinize. Angus's way out of the conundrum takes him through modern cultural history into the postmodern present, wherein, he alleges, critical theory can be relegitimated through an invention he calls 'comparative media theory'.

In Part II, these issues resurface, but this time in analyses of a wide variety of cultural objects and practices. Lather and Simons take up similar problematics as regards a major arena for ideology critique these days, that of the schools and colleges. As Simons notes, the cultural left in the United States has been the recipient of intense criticism for allegedly foisting its ideas of 'politically correct' thinking on to unsuspecting students, in the guise of 'liberating' them from their oppressive (i.e. racist, classist, sexist, Eurocentric, homophobic, etc) practices and prejudices. A major dilemma for the cultural left, Lather observes, is that its promotive efforts are at variance with its commitments to egalitarianism in the classroom.

This is a central ideological dilemma in democratic liberalism, compounded by simultaneous commitments to postmodern scepticism and multivocality (see Billig et al., 1988, for a discussion of the concept of 'ideological dilemma'). Lather writes self-reflexively as a feminist and a deconstructionist, producing her own multi-voiced approach both to liberatory pedagogy and to research on pedagogy. Her text is filled with different discourses, different stories. Simons offers what he calls a dialectical approach to the dilemma, in which the teacher's problems are placed before the students for their consideration.

Even if the desirability of ideology critique were to be affirmed by postmodern theory, there would still be the question of how it should be textually inscribed. Postmodernism may be marked by textual experiments, but these experiments need to be examined through the use of further experiments. This is an underlying thesis of Billig's chapter, which confronts the ideas and rhetoric of Jean Baudrillard. Billig accepts the need for new ways of doing critique, but he rejects the élitism of Baudrillard's analysis of hyperreality. Taking a visit to Disney World as his topic, Billig plays with the idea of 'fiction-theory', suggesting that, in order to explore critically the contentments of contemporary society, an ironic sense of fiction should be employed. Thus, his piece is filled with a multiplicity of voices, ending with a voice which hints at the economic basis of critique itself.

Stanley Deetz continues the attack upon élitist cultural critique. He sees a pressing need for critique of workplace ideology, but finds the premises of traditional ideology critique to be inadequate to account for situations 'where compliance and consent are a result of clear member understanding of the material conditions for their success'. Thus, the loyalty which employees in the typical large company are required to feel for their organization is not to be dismissed as irrational or false. In his proposals for moving beyond traditional ideology critique, Deetz draws upon both modern and postmodern phenomenology. If the critic ignores the phenomenology of contemporary experience, and criticizes from a supposedly superior position the irrationality of ordinary people, the result will be a critique which resounds with the voices of élitism.

Dwight Conquergood's moving essay on street gangs depicts a world far removed from Deetz's loyal employee. Another sort of loyalty is described. Conquergood is concerned with the voices of discontent, rather than contentment, and he recreates textually the lives of those living in the extremes of urban poverty. His prose expresses the hermeneutics of affirmation by way of a sympathetic 'counter-narrative' of the lives of Chicago gang members. At first sight, here seems to be a classic ethnography, with the ethnographer telling 'a realist's tale', presenting truths about life in another place. However, Conquergood's rhetoric is more reflexive, more rhetorically self-aware than that. In contrast with Gergen, Conquergood does not draw back from attacking critics directly. Indeed, he is savage in his response to sociologists who have textually assaulted the dignity of gang members. By writing in this way, Conquergood is doing more than offering ethnographic realism, or engaging in academic critique. He is also affirming rhetorically his community with the gang members themselves. His own textual practices attack and assault, just like the gang members, whose lives Conquergood celebrates. In this way, Conquergood's own text is not claiming for itself a higher morality than that held by the gang members.

Conquergood's narrative illustrates the poverty of the world's wealthiest capitalist democracy. In doing so, he provides support for the book's concluding contribution. Dana Cloud is alone among the contributors in putting forward an unequivocal case for the class-oriented tradition of Marxist ideology critique. She does this at a time when, as she observes, many self-styled Marxists, having succumbed to postmodern scepticism, advocate a reduced, thera-peutic vision of counter-hegemonic resistance. Cloud likens the post-Marxist radical democratic politics championed by Laclau and Mouffe to the New Age movement, a congeries of discourses and practices ranging from vegetarian evangelism to crystal worship. These seemingly different ideologies turn out, on her analysis, to be strikingly similar and not altogether unattractive in their democratic acceptance of a plurality of voices. Ultimately, she concludes, there is a fundamental incompatibility between aspects of the democratic imaginary and radical political goals. Capitalism is still inimical to the interests of the poor and dispossessed, and, in consequence, traditional class-oriented ideology critique needs to be preserved.

Looking back on this brief Introduction we see consistent confrontation with the postmodern problematic but no clear consensus. There are hints of the possibilities for emancipatory postmodern critiques which resist epistemological certitude and critical dogmatism. These seek to open the way for a recovery of ideology critique's moral stance and exposure, sometimes in a voice (or voices) that is (are) dialectically ironic, and performatively self-reflexive. Yet there is no uniformity in the present text itself. The authors may be struggling with the same dilemmas of ideology critique, but their textual reactions are different. Some experiment with forms of multivocality; some, like Gergen and Conquergood, adapt familiar rhetorical formats in order to accomplish a textual self-reflexivity. In short, there is no common format, as the collected text itself displays a multivocality.

This multivocality requires more than authorial production and editorial connivance. Publishers, with their eye for the market, are also involved in the creation of texts, including this one. There is an additional factor, without which the various voices of the authors would be condemned to marginal silence. The embodied reader is required. Unless there now is a hand to turn the page, all will remain quiet.

References

Adorno, T.W. and Horkheimer, M. (1973) *Dialectic of Enlightenment*. J. Cumming, trans. London: Allen Lane.

Bauman, Z. (1992) *Intimations of Postmodernity*. London: Routledge.

Billig, M., Condor, S., Edwards, D., Gane, M., Middleton, D. and Radley, A.R. (1988) *Ideological Dilemmas: a Social Psychology of Everyday Thinking*. London: Sage.

Eagleton, T. (1991) *Ideology: an Introduction*. London: Verso.

Fiske, J. (1990) *Introduction to Communication Studies*. London: Routledge.

Giroux, H.A. (1988) *Schooling and the Struggle for Public Life: Critical Pedagogy in the Modern Age*. Minneapolis: University of Minnesota Press.

Gramsci, A. (1971) *Selections from the Prison Notebooks*. Q. Hoare and G. Nowell Smith, ed. and trans. London: Lawrence & Wishart.

Hall, S. (1988) 'The toad in the garden: Thatcherism among the theorists', in C. Nelson and L. Grossberg (eds), *Marxism and the Interpretation of Culture*. London: Macmillan.

Kontopoulos, K. (forthcoming) 'The dark side of fire: postmodern critique and the elusiveness of the ideological', *Argumentation*.

Lyotard, J.-F. (1984) *The Postmodern Condition: a Report on Knowledge*. G. Bennington and B. Massum, trans. Manchester: Manchester University Press.

Mannheim, K. (1960) *Ideology and Utopia*. London: Routledge.

Marx, K. and Engels, F. (1970) *The German Ideology*. London: Lawrence & Wishart.

Ricoeur, P. (1986) *Lectures on Ideology and Utopia*. G.H. Taylor (ed.), New York: Columbia University Press.

Rose, G. (1978) *The Melancholy Science*. London: Macmillan.

Smith, B.H. (1992) 'Introduction: the public, the press, and the professors', in D.J. Gless and B.H. Smith (eds), *The Politics of Higher Education*. Durham, N.C.: Duke University Press. pp. 1–12.

Williams, R. (1974) *Television*. London: Fontana.

PART I THE POSTMODERN PROBLEMATIC

1

Reconstructing Social Theory after the Postmodern Critique

Richard Harvey Brown

In recent decades there have been profound changes in global politics, academic knowledge and the Western moral order. The modern academic disciplines – especially the social sciences – were largely formed *as* disciplines, professionalized and institutionalized, during the proud days of nineteenth-century industrial expansion, state formation and imperialism. The optimism of this earlier era began to falter in the twentieth century, which has experienced two global wars, the rise of Nazism and Stalinism, the end of empires, and the threat of ecological collapse.

The expansion and then relative decline of the West was reflected within the academic disciplines, earlier in Europe, later in the United States. The very success of academic knowledge contributed to this. Comparative history, religion, anthropology and sociology relativized claims to positive knowledge and showed how all truths are constrained and shaped by their historical, social and linguistic contexts. In the United States, however, military victory, economic success and global hegemony discouraged such critical self-reflection in the two post-war decades. Instead, this was the heyday of academic and popular discussion of the affluent society, the end of ideology, and the post-industrial society. Around 1970, however, the United States began to experience declines in economic growth ('stagflation'), political empire ('Vietnam') and cultural legitimacy ('the sixties'). This loss of stature and self-confidence elicited jingoism and reaction. But it also created space within American academia for critical and self-reflective discourses, such as Marxism, critical theory, phenomenology, ethnomethodology, existentialism, feminism and, most recently and comprehensively, postmodernism.

These tendencies in academic knowledge have matured within the past decade to become an important intellectual movement. The unifying perspective of this movement has variously been called social constructionism, the rhetorical turn, society as text, deconstructionism and postmodernism. Within the postmodern perspective, it is taken for granted that social and cultural reality, and the social sciences themselves, are linguistic constructions. Not only is society increasingly viewed as a text, but scientific texts themselves are seen as rhetorical enactments, with no ultimate logical or empirical warrant. In such a view, the distinctions between fact and fiction become blurred, as both are seen as products of and resources for communicative action; both are viewed as representations of a constructed reality that also represent various groups, interests and ideologies.

Many analysts have attempted to define postmodernism and to eliminate the confusion surrounding this term. Others argue that confusion is the pre-eminent characteristic of postmodernism, not only because it eschews the linearity, order and rationality of modernity, but also because postmodernism has left the modern but has not yet arrived at a historical destination of its own. Indeed, this ambiguous temporal and terminological status is implied in the very name '*post*modernism' as relational to the 'modernism' from which it departs. Hence, a number of difficulties are encountered in the analysis of modernity and postmodernity, notably a constellation of vague concepts and ambiguous and conflicting historical referents and periodizations. At the edge of that unnamed newness, we are like our forebears at the edge of modernization. In our present passage, like theirs before us, there is a hiatus between the word and the world. To find the word – those words by which we can truly know ourselves and guide our collective affairs – that is the challenge of the 'postmodern' to which we must respond.

The Exhaustion of Modernism and the Postmodern Confusion

Some have argued that there have been two great events in human history: first, the emergence of horticultural states about six thousand years ago and with this the appearance of what we call 'civilization'; second, the emergence of 'modern' societies with their industrial economies, territorial states and mass cultures. Perhaps we are on the brink of a third such 'event' – the appearance of an as yet unnamed 'postmodern' social and cultural formation (Boulding, 1966; Kahn and Wiener, 1967). More and more people recognize that late capitalism, post-industrial society or postmodern culture are qualitatively different from what has come before. Whether such changes are conceptualized in terms of a late, consumer, global capitalism bearing a hyper-modern culture, or of a post-industrial information society embodying a postmodern sensibility, it seems clear that things are no longer as once they seemed and that these changes, though only bleakly understood, are of epochal proportions.

The idea of the present as postmodern has been hotly debated for over a decade, at least by intellectuals. Perhaps this is because the complex shifts and transformations that constitute our present world are not adequately articulated in prevailing forms of social theory, which emerged from and is still too rooted in the fading modern world. Most of the key concepts that we use to describe modern societies emerged with modernity itself in the early nineteenth century. Terms like industry, revolution, intellectual, ideology or alienation did not exist, or did not have their current meanings, until during and after the political and industrial revolutions of England, France and the United States. Montesquieu is closer to Deuteronomy than to Durkheim. In 1850 Carlyle still referred to 'the Continental nuisance called "Bureaucracy"'; not until Weber's theories was the concept generalized successfully. By the late nineteenth century, however, the great transformation to modernity eventually yielded social theories to explain it. But in the early transitional period, these theories did not yet exist, and so the emerging modern experience was literally unaccountable. The confusion and intensity of debates on postmodernity suggest that we may be in a similar situation today.

The distinction between 'industrial' and 'post-industrial' society also has been employed to conceptualize a range of changes in social life, technological innovation and late capitalist modes of production. Many writers assume a close relationship between 'post-industrial' and 'postmodern' forms. They focus on the emergence of a knowledge-dependent service sector, the new meaning and significance of information, the globalization, commodification, rationalization and massification of both public and private life, the search for an authentic (or narcissistic) self, and the increased importance of the state both as a protector and regulator of the market and as an economic actor in its own right. For example, Jean-François Lyotard argued that the status of knowledge alters as 'societies enter what is known as the postindustrial age and cultures enter what is known as the postmodern age' (1984: 3). Similarly, Frankel noted that the debate over modernism and postmodernism 'has in many ways become an explicit debate over the nature of culture and social production in the emerging "postindustrial" society' (1987: 10). Yet the exact character of the relationship between post-industrial society and postmodern culture is still to be established.

Another way of understanding postmodernism is to see it as a response to the entropy of Eurocentric discourse. The goals and values that have been central to Western civilization can no longer be considered universal, and the associated 'project of modernity' is unfinished because its completion would be disastrous, even if possible, particularly on the current Euro-American model. Thus the advent of the 'postmodern' may be a code-word for the emergence of a 'post-Western' era. As Feher commented,

> True to the spirit of declining worlds, which learn to relativize their deities in the face of imported foreign gods, 'Europe' humbly inserts itself and its culture in yet another postmodernist innovation, in a 'wider context' of all cultures which are supposedly all equivalent. (1987: 44)

Contrary to the view that America represents the form of civilization 'best adapted to the probability . . . of the life that lies in store for us' (Baudrillard, 1988: 10), the waning of Europe's economic and cultural hegemony has been followed by a 'crisis of the Pan Americana' (Eco, 1978: 76). If the Old World of Europe no longer seems to be the bearer of universal values and the model for enlightenment and material progress, the New World of America, in its turn, has encountered a relative economic decline, military ineffectiveness in relation to terrorist or political resistance, and a political and social crisis of legitimation. Moreover, the demise of the Soviet Union, far from ensuring the continued hegemony of America, has created a more polycentric, less controllable world in which American ideologies are increasingly anachronistic. Thus, the preoccupation with the postmodern may be a symptom not so much of the exhaustion of the modern, as of a belated recognition of its geo-political relocation, the shift of its creative momentum away from the West.

The term 'postmodernism' was first used in the 1960s by literary critics such as Leslie Fiedler and Ihab Hassan, who noted the entropy of the modernist movement and tried to characterize what was coming next. During the early and mid-1970s the term gained a much wider currency, encompassing first architecture, then dance, theatre, painting, film and music, and then contemporary culture and society as a whole. While the postmodern break with modernism was fairly visible in architecture and the visual arts, the notion of a postmodern rupture in literature has been much harder to ascertain. At some point in the late 1970s, 'postmodernism' migrated to Europe via Paris and Frankfurt. Julia Kristeva and Jean-François Lyotard took it up in France, Jürgen Habermas in

Germany. In the United States, meanwhile, critics had begun to discuss the interface of postmodernism with French post-structuralism, and with that peculiar American adaption, deconstructionism. By the early 1980s the modernity/postmodernity constellation in social theory had become hotly contested. And it was contested precisely because there is so much more at stake than the existence or non-existence of a new artistic style or a 'correct' theoretical line.

In much of the debate on postmodernism, either it is said that postmodernism is continuous with modernism, in which case the whole 'debate' is specious; or it is claimed that there is a radical rupture, a break with modernism, which is then evaluated in either positive or negative terms. The various discussants can be grouped into four major camps. First, those who see postmodernism as a rupture with modernism, and who, like Georges Bataille, Michel Foucault or Jacques Derrida, characterize it in terms of 'a decentered subjectivity, emancipated from the imperatives of work and usefulness' (Habermas, 1987: 14). Second, those who decry postmodernism because it reinforces 'the logic of consumer capitalism' (Jameson, 1984: 125), or because it parodies the formal resolution of art and social life, 'while remorselessly emptying it of its political content' (Eagleton, 1990: 61). Third, those who see postmodernism as positive, and welcome it as a triumph of heterogeneity over consensus. They envision artists and writers 'working without rules in order to formulate the rules for what *will have been done*' after the event has happened, and thereby able to resist capture by any form of ideology (Lyotard, 1984: 81). Finally, Jürgen Habermas (1987) eschews literary Marxism even as he criticizes postmodernists for overlooking political economy and thereby drifting unwittingly into the neo-conservative camp.

Habermas is joined by many others who are of a more openly 'left' persuasion. These writers view Nietzsche not only as the great critic of Enlightenment pretensions, but also as the harbinger of a new order whose values would be self-consciously invented 'myths'. Thus they seek a concept of the normative that avoids both absolutism and its nihilistic counterparts; and instead of rejecting the political, they seek to redefine it (e.g. Agger, 1989; Aronowitz, 1981; Huyssen, 1984). For example, Agger (1990) asserts that 'postmodernity is a myth', not a new historical epoch where 'class, race, gender and geographic inequalities' have been overcome, but, on the contrary, merely a way of 'casting doubt on the standard left-wing attempts to specify definitive values' and of undermining the Marxist historical project. None the less, Agger takes postmodernism with great seriousness. He wants to appropriate it for his own Marxist and feminist project: 'One might well disqualify the death penalty as barbaric but recognize that the very discourse of "death penalty" is an artifact of a society legitimizing certain kinds of death (e.g. from starvation or war)' (1990: 18).

Thus postmodern social theory implies a larger set of questions. How can we recover the central role of old-fashioned social science in forming a democratic public space? How can we create a politically constructive moment for an intellectually deconstructive critique? Accepting that some forms of rationality bring advantages for certain groups over others (e.g. colonial anthropology, feminism, expertise), how can we form a discourse that would include more of society or humanity as its implicit public? How can we develop a more liberating textwork in relation to the institutionalized interests and ideologies of scholars, the contexts of public presentation (press, museums, policy councils), and the larger political economy? Many textual leftists responded to an era of conservative politics by retreating into deconstructive hermeneutics and eschewing civic engagement. But what basis for political action, rather than retreatism, could be established within the consciousness engendered by deconstructive criticism? How can textual reflectiveness within disciplines yield greater empowerment of citizens? If all forms of truth are ultimately fictions or myths, what might be more adequate myths for our polity and how might textwork contribute to their creation?

The notion of postmodernism as resistance to any form of reified meaning is central for those who believe in its radical potential. But is this enough? Is it sufficient to stress the marginal against any sense of collectivity? For example, the feminist critique of patriarchy and the postmodernist critique of representation intersect most fruitfully when they go beyond a mere critique of masculinist representation. Alternately, if we agree that *everything* is representation, that there is nothing outside the text, then postmodernism becomes a metaphysic so broad that it tells us little about anything in particular. Indeed, the debate over pros and cons of representation as such has impeded a postmodern politics in which 'the power of representation is something sought, indeed passionately struggled for, by groups that consider themselves dominated by alien and alienating representations' (Arac, 1986: 31–2). Conversely, if the postmodern is discussed as a new historical condition, it becomes possible to sharpen its critical edge. Thinking historically and practically, we would no longer either eulogize or ridicule postmodernism 'as a whole'. For this project, the postmodern must be salvaged from both its champions and its detractors. An important step in this direction is taken by Jürgen Habermas.

Jürgen Habermas on the Modern, the Postmodern and the Political

Jürgen Habermas was the first thinker of philosophic sophistication to address the question of postmodernism's relationship to politics and especially to neo-conservatism. Habermas's project may be seen as a defence of enlightened modernity, which is *not* identical with the aesthetic modernism of literary critics and art historians. Instead, Habermas's critique is directed simultaneously against political conservatism and against the cultural anti-rationalism of post-Nietzschean aestheticism.

In his 1980 lecture for the Adorno Prize, Habermas identified the postmodern with some forms of conservatism and criticized both for not coming to terms either with the exigencies of culture in late capitalism or with the success and failures of modernism itself. Habermas's attack on postmodern conservatism took place on the heels of the conservative political backlash of the mid-1970s and 1980s, when American, British, French and German neo-conservatives sought to regain hegemony and to wipe out the effect of the 1960s in political and cultural life. But the particularly German contingencies of Habermas's argument are at least as important. He was writing after '1968' when both the utopian hopes and the pragmatic promises of the modernization of German cultural and political life were giving way to disillusion. Against the growing cynicism – a kind of enlightened false consciousness – Habermas tried to salvage the emancipatory potential of reason which to him is the sine qua non of political democracy. Habermas defended a substantive notion of communicative rationality, especially against those who would collapse reason into domination, or who believed that by abandoning reason they become free.

One does not have to share Habermas's positions to see that he raised the most important moral and political issues at stake in a form that avoided the usual apologies and facile polemics about modernity and postmodernity. Habermas's questions were these: How does postmodernism relate to modernism? How are political conservatism, cultural eclecticism or pluralism, tradition, modernity and anti-modernity interrelated in contemporary Western culture? To what extent can the cultural and social formation of the 1970s be characterized as postmodern? And further, to what extent is postmodernism a revolt against reason and enlightenment, and at what point do such revolts become reactionary?

However, there were problems not so much with the questions Habermas raised as with some of the answers he suggested. Thus his attack on Foucault and Derrida as conservatives drew immediate fire from post-structuralists who reversed the reproach and labelled Habermas himself a conservative. This debate between 'Frankfurters and French fries' quickly reduced to one of political correctness – who is the least conservative of us all? And yet, the battle remains instructive because it highlights two fundamentally different visions of modernity. The French vision draws on Nietzsche and Mallarmé and thus is quite close to what literary critics describe as modernism. Modernity for the French is primarily, though not exclusively, an aesthetic question relating to the energies released by the deliberate destruction of fixed meanings in language and other forms of representation. By contrast, for Habermas, modernity goes back to the best traditions of the Enlightenment, which he tries to salvage and to reinscribe into the present philosophical discourse in a new form. In this, Habermas differs radically from an earlier generation of Frankfurt School critics. In *The Dialectic of Enlightenment* (1972), for example, Adorno and Horkheimer developed a view of modernism that seems to be much closer in sensibility to current French theory than to Habermas. But even though Adorno and Horkheimer's assessment of the Enlightenment was so much more pessimistic than Habermas's, they also held on to a substantive notion of reason and subjectivity which much of French theory has abandoned. It seems that in the context of the French discourse, enlightenment is simply identified with a history of terror and incarceration that reaches from the Jacobins via the meta-theories of Hegel and Marx to the Soviet gulag (e.g. Derrida, 1978: 282; Mortley, 1991: 104). Habermas is right in rejecting that view as too limited and as politically dangerous. Auschwitz, after all, did not result from too much enlightened reason (even though it was organized as a perfectly rationalized death factory), but from a violent anti-enlightenment and anti-modern affect, which exploited modernity ruthlessly for its own purposes. At the same time, Habermas's characterization of the French post-Nietzschean vision of *modernité* as simply anti-modern or, as it were, postmodern, itself implies too limited an account of modernity, at least as far as aesthetic modernity is concerned.

Jean-François Lyotard contra Jürgen Habermas

Postmodernists, of course, have countered Habermas's attacks. For example, Jean-François Lyotard argued that Habermas's commitment to communicative rationality and evolutionary ethics is a mythical narrative of emancipation (Redding, 1986; Rorty, 1985). For Lyotard, the disillusionment of our culture is caused by an incredulity toward meta-narratives. This analysis is based on a distinction between narratives and science, a distinction which is shared by Habermas himself. In this view, narratives are myths that provide a legitimation of a social matrix of power. Hence, they are tools for excluding alternate language games. Conversely, science is seen as having demythologized such meta-narratives. But now, according to Lyotard, science has become a mythical narrative itself. In order to legitimate a scientific society, science is being used to delegitimate all other language games. This attempt at intellectual hegemony takes the form of a myth of emancipation, through rationality, as developed by Habermas.

Lyotard accuses Habermas of delegitimating other language games by defining truth in terms of a timeless universal pragmatics. Truth is based on the consensus of a collective universal subject. This notion of an ideal truth devalues the actual truths of the expressions of particular historic subjects, based on their own creative activity. In addition, according to Lyotard, by requiring a consensus for a statement to count as truth, universal pragmatics stifles the new expressions of those without a voice. Thus postmodern thought rejects the meta-narrative of emancipation, and sees a continuous conceptual revolution as the only way to give a voice to all human expressions. Legitimate truth resides in the particular language games that create the heteromorphous, popular, local narratives of everyday life, subject to heterogeneous sets of pragmatic rules. 'For this reason', says Lyotard, 'it seems neither possible, nor even prudent, to follow Habermas in orienting our treatment of the problem of legitimation in the direction of a search for universal consensus through what he calls *Diskurs*, in other words, a dialogue of argumentation' (1984: 65).

Habermas's response to this critique is complex, and much of it has not yet appeared in English. However, a provisional discussion of his rejoinder to Lyotard is possible (Dews, 1987). It contains three basic arguments. First, Lyotard confuses language games with validity claims. This leads him to conclude that universal pragmatics defines the content of a language game that seeks to hegemonize thought. However, this ignores the character of universal pragmatics as a procedure for argumentation that cuts across all language games. Because any language can be translated into others, language games have a common structure that universal pragmatics seeks to identify. Because of this common structure, we are not in a completely relative world of incommensurable realities. Rather, we can enter into discourse with these other language games and, in principle, come to agreement.

Habermas's second argument is that Lyotard's analysis of modern society is historically inaccurate. The coordination of activity in modern society is based on the dissolution of traditional norms and a reintegration through the development of abstract norms. Because Lyotard fails to recognize the difference between tradition-al and modern forms of social integration, he views modernity as just another tradition. Finally, according to Habermas, Lyotard's position is ethically and politically bankrupt. It cannot provide grounds for choosing a particular language game or form of life.

Another objection that Lyotard raises against Habermas's for-mulation is perhaps more serious: Habermas's assumption that the goal of dialogue is consensus. Instead, for Lyotard,

> consensus is only a particular state of discussion, not its end. Its end, on the contrary, is paralogy. This double observation (the heterogeneity of the rules and the search for dissent) destroys a belief that still underlies Habermas's research, namely, that humanity as a collective (universal) subject seeks its common emancipation through the regularization of the 'moves' permitted in all language games and that the legitimacy of any statement resides in its contributing to that emancipation. (1984: 65–6)

A Habermasian reply to this second criticism would be much like his answer to the first: Lyotard is confusing different registers of rationality. These might be called the rules *from which* we reason and the rules *with which* we reason. The former are heterogeneous and may or may not encourage consensus. The latter – the rules *with which* we reason – provide the framework of intelligibility and the possibility of consensus *or* dissensus.

Such a response brings contradictions of its own, however, insofar as it is an epistemological or linguistic version of the traditional liberal method of maintaining order and achieving consensus in an open, pluralistic society. That is, the *Diskursethik* is a philosophic version of the liberal values of fair play and procedural justice. But Habermas wants to be more than a liberal; he wants to move reason in society beyond instrumental utility to a substantively emanci-pated polity.

We might add that both Habermas's and Lyotard's positions are based on a dubious distinction between science and narration. As many thinkers have argued, science has a narrative structure (Brown, 1991; MacIntyre, 1980; Rouse, 1987), everyday life has its own structure of rationality (Fisher, 1992; Garfinkel, 1967; Schutz, 1964), and truth in both is generated through discursive practices. All discourses of knowledge have a narrative form, and to deny this is to mystify critique. Lyotard's argument could thus be turned back at him to show that what he provides is a meta-narrative of nihilism. To assert that all discourses of social relations are equally arational and amoral is also to view them as equally rational and moral. Thus Lyotard's pessimism is not only politically irresponsible; it is also intellectually incorrect, since the fact that a truth is socially constructed does not make it untrue.

Habermas's solution to this dilemma is also inadequate: he establishes hypothetical or transcendental standards of rational speech that can only exist *exterior* to any possible political community (Habermas, 1990a). His *Diskursethik* is thus a kind of contract theory (or, later, an evolutionary ideal) of discourse that may provide general standards for critique, but tells us little or nothing about what the title of Habermas's masterwork once promised – a moral and political *pragmatics* of human communication (see Habermas, 1990b, for rejoinder). In the end, then, the theories of Lyotard and Habermas have another trait in common: both of them eschew the moral political realm, one through relativistic reduction, the other through idealistic transcendence.

In addition, both Lyotard and Habermas radically segregate truth from desire. They are thus unable to address adequately the *will* to truth nor explain why *Diskursethik* or paralogy would yield more than a contractual kind of solidarity. And because truth in either case is separated from will, politics, or compassion, neither bears any necessary relation to practice. Indeed, Habermas (1971: 32–3) rejects as 'mystical' the effort of the earlier Frankfurt School to develop a concept of rationality that is both libidinal and cognitive. Postmodernists often have an equally constipated conception of reason, equating it with control (Foucault) or, alternately, relating it negatively or positively to aesthetic pleasure or play (respectively Barthes or Baudrillard, and Lyotard).

What is the main implication of this discussion for the task of reconstructing social theory after the postmodernist critique? I believe it is to clarify the limits of two principal alternatives: a modernist theory of postmodernity and a postmodernist social theory. Critics like Featherstone or Bauman urge us to 'relinquish the attraction of a postmodern sociology and work towards a sociological account of postmodernism' (Featherstone, 1988: 205). Such a social theory of the postmodern risks being inappropriate to its subject matter if we mean by social theory a systematizing, generalizing social science. Can a modernist social theory of postmodernity remain impervious to the dissipation of objectivity, to the existence of a multiplicity of competing or even incommensurate life-worlds, traditions and language games, and to the crisis of foundations and the decomposition of Eurocentric cognitive hierarchies associated with the advance of a postmodern worldview? The proposal that it is necessary to move beyond a 'postmodern sociology' to a 'sociology of postmodernity', as in Bauman (1988: 235) and Featherstone (1988: 205), may be a step backward.

This is because such a proposal implies a return to the very 'business as usual' that was earlier rejected, only now the business has somewhat different customers and concepts. That is, it suggests the possibility of simply moving beyond 'false' methodological and epistemological oppositions to a direct address of postmodern phenomena, effecting thereby a return to 'the real as referential'.

To question the possibility of a simple return to an orthodox social science investigation of postmodernity as a new object is not to support the cultivation of social theory that itself expresses and is limited to the cultural climate of postmodernity. This second alternative also has all the limits highlighted by Habermas's critique of Lyotard. Thus, we still must ask precisely what alternative forms of social thought and civic discourse might be open to us beyond the critique of postmodernism *and* the postmodern critique.

Postmodernism: Resistance, Relativism and Renewal

Contacts and conflicts between peoples and nations increasingly challenge us to create discourses that are more global and embracing. Yet these same contacts and conflicts have also relativized formerly privileged canons of truth and ethics by which more inclusive communities might be created. Indeed, such canons are now rendered parochial or even absurd. In the presence of this relativization of knowledge and value, many feel nostalgia for a lost foundation for fixed and certain rules of conduct and belief. This accounts in part for the often hostile reception of postmodern thought, because postmodernism suggests that the limits of modernism have been reached, at least in the West, and that the pursuit of unshakeable foundations for analytic truth is fruitless (Feather-stone, 1988; Kellner, 1988). In addition, it appears to many that the promise of modernity to achieve the emancipation of humanity from poverty and prejudice is no longer feasible (Krugman, 1991; Lyotard, 1984: 302), and that politics of revolution, forms of knowledge, and subjective experiences have less liberating potential than once was thought. Postmodernism also undermines the position of modern intellectuals and their universal meta-narratives of progress or emancipation.

For all these reasons, the practical scope of postmodern ideas seems limited to a politics of resistance, since the grounds, goals or even stable meaning of any positive social historical project are radically relativized by postmodern thought. As Lyotard suggested,

> The real political task today, at least in so far as it is also concerned with the cultural . . . is to carry forward the resistance that writing offers to established thought, to what has already been done, to what everyone

thinks, to what is well known, to what is widely recognized, to what is 'readable', to everything which can change its form and make itself acceptable to opinion in general . . . The name most often given to this is postmodernism. (1984: 302)

Can we not go beyond such negative criticality, to an affirmative one? This would require us to reformulate key aspects of postmodernism itself. For example, the notorious Derridean aphorism 'il n'ya pas de hors-texte', may be invoked to abet an escape from the determinate necessities of history, a self-abandonment to the indeterminate pleasures of the text (Barthes, 1975; Baudrillard, 1983). However, it may also be construed as an insistence upon the ideological force of discourse in general and especially of those discourses that claim to reflect an essential pre-given truth (Montrose, 1989). In this spirit, postmodernists insist that much of the import of a message is contained in what it does *not* say. The dominant discursive practices of a group or society define not only what is to be said, but, more importantly, what cannot be stated and what goes without saying. Regimes of truth marginalize certain kinds of knowledge and move others to centre-stage. For example, in policy-oriented research on alcohol use, the total framework of silent assumptions and interests persuades the audience by constructing the object of study and constraining the ways in which it may be described. In the case of alcohol studies, a historic shift has been effected in America since 1950 in the definition of the research object and of social reality from 'habitual drunkard' to 'alcoholic'. In this movement from a moral vocabulary of sin and redemption to a scientific vocabulary of sickness and cure, the sociology of social problems became a new version of the theology of evil, personal identities were transformed, and power shifted from church and community to medical institutions and the state (Gusfield, 1992). By uncovering such silences, postmodern social theory is no longer 'merely theoretical'. Instead, it makes something happen. It disables the power of the words to go on blindly proliferating the ideologies and the canonical readings that they impose. In this way, postmodernism can earn the adjective 'critical'. It becomes an indispensable means of unmasking ideological assumptions (Miller, 1982: 89).

After postmodern awareness and deconstructive criticism have done their work of resistance, we still are faced with the challenge of establishing moral authority and inventing positive values as central elements of any polity. In addition to a postmodern hermeneutic of suspicion (Ricoeur, 1983, 1986), then, we also need a 'hermeneutic of affirmation'. Accordingly, some postmodernists shift the image of discourse on social issues from one of explanation and verification to that of a conversation of scholars and citizens who seek to guide and persuade themselves and each other. Cognitive, moral and civic truths are no longer seen as fixed entities discovered according to a meta-theoretical blueprint of linearity or hierarchy; instead, they are invented within an ongoing self-reflective community in which 'critic', 'social scientist' and 'citizen' become relatively interchangeable (Burke, 1984; Rorty, 1979). Critique of theory, method and practice remain permanently immanent precisely because they cannot be universalized. We too are required to acknowledge the permanent immanence of our own role and identity – the rhetorical constitution of ourselves as subjects and of our fields as disciplinary objects. And then we are obliged to maintain and apply this consciousness and practice of rhetorical awareness to our common civic life.

Through postmodern awareness and criticism, norms of cognition and of conduct can be relocated in the act of symbolic construction, and no longer regarded as sacred or natural laws that symbols subserviently convey. In such a postmodernism, norms are not viewed merely as objective products, but also as symbolic processes that are inherently persuasive. Humans enact truth and justice not merely by rational legislation, but also by rhetorical performance. In this view, standards for knowledge and conduct are not based on some extra-linguistic rationality, because rationality itself is demystified and reconstituted as a historical construction and deployment by human rhetors. Logic, reason and ethics all are brought down from their absolute, pre-existent heights into the creative, contextual web of history and action (Brown, 1987: 64–79).

Postmodern criticism subverts dogmatic claims in science, ethics and politics. But as scholars and as citizens we still need to justify the truth of our scientific statements and the morality of our political actions. Indeed, we must do this if we are to establish rational and ethical standards for our collective life. Thus rhetorical analysis of scholarly and social texts has a positive, constructive task as well as a negative, deconstructive one. This positive task begins with the human authorship of human worlds: it requires us to imagine more adequate narratives for our political community, and to show how academic writing can help create these narratives. This is not purely a product of textual criticism, however. Interpretive openness and moral sensibility through critical rhetorical methods are possible only within the context of certain social and historical conditions. Thus the reform of knowledge requires more than the replacement of positivistic constructions with rhetorical deconstructions or reconstructions. More importantly, it requires a new vision and new practices of the public space.

In this sense, the arcane academic struggle over postmodernism articulates a broader struggle for the soul of democratic peoples. Traditional social science gave an implicit account of the public space and a model of the ideal citizen. Disciplined inquiry into the laws of society provided an ideal of general political discussion; the scholar's suspension of self-interest provided a model of the citizen, who would make judgements about the social whole according to general reason instead of partisan passions. In short, ideals implicit in social science became interwoven with the very fabric of the liberal polity. Science, in the words of Walter Lippman, was 'the discipline of democracy'.

For these reasons, however brilliantly positivism and foundationalism have been criticized by dissident academics, they remain powerful supports for institutions and practices that few of us are willing to abandon: academic freedom, professional judgement, civil liberties and due process of law (Peters, 1990). As a child of liberalism and the Enlightenment, social science has been a major ideological force in the victory of civility over violence, reason and evidence over passion and prejudice, clear communication over cloudy commitment. In the social thought of the Progressive Era in particular, social science was held up as a paradigm of a democratic public discourse. The ideal practice by professional social scientists – of value-neutrality, objectivity and dispassionate, reasoned argumentation – was taken as a model of conduct, communication and inquiry for the rest of the citizenry. This vision is still with us institutionally, however much we have been soured on it by subsequent history and theory. Thus, we should not dismiss modernist social science too blithely, nor imagine that all one needs is a more congenial vocabulary. Instead, if we are to make deconstructive social theory consequential in the public and political arenas, we must consider its ramifications outside the halls of academe.

Despite its profound achievements, foundationalism has become philosophically untenable and liberalism politically exhausted, at least in the West. What, then, might be a substitute way of conceiving the moral nature and political functions of social science? Clearly, any response entails relativism and, with this, the fear that usually accompanies the view of the world as uncertain. Acceptance of rhetoric, social constructionism and relativity undermines absolutisms and invites a broader tolerance for alternative perspectives. In an increasingly diverse and conflictual world, the need for such an openness of discourse is greater than ever. But politics is also about closure, and power about exclusion. We still need moral criteria to make and measure actions and decisions.

Whose discourse and which moral criteria shall we use? Does not postmodern social theory relativize any possible moral political practice? And is not such relativism therefore an 'ideology of helpless surrender' (Lukács, 1981: 89).

Several answers to the fear of relativism can be made. First, fewer atrocities in the history of the world have happened as a result of excessive tolerance than as a result of absolutism. Which is worse, the possibility that evil will be tolerated in the name of cultural relativism, or the promise that future atrocities will be justified by some group's assurance that they are absolutely right? Whereas tyranny is or depends on absolutism, in a democratic polity we are and must be relativists in practice because we exercise judgement as citizens in shaping or finding ethical truth. Democratic practice requires prudent judgement, and such judgement presupposes critical, even deconstructive, reflection on political experience that is inherently contingent.

It also is useful, following Bhaskar (1979), to distinguish between epistemic relativism and judgemental relativism. Epistemic relativism asserts that all knowledge emerges from and is shaped by particular historical and social circumstances and that, therefore, there is no realm of 'pure data' describable either extra-linguistically or in a non-indexical language (Barnes and Law, 1976; Collins, 1983: 102). By contrast, judgemental relativism makes the further claim that because all forms of knowledge are epistemically relative they are therefore all equally valid (or invalid). They are all embedded in local historical, social and linguistic practices and, therefore, we cannot compare different forms of knowledge and discriminate among them. But these latter assertions of *judgemental* relativism are not in the least entailed by the position of *epistemological* relativism. Indeed, in some ways the two are opposite. First, judgemental relativism assumes that standards must be absolute or universal to be valid, whereas epistemological relativism identifies alternative forms of valid knowledge. Second, epistemological relativism is a stance one may assume when *talking about* forms of knowledge. But it usually is quite inappropriate when *actually using* one of them. Thus, for example, the fact that any explanatory category can be analysed sociologically does not count, by itself, as a criticism of the usability of that category (Collins, 1983: 101). Nor could we very well analyse the category sociologically *and simultaneously* deploy it as an explanation within its specific domain. Concepts can be treated as *topics of* research or *resources for* research. The epistemological relativism implied in the former does not of necessity justify a judgemental relativism about the latter.

Finally, and accordingly, epistemological relativism appears to be a precondition for the need and possibility of making determinations about the validity of knowledge systems. This is far from the disavowal by judgemental relativists of such determinations. As Knorr-Cetina and Mulkay put it,

> The belief that scientific knowledge does not merely replicate nature *in no way* commits the epistemic relativist to the view that therefore all forms of knowledge will be equally successful in solving a practical problem, equally adequate in explaining a puzzling phenomenon or, in general, equally acceptable to all participants. Nor does it follow that we cannot discriminate between different forms of knowledge with a view to their relevance or adequacy in regard to a specific goal. (1983: 6)

We might take copies of both *Moby Dick* and *Celestial Navigation* on our sailboat, respecting the validity of each for their specific purposes, both of which may serve the larger purpose of our voyage.

This also illuminates the debate between Lyotard and Habermas previously discussed: different forms of knowledge are not merely competing *or* subsumable language games, because each of them implies a different moral affirmation. For a purely language-analytic philosophy, all interpretations are equally valid within the limits of the theory that provides their given rules of reading. But each such set of rules also has its own particular utilities and existential functions (Ricoeur, 1980: 107). Thus the telos of psychoanalysis is an archaeology of the subject, the telos of the phenomenology of religion is an eschatology, the telos of positive social science is the technical direction of society. The telos of a textualist analysis of society is the human authorship of the world.

In short, relativism does not entail a society without standards. Rather, the conjoining of deconstruction and epistemology helps us to recognize when, where and how the standards are to be established cooperatively, constantly renewed and periodically reshaped. Hence, unlike absolutism, relativism is reflective about its own limits. This can be shown through the work of Alisdair MacIntyre. MacIntyre deplores the multiplicity of incommensurable local discourses that characterize our postmodern condition. Insofar as incommensurability reigns, a community beyond the local must remain a distant and perhaps impossible dream. But is the picture really as bleak as MacIntyre paints it? Incommensurability is largely a product of people's certainty about their own version of truth and their own particular vocabulary and grammar (MacIntyre, 1981: 69ff.; 1988: 326–48). For most practical purposes, however, such competing advocates do not need to persuade one another. Instead, they must only gain the adherence of a relevant audience –

one usually composed of *others* who are affected by the matter at hand but whose values are still open to discussion and debate. Protesters, as MacIntyre notes in *After Virtue* (1981: 66), talk past one another, as one side grounds arguments in 'rights' and the other in 'law'. But they do not talk past those who will decide the outcome of the controversy. This public assesses the coherence and fidelity of the rival stories told by these factions and makes decisions usually for good reasons (Fisher, 1992: 204). This sort of rationality will not satisfy those who demand consensus based on strict logical computation. But it does comply with another notion of rationality, the idea of rationality as a social process, of rationality as the civic intelligence that is displayed when people are open to argument and willing and able to take good reasons into account. Such rationality can be textually deconstructive, but only because it can be, and is, socially constructed.

Thus the fear of relativism can be partly allayed by shifting from a conception of truth as discovery or product, towards a view of truth as invention or process. In their different ways, this shift characterizes the writings of Walter Fisher, Jürgen Habermas, Michel Foucault, Kenneth Burke and Richard Rorty. For example, Rorty has argued that it 'is the vocabulary of practice rather than of theory, of action rather than contemplation, in which one can say something useful about truth' (1982: 162). Rorty establishes the centrality of language, allowing the 'text' and conversation to become loci of inquiry. He thereby orients us towards communicative *process* with respect to the practical life of a civic or scholarly community. In this sense, pragmatism does not collapse into relativism, nor is it transcendental as in Habermas's sense of pragmatics. Instead 'the pragmatist knows no better way to explain his convictions than to remind his interlocutor of the position they both are in, the contingent starting points they both share, the floating, ungrounded conversations of which they are both members' (Rorty, 1982: 173–4; see Cheney, 1987). Even if we accept Rorty's deconstruction of epistemology and ethics, however, the consequences of such a move are open. And, for better or worse, it does make it harder to isolate any general or transcultural standards of judgement (Hacking, 1986; Rabinow, 1986: 236).

Michel Foucault explored this problem by showing how Western notions of reason, ethics and identity are historically embedded in institutionalized patterns of discourse. Thus, despite pressures from the French left, Foucault was reluctant to designate utopian goals or even a particular social arrangement as *the* ideal implied by his historical and social criticism. Instead, he argued that social criticism of institutions should itself be institutionalized. In his historical genealogies of major institutions of society, such as mental health, criminal justice and the human sciences, and in his later analyses of power, Foucault sought to expose various modes of domination. He conceived of power as interactive and enabling, and best understood through analysis of both resistance and empowerment. In this sense, Foucault promoted a critique of knowledge/power that would treat it *in action*, for that is the only place it truly exists (Foucault 1980; see Cheney, 1987; Dallmayr, 1984). Thus Foucault also responds to relativism by focusing on the *how* rather than the *what* of truth or virtue, and he implies a form of knowledge/power that may be more open and democratic than existing ones.

Kenneth Burke also speaks of critical rhetoric as a civic discourse. Unlike most literary theorists, Burke never separated action from contemplation, willing from imagining, or poetry from power. Instead, he held that all intellectual activity (even the most theoretical sort that disdains politics) is itself a kind of praxis, first and foremost an *act* (Cheney 1987; Lentricchia, 1983: 87). Burke thereby helps us to recover the classical relationship of *theoria* and *praxis* through a realization of criticism's practical power. By concerning itself with the ways we make and change allegiances to key symbols of authority such as family, employer, religion or nation, rhetorical criticism participates in the ongoing moral and practical re-creation of society. As early is 1937, Burke acknowledged this dimension of his activity:

> Our own program, as literary critic, is to integrate technical criticism with social criticism . . . by taking the allegiance to the symbol of authority as our subject. We take this as our starting point and 'radiate' from it. Since the symbols of authority are radically linked with [material social] relationships, this point of departure automatically involves us in socio-economic criticism. And since the whole purpose of a 'revolutionary' critic is to contribute to a change in allegiance to the symbols of authority, we maintain our role as 'propagandist' by keeping this subject ever uppermost in our concerns. (1937: 234–5)

More specifically, as Cheney (1987) has noted, what Burke seeks is a continual shift toward humane symbols of authority as devices 'for spreading the areas of allegiance' (Burke, 1935: 89). Such symbols must enlist our sympathies and hopes by articulating ideals 'which we should like to share' (1937: II, 78). Consequently, for Burke, the ideal society is one of *communion*, where the reciprocity of identification is maximized, where all have a 'common stake in both cooperative and symbolic networks' (1937: II, 247–8), where 'we the people' includes all of humanity (1935). With the broadening of loyalties, a new kind of transcendence might be achieved in which opposing groups would stress and enhance their similarities and not their differences. This is the locus of social praxis for Burke – one in which ethics and politics meet on rhetorical ground (Cheney, 1987).

These considerations of relativity also imply a reconceptualization of ideology: if there is no foundational reality exterior to those created in language, how are truth and power to be distinguished, much less separately judged? Again a partial response can be found by focusing on the process of construction and not just the product that is constructed: How open is this process to criticism, self-criticism and practical transformation by people in light of their own experience? In Louis Althusser's (1970) view, for example, ideology is not so much a system of abstract ideas as a set of practices that shape people's lived relation to the real. Althusser shifts the conception of ideology as false consciousness by rendering ideology practical and social. Consciousness is no longer the locus of ideology. Instead,

> Althusser speaks of misrecognition, arguing that in the very process in which subjects are able to recognize themselves in social relations there exists also a misrecognition, a failure to see that their subjectivity is produced historically and materially by forces beyond their control . . . Persons learn to objectify themselves, regarding their identities as natural and ethically appropriate rather than as impositions representing social practices. (Shapiro, 1988: 3)

Pierre Bourdieu (1977) offers a similar formulation in his analyses of how orthodox practices of discourse classify some views as true and others as false, some as admissible and others as marginal. While the 'universe of discourse' gives us access to its explicit contents, it also renders inaccessible what is unthinkable, 'doxa' or the 'universe of the undiscussed'. Thus, for Bourdieu, ordinary discourse can provide only a politicized, ideological version of the real – that is, a version which suppresses awareness of its own partiality.

To counter the ideological character of realism, an extraordinary discourse is needed. Such a discourse will not be found outside of language. Instead, I believe it can be built from the rhetorical model itself. The postmodern metaphor of aesthetic, scientific and social realities as rhetorical construction allows us to abandon the views both of social structures as objective entities acting on individuals, and of subjective agents inventing their worlds out of conscious intentions. Instead, both structures and consciousness, as well as public and private worlds, are seen as practical, historic accomplishments, brought about through everyday communicative action, through poetic and political struggles over the nature and meaning of the real (Brulle, 1993).

To the extent that modern social science ignores such critical perspectives and remains linguistically unreflective, it becomes part of society's mechanisms for legitimation, marginalization and punishment. In reproducing prevailing discursive practices, an unreflective social science helps to fix persons, objects and relations in the categories already established through institutionalized social control. By contrast, a social science informed by postmodern thought would make it evident that objects, norms, persons and events are inseparable from the processes of representation by which they are formed. The activities of the imagination that produce facts and meanings are not acts of a disembodied cogito; instead, they are historically developed practices that reside in the very style in which statements are made, in the grammatical and narrative structures that compose even the discourses of science. The *what* of any system of knowledge and value is radically entangled in the *how* of its writing and speaking. For this reason, the text that is self-conscious about its own rhetorical structure is the exemplar of a non-delusional mode of writing for social scientists (Shapiro, 1988: 7–8) and, by extension, for citizens as well.

These observations also suggest that such a critical social science would have an uneasy relation to its own institutionalization. This is because rhetorical criticism is transgressive, more profane than pious. It demands a generalized displacement and re-articulation of established discourses or disciplines, not a quarantined place at their margins (LaCapra, 1987: 236). This demand accords with a politically serious, and not only intellectually playful, aspect of postmodern social thought. The relativity of rhetorical deconstruction and its ambiguous relation to practice implies not the endless proliferation of variety, but the agonistic elimination of error, the marginalization of trivial contentions and the clarification of fundamental and irreducible differences. It is not a 'liberal toleration of opposing views from a neutral ground, but transformation, conversion, or at least, the kind of communication which clarifies exactly what is at stake in any critical conflict' (Mitchell, 1982: 613–14; see Farrell, 1976; Johnstone, 1980). Postmodern social theory thus ideally is our self-consciousness through civic discourse.

The tensions between postmodern reflexivity and moral political relevance can be fruitfully exploited by viewing the rhetoric of the social sciences as a critique that empowers peoples and enables actions. Postmodern analysis can be more than a game of 'the emperor has no clothes', especially when we realize that none of us is securely clothed. Indeed, the epistemological undressing of emperors and absolutes might also be politically prudish, for it keeps us from asking the more messy practical question of how, literally, to clothe the masses. Postmodern analysis need not rest in smugness or unease, having dispatched the philosophic problems of moral essences, universals and foundations. The interesting question is not *whether* there is a truth, reality or virtue independent of all possible accounts of it, but *how* such accounts are made adequate to their respective purposes and practices of poetic and political representation. The insight that everything is a sign for some other sign can have a practical import. One can shift Saussure's question, 'What stands for what?', to Lenin's question, 'Who stands for whom?' And from there, to the question, 'What discursive and cultural practices would support each person standing for themselves, and each standing for each other?' To pursue such questions is to be as knights in search of a Holy Grail, only now we do so ironically, knowing that the quest itself is our telos, our truth, our communion. The ideal republic did exist for Plato and his friends – in their quest, in their actual practice of talking about it.

Such an ironic practice is both dialectic and dynamic (Brown 1989: Ch. 5; Woolgar, 1983: 259–60). It acknowledges the contradictions between the reflection of reality *in* language and the constitution of reality *by* language. It recognizes that the literal and the metaphoric are reciprocally defining and mutually transforming. Indeed, the very effectiveness of such a practice *as* ironic depended on its constituting at least part of the world as literally true in order to unmask false versions. Such an irony also builds solidarity between speaker and audience since the latter is presumed, unlike naïve outsiders, to be capable of *noting* the irony itself. Such irony also fosters agency and enlightenment, because it never states absolutely which of the terms of opposition is intended to be the truer or better one – the telos of the quest or the quest as telos. This must be decided by the auditor. Contrary to Lyotard, the ironicist plays two language games at once, making opposites seem (almost) commensurable within a single frame. But unlike Habermas, the ironicist does *not* want to be universally understood (Capel, 1965: 32). In deploying the dialectics of irony, in *seeing* the irony or in *being* ironic, we take more seriously the deep ambiguities of all modes of representation, all quests, all truths, all universals.

I believe that, if practised in this dialectical, ironic mode, a postmodern social science can be a discourse of both resistance and of affirmation. What is affirmed is the will towards knowledge and experience of the good, and this affirmation is contained in the practice of resistance, including resistance to that easy postmodernism of either complacent self-endorsement or nihilistic 'anything goes'. Resistance will always have to be specific and contingent upon the cultural field within which it operates. It cannot be defined simply in terms of negativity or non-identity, à la Adorno, nor will the litanies of a totalizing, collective project suffice. At the same time, the very notion of resistance may itself be problematic in its simple opposition to affirmation. After all, there are affirmative forms of resistance and resisting forms of affirmation. The space of fruitful tensions between a hermeneutic of suspicion and a hermeneutic of affirmation is always shifting. But this need not and should not keep us from making moral judgements. There are more important things to do with paradoxes than resolve them.

We need neither suppress nor overcome the tensions of rhetorical deconstruction and political reconstruction. Instead, we should heighten these tensions, continually rediscover and refocus them in criticism and in practice (Baker, 1990). No matter how troubling it may be, the landscape of the postmodern surrounds us. It simultaneously delimits and opens our horizons. It is our dilemma. It is our hope.

Note

This essay emerged from several seminars on 'Postmodern Social Theory' held at the University of Maryland since 1988. We rewrote this shared text so often that some citations to works drawn upon were lost in the process, making the present essay something of a pastiche. The section titled 'Jürgen Habermas on the Modern, the Postmodern, and the Political' is co-authored with Robert Brulle. Several of the paragraphs in the final section have appeared previously in other of my works. I thank Herbert Simons for his editorial guidance, and my students for their ideas and criticisms.

References

Adorno, T.W. and Horkheimer, M. (1972) *Dialectic of Enlightenment*. J. Cumming, trans. New York: Herder & Herder.

Agger, B. (1989) *Fast Capitalism: A Critical Theory of Significance*. Urbana: University of Illinois Press.

Agger, B. (1990) *The Decline of Discourse: Reading, Writing and Resistance in Postmodern Capitalism*. New York: Falmer.

Althusser, L. (1970) *For Marx*. Ben Brewster, trans. New York: Random House.

Arac, J. (1986) *Postmodernism and Politics*. Minneapolis: University of Minnesota Press.

Aronowitz, S. (1981) 'Postmodernism and politics', in A. Ross (ed.), *Universal Abandon? The Politics of Postmodernism*. Minneapolis: University of Minnesota Press. pp. 46–62.

Baker, S. (1990) 'Reflection, doubt and the place of rhetoric in postmodern social theory', *Sociological Theory*, 8 (2): 232–45.

Barnes, S.B. and Law, J. (1976) 'Whatever should be done with indexical expressions?', *Theory & Society*, 3: 223–37.

Barthes, R. (1975) *The Pleasures of the Text*. R. Miller, trans. New York: Hill & Wang.

Baudrillard, J. (1975) *The Mirror of Production*. M. Poster, trans. St Louis, MO: Telos Press.

Baudrillard, J. (1981) *For a Critique of the Political Economy of the Sign*. C. Levin, trans. St Louis, MO: Telos Press.

Baudrillard, J. (1983) *In the Shadow of the Silent Majorities*. P. Foss, P. Patton and J. Johnston, trans. New York: Semiotext(e).

Baudrillard, J. (1988) *America*. London: Verso.

Bauman, Z. (1988) 'Is there a postmodern sociology?', *Theory, Culture & Society*, 5, (2–3): 217–38.

Bhaskar, R. (1979) *The Possibility of Naturalism: a Critique of the Contemporary Human Sciences*. Brighton: Harvester Press.

Boulding, K. (1966) *The Image*. Ann Arbor: University of Michigan Press.

Bourdieu, P. (1977) *Outline of a Theory of Practice*. R. Nice, trans. Cambridge: Cambridge University Press.

Brown, R.H. (1987) *Society as Text: Essays on Rhetoric, Reason, and Reality*. Chicago, IL: University of Chicago Press.

Brown, R.H. (1989) *A Poetic for Sociology: Toward a Logic of Discovery for the Human Sciences*. Chicago, IL: University of Chicago Press.

Brown, R.H. (1991) 'Narrative in scientific knowledge and civic discourse', in B. Agger (ed.), *Current Perspectives in Social Theory*, Vol. 11. Greenwich, CT: JAI Press. pp. 313–29.

Brulle, R.J. (1993) 'Power, discourse, and social problems', in G. Miller and J.A. Holstein (eds), *Current Perspectives on Social Problems*. Vol. 4. Greenwich, CT: JAI Press.

Burke, K. (1935) 'Revolutionary symbolism in America', in H. Hart (ed.), *American Writers' Congress*. New York: International Publishers. pp. 87–94.

Burke, K. (1937) *Attitudes toward History*, 2 vols. New York: The New Republic.

Burke, K. (1984) *Permanence and Change: an Anatomy of Purpose*, 3rd edn. Berkeley: University of California Press.

Capel, L.M. (1965) 'Historical introduction', to S. Kirkegaard, *The Concept of Irony*. L.M. Capel, trans. Bloomington: University of Indiana Press. pp. 7–41.

Carlyle, T. (1850) *Latter-day Pamphlets*. London: Chapman and Hall.

Cheney, G. (1987) 'On communicative praxis and the realization of our discipline's potential'. Paper presented to the Central States Speech Communication Association, Columbus, OH.

Collins, M. (1983) 'An empirical relativist programme in sociology of scientific knowledge', in K.D. Knorr-Cetina and M. Mulkay (eds), *Science Observed: Perspectives on the Social Study of Science*. Beverly Hills, CA: Sage. pp. 85–113.

Dallmayr, F.R. (1984) *Polis and Praxis: Exercises in Contemporary Political Theory*. Cambridge, MA: MIT Press.

Derrida, J. (1978) 'Structure, sign, and play in the discourse of the human sciences', in *Writing and Difference*. Alan Bass, trans. Chicago, IL: University of Chicago Press.

Dews, P. (1987) *Logics of Disintegration: Post-structuralist Thought and the Claims of Critical Theory*. London: Verso.

Eagleton, T. (1990) *The Ideology of the Aesthetic*. Oxford: Basil Blackwell.

Eco, U. (1978) *La definizione dell'arte*. Milan: Ganzanti.

Farrell, T.B. (1976) 'Knowledge, consensus, and rhetorical theory', *Quarterly Journal of Speech*, 62 (1), February: 1–14.

Featherstone, M. (1988) *Consumer Culture and Postmodernism*. London: Sage.

Feher, F. (1987) 'The Status of Post-Modernity', *Philosophy and Social Criticism*, 13 (2).

Fisher, W.R. (1992) 'Narration, reason, and community', in R.H. Brown (ed.), *Writing the Social Text: Poetics and Politics in Social Science Discourse*. New York and Berlin: Aldine de Gruyter. pp. 199–218.

Foucault, M. (1980) *Knowledge/Power: Selected Interviews and Other Writings, 1972–1977*. C. Gordon, trans. New York: Pantheon.

Frankel, B. (1987) *The Post-Industrial Utopians*. Cambridge: Polity Press.

Garfinkel, H. (1967) *Studies in Ethnomethodology*. Englewood Cliffs, NJ: Prentice-Hall.

Gusfield, J.R. (1992) 'Listening to the silences: the rhetorics of the research field', in R.H. Brown (ed.), *Writing the Social Text: Poetics and Politics in Social Science Discourse*. New York and Berlin: Aldine de Gruyter. pp. 117–34.

Habermas, J. (1971) *Knowledge and Human Interests*. J.R. Shapiro, trans. Boston: Beacon Press.

Habermas, J. (1987) *The Philosophical Discourse of Modernity: Twelve Lectures*. F. Lawrence, trans. Cambridge, MA: MIT Press.

Habermas, J. (1990a) *Moral Consciousness and Communicative Action*. Cambridge, MA: MIT Press.

Habermas, J. (1990b) 'Justice and solidarity: on the discussion concerning "stage six"', in M. Kelly (ed.), *Hermeneutics and Critical Theory in Ethics and Politics*. Cambridge, MA: MIT Press. pp. 32–52.

Hacking, I. (1986) 'Making up people', in T.C. Heller, M. Sosna and D.E. Wellberg (eds), *Reconstructing Individualism: Autonomy, Individuality, and the Self in Western Thought*. Stanford, CA: Stanford University Press. pp. 222–36.

Huyssen, A. (1984) 'Mapping the postmodern', *New German Critique*, 33, Fall: 5–52.

Jameson, F. (1984) 'The politics of theory: ideological positions in the postmodernism debate', *New German Critique*, 33, Fall: 52–66.

Johnstone, C.L. (1980) 'An Aristotelian trilogy: ethnics, politics, and the search for moral truth', *Philosophy and Rhetoric*, 13 (1), Winter: 1–24.

Kahn, H. and Wiener, A.J. (1967) *The Year 2000: a Framework for Speculation on the Next Thirty-three Years*. New York: Macmillan.

Kellner, D. (1988) 'Postmodernism as social theory: some challenges and problems', *Theory, Culture & Society*, 5 (2–3): 329–70.

Knorr-Cetina, K. and Mulkay, M. (1983) 'Introduction: emerging principles in the social study of science', in K. Knorr-Cetina and M. Mulkay (eds), *Science Observed: Perspectives on the Social Study of Science*. Beverly Hills, CA: Sage. pp. 1–18.

Krugman, P. (1991) *The Age of Diminished Expectations: US Economic Policy in the 1990s*. Cambridge, MA: MIT Press.

LaCapra, D. (1987) 'Criticism Today', in M. Krieger (ed.), *The Aims of Representation: Subject/Text/History*. New York: Columbia University Press. pp. 235–55.

Lentricchia, F. (1983) *Criticism and Social Change*. Chicago, IL: University of Chicago Press.

Lukács, G. (1981) *The Destruction of Reason*, Vol. 3. P. Palmer, trans. Atlantic Highlands, NJ: Humanities Press.

Lyotard, J.F. (1983) *La Differend*. Paris: Éditions de Minuit.
Lyotard, J.F. (1984) *The Postmodern Condition: a Report on Knowledge*. G. Bennington and B. Massumi, trans. Minneapolis: University of Minnesota Press.
Lyotard, J.F. (1985) *Just Gaming*. W. Godzich, trans. Minneapolis: University of Minnesota Press.
MacIntyre, A. (1980) 'Epistemological crisis, dramatic narrative, and the philosophy of science', in G. Nutting (ed.), *Paradigms and Revolutions*. Notre Dame, IN: University of Notre Dame Press.
MacIntyre, A. (1981) *After Virtue: a Study in Moral Theory*. Notre Dame, IN: University of Notre Dame Press.
MacIntyre, A. (1988) *Whose Justice? Which Rationality?* Notre Dame, IN: University of Notre Dame Press.
Miller, J.H. (1982) 'The function of rhetorical study at the present time', in *Teaching Literature: What is Needed Now*. Cambridge, MA: Harvard University Press.
Mitchell, T.J. (1982) 'Critical inquiry and the ideology of pluralism', *Critical Inquiry*, 8 (3), Summer: 604–18.
Montrose, L.A. (1989) 'Professing the renaissance: the poetics and politics of culture', in H.A. Veesen (ed.), *The New Historicism*. New York: Routledge. pp. 15–36.
Mortley, R. (1991) *French Philosophers in Conversation: Derrida, Levinas, Schneider, Serres, Irigaray, LeDoeuff*. London: Routledge.
Peters, J.D. (1990) 'Rhetoric's revival, positivism's persistence: social science, clear communication, and the public space', *Sociological Theory*, 8 (2), special issue: R. H. Brown (ed.), *The Postmodern Turn in Sociological Theory*: 224–31.
Rabinow, P. (1986) 'Representations are social facts: modernity and postmodernity in anthropology', in J. Clifford and G. Marcus (eds), *Writing Culture: the Poetics and Politics of Ethnography*. Berkeley: University of California Press. pp. 194–233.
Redding, P. (1986) 'Habermas, Lyotard, Wittgenstein: philosophy at the limits of modernity', *Thesis Eleven*, 14: 9–25.
Ricoeur, P. (1980) 'Existence and hermeneutics', K. McLaughlin, trans, in J. Bleicher (ed.), *Contemporary Hermeneutics: Hermeneutics as Method, Philosophy and Critique*. London: Routledge and Kegan Paul.
Ricoeur, P. (1983) *Time and Narrative*, Vol. 1. K. McLaughlin and D. Pellaner, trans. Chicago, IL: University of Chicago Press.
Ricoeur, P. (1986) *Lectures on Ideology and Utopia*. G.H. Taylor ed. and trans. New York: Columbia University Press.
Rorty, R. (1979) *Philosophy and the Mirror of Nature*. Princeton, NJ: Princeton University Press.
Rorty, R. (1982) *Consequences of Pragmatism*. Minneapolis: University of Minnesota Press.
Rorty, R. (1985) 'Habermas and Lyotard on postmodernity', in R.J. Bernstein (ed.), *Habermas and Modernity*. Cambridge, MA: MIT Press. pp 161–76.
Rouse, J. (1987) *Knowledge and Power: Toward a Political Philosophy of Science*. Ithaca, NY: Cornell University Press.
Schutz, A. (1964) *Collected Papers II: Studies in Social Theory*. A. Broadersen (ed.). The Hague: Nijhoff.
Shapiro, M.J. (1988) *The Politics of Representation: Writing Practices and Biography, Photography, and Policy Analysis*. Madison: University of Wisconsin Press.
Woolgar, S. (1983) 'Irony in the social study of science', in K.D. Knorr-Cetina and M. Mulkay (eds), *Science Observed: Perspectives on the Social Study of Science*. Beverly Hills, CA: Sage. pp. 239–66.

2

Evading the Subject:
the Poverty of Contingency Theory

Steven E. Cole

The rejection of normative argument in contemporary cultural theory has generally been seen as the consequence of an awareness of the intractable contingency of experience. Indeed, what stands behind the oppositional political agenda which now defines current discussion of personal and social identity is a widespread belief that an appeal to contingency (or, more accurately, an exposure of the omnipresence of contingency) can be tied directly to a political resistance to dominant forms of oppression, the assumption being that the self-evident oppositional power of contingency can stand as the basis of nuanced accounts of how contingency can itself undermine pretensions to power and authority.[1] What follows from such an assumption at the level of discourse is an intractable suspicion towards any discussion which seems to rely upon the now discarded resources of a philosophical tradition determined by what Christopher Norris calls 'the quest for epistemological certitude, for a truth not merely "good in the way of belief" but good for all time and all possible modes of experience' (1985: 142). A consequence of what I want to call contingency theory is the belief that discourse should itself be motivated by strategic interests and should thus frame its discussions in terms of pragmatic questions about the local effectiveness of particular kinds of argument.[2] Analysis of the logical coherence of an argument is accordingly a discarded relic of the 'quest for epistemological certitude', and what remains is finally gossip writ large: an infinitely proliferating intertextuality that has as its object the exposure of the minute dependencies and evasions which determine the relations among particular discourses.

An unintended virtue of recent arguments in defence of contingency theory by Stanley Fish (1989), Barbara Herrnstein Smith (1988) and Richard Rorty (1989) is that each holds open the possibility of precisely the kind of analysis which is precluded if contingency theory is itself accepted as the basis of discourse. By insisting both on the possibility of public argument about the nature of the subject, and on the ultimate contingency of the subject which such argument seeks to define, these writers unintentionally expose the incoherence of contingency theory when it is understood as a publicly accessible argument about the nature of identity. That the very notion of publicly accessible argument draws upon the resources of the discarded 'quest for certainty' which contingency theory seeks to surmount is unimportant here: what matters is that it is precisely the impossibility of offering a coherent *public* account of the contingent subject which will expose the confusions attendant upon the claim of contingency theory that it is possible to derive an account of political and social interests from a contingently defined subject.

My central argument is that far from it being the case that we now know the contingency of our own subjectivity, in fact this claim is both logically deluded and pragmatically disastrous. From both perspectives, what we will find is that the implicit claim of contingency theory that knowledge and value are reducible to privately defined interests will help to show the emptiness of the theory itself; the denial that ends have anything more than a contingent relation to the interests and desires of a subject leaves contingency theory unable to account for the very existence of the subject to which it appeals in its account of contingency. From a logical perspective, contingency theory makes sense only if subjects are privately constituted sets of interest who stand intractably outside any further description, but, as we shall see, such an account of the subject could not be true for anyone other than one's self. It is simply not coherent to claim both that all knowledge and value are reducible to the contingent interests of a subject, and that one knows that this is the case for all subjects, for such knowledge would be possible only if the claim were itself not true. To see this, consider how odd it would be to claim that one has contingently produced certainty of what is always the case for other subjects: contingency and universal certainty simply can't be yoked together in this way. This logical difficulty might be evaded by claiming that what is at stake is less an ontology of the subject than a pragmatic description of what sorts of interests might be sustained by a given form of subjectivity; what would be required here is a description of what subjectivity would be like if social experience were constituted in such a way that subjects were believed to be (or regarded as) nothing more than a privately defined bundle of interests, regardless of whether that was in fact all that they could be. But such an assessment would then need to explain its own interest in describing subjectivity in this way, and as soon as the possibility of such description was granted, the appeal to privately defined contingency would necessarily fail, since what is at issue is precisely the social status of those private contingencies. Paradoxically, the very privacy of subjectivity which is demanded by the logic of contingency theory becomes impossible if contingency theory takes seriously the social consequences of its position, for as soon as some form of social identity is granted, then the claim that identity is reducible to contingency becomes impossible to sustain without reducing the social itself to privately defined contingencies. Accordingly, my aim here will be to show not merely that the account of the subject presupposed by contingency theory is logically incoherent as an ontology of the self; I also want to show that as social description, the minimalist definition of the subject results in a world which is so impoverished that it quite literally can be the basis of nothing that we would want to do or say.

Stanley fish and the Situational Subject

Few contemporary critics would reject more vehemently than Stanley Fish the idea that subjectivity is in any important sense private. Indeed, a central target of *Doing What Comes Naturally* is how agency is understood within what Fish calls 'left critical theory', roughly the claim that 'the insight that the present order of things is neither natural nor inevitable is itself an indication that the totalizing claims of that order can be resisted' (1989: 447). Fish argues that this conclusion is mistaken because it appeals to an absence of constraint which is completely at odds with what it means to be a subject:

> the degree of constraint – at least in relation to an ideal condition of freedom – is always the same and always total. By this I do not mean that we are never free to act, but that our freedom is a function of – in the sense of being dependent on – some other structure of constraint without which action of any kind would be impossible. (p. 459)

For Fish, constraint is omnipresent in the sense that simply to be an agent, to be a subject, is to be constrained by the forces which constitute one's identity *as* agent or subject: 'anti-foundationalism . . . is an argument for the situated subject, for the individual who is always constrained by the local or community standards and criteria of which his judgment is an extension' (p.323). Since he clearly here repudiates the very idea than an individual might exist outside the public constituents of his or her identity, it might seem perverse to suggest that Fish's account of social practice entails an essentially private notion of the subject. However, as I trust we shall see, Fish's position is hopelessly confused: the 'situated subject' constrained by public meaning which he describes is precisely what cannot occur within practices as Fish describes them.

Repeatedly, Fish defines practices as a set of rules or procedures which are the conditions of intelligibility for anything we might claim to know, and he argues that these rules and procedures are embedded in the very act of knowing:

> the lesson of anti-foundationalism is not only that external and independent guides will never be found but that it is unnecessary to seek them, because you will always be guided by the rules or rules of thumb that are the content of any settled practice, by the assumed definitions, distinctions, criteria of evidence, measures of adequacy, and such, which not only define the practice but structure the understanding of the agent who thinks of himself as a 'competent member'. That agent cannot distance himself from these rules, because it is only within them that he can think about alternative courses of action or, indeed, think at all. (p. 323)[3]

At the heart of Fish's argument here is the claim that traditional accounts of knowledge and value have been vitiated by their acceptance of distinctions between what he variously calls the indeterminate and the determinate, the uninterpreted and the interpreted, and the given and the conventional. Fish's claim is that in each of these pairs, the putative ontology of the first term can be exposed as a chimera by showing its derivation from, or evasion of, the constitutive power of the second. Thus, the determinate, the interpreted and the conventional all designate a kind of knowledge or value which emerges from within varying practices, and which cannot be identified independently of those practices:

> there is no subjectivist element of reading because the observer is never individual in the sense of unique or private, but is always the product of the categories of understanding that are his by virtue of his membership in a community of interpretation. It follows, then, that what our experience in turn produces is not open or free, but determinate, constrained by the possibilities that are built into a conventional system of intelligibility. Earlier I concluded that the distinction between what is given and what is supplied won't hold up because everything is supplied, both the determinate and the indeterminate poles of the 'aesthetic object'; now I am arguing that the same distinction won't hold because everything is given. There is no paradox here. It is just that 'supplied' and 'given' will only make sense as fundamental categories of classification if the entities to which they refer are pure, if, at some level, we can speak meaningfully of a text that is simply there, waiting for a reader who is, at least potentially, wholly free. (p. 83)

What we can see here is that Fish's account of practices is designed to preclude any appeal to some entity which stands outside our activity as mediated subjects; Fish wants to argue that our ability to construe such an entity presupposes the very practices which the entity was assumed to stand outside of, and he argues further that practices themselves require no further identification in that such identification would itself be enabled by, and thus part of, the practice which it sought to identify. There is, in Fish, no transcendental perspective which allows further precision about what it means to be engaged in a practice, in part because he would deny Kant's distinction between the transcendent and the transcendental:[4] in both cases, the search for a determinant outside of practices themselves must fail, since that search presupposes an access to determinants independent of practices, while it is in fact practices themselves which determine determinants. There is nothing outside of practices which can be appealed to as the ground of what practices allow us to know, since it is only *through* practices that we know anything at all.

We began by considering Fish's claim that 'anti-foundationalism . . . is an argument for the situated subject' (p. 323), but we are now in a position to see that the very description of practices makes it impossible to explain what it might mean to *be situated*. A standard argument against the situated subject is the sceptical denial that subjects have any real relation to the world which they experience, and Fish's central assertion is that this sceptical denial is unreal because it is grounded in an assumption about the possibility or even the necessity of getting outside of a practice while failing to recognize that that very assumption is itself the consequence of a practice, and thus a necessary part of that which it wants to question.[5] Scepticism would be coherent only if the sceptic could find a way of expressing doubt which did not presuppose the existence of that which the sceptic wants to question. The relation the sceptic wants to question about the inside and the outside of knowledge is inconceivable because there is no outside that is not presupposed by the inside. But the obvious question is why the denial that a distinction can be drawn between the inside and the outside of a given practice (a denial which we have seen makes it impossible to reflect upon what constitutes a practice itself) is not extended to the relations of an individual to a given practice. For the very argument that the sceptic is deluded in claiming that he or she can express what it means to be outside of a practice makes sense only if literally everything that the sceptic said counted as evidence for the existence of a practice. But it would then follow from this that any individual's questions about whether he or she were situated in a practice has a similarly circular answer: the question itself presupposes the answer being sought. But the problem here is that just as I have no way of knowing what constitutes a given practice (since such knowledge would itself have to be constituted by a practice), so I have no way of knowing whether my belief that I am engaged in a practice is anything more than a description of privately defined interests and purposes which were only illusorily being claimed to have a public determination. What would prevent such a reduction of public meaning to private desire is some way of explaining why such meaning neither presupposes, nor is reducible to, such desire, but such an explanation would require the very distinction between the act of knowing and what is known which the argument against scepticism denied. Fish's argument thus entwines him on the horns of a dilemma: the very defence of practices as constitutive of both knowledge and the known presupposes an indeterminacy of apprehension which, if granted, would vitiate the possibility of identifying the very object which is being defended. What would allow us to know that we are situated within practices is fundamentally the same as what would allow us to know what practices are *about*: in both cases, a distinction is required between the act of knowing and the object of knowledge. Crucially, if this distinction is denied, then the situated subject becomes an impossibility, for what we might call the locus of the idealist claim that we can know nothing but our own creations is finally the private self, for it is only there (but where?) that an argument against externality can be located.

As Thomas Nagel (1986: 54–66) has shown, a fundamental fact of where we are in the world is that we are able to understand ourselves as both subject and object of what we understand, and there is finally no limitation to the oscillation between these points of view. Insofar as we are part of the world, we are absolutely constrained, and Fish is right to point out that it is the very absoluteness of that constraint which makes it somehow beside the point to ask of our involvement in the world, 'How are we constrained?' But the very fact that we have a knowledge of that involvement points to a question about our relation to the world which Fish's description of practices cannot account for. If nothing constrains us because everything is part of a practice, then the subject of those practices has no reason to ask questions about how it is related to those practices, and the clear implication here is that if nothing the subject does or thinks raises problems about the objects of that doing or thinking, then the subject itself is absolutely unconditioned since the conditions of its experience are transparently connected with what it does or thinks. Fish wants to claim that the description of practices presupposes a social subject, but what Nagel allows us to see is that the social view of the subject makes sense only if the subject has the possibility of not being social. What makes our questions about where we are in the world urgent is both that the answers are not obvious, and that there are consequences to the answers we come up with. A Fishian subject has no capacity to reflect upon the relations of its interests to the world, precisely because those interests are transparently a part of the world. But if the world and the subject are inextricable, then nothing can be said about the relation of particular subjects to the world, nor can anything be said about the different kinds of positions subjects might have within the world. Ethics and politics presuppose the possibility of saying something about what a subject is, and where a subject is located, and accordingly it is perfectly fair to attack Fish for leaving ethical and political questions as either unanswerable, or as already answered. Why are things as they are? Ethical or political discourse assumes that we can answer this question only if we can stand outside of how things are; Fish's Leibnizian response would have to be that things are as they are because they are the consequence of practices which are only and always sufficient, and which accordingly not only do not require, but positively preclude, any further reason.

Richard Rorty and the Ironized Subject

Fish's polemic against theory is motivated by the claim that 'doing what comes naturally' is sufficient for our experience of the world. I have argued that this claim makes sense only if subjects are essentially private, and I have tried to show that, despite his own assertions, such is the view of the subject which Fish in fact holds. I have also suggested that contingency theory's view of the subject leaves it unable to offer anything like an account of ethical or political experience, and I would now like to examine this issue more closely. My specific focus will be how Richard Rorty and Barbara Herrnstein Smith try to account for political and ethical discourse within a general description of beliefs as contingently determined by private interests. Rorty and Smith are unapologetic in insisting that our experience is indeed constituted by private interests; thus, while they share with Fish a belief that we have no foundations for our claims about the world, they reject his idea that social practice can in some sense serve as a substitute for foundations. Instead, they argue for precisely the private subject which I have tried to show is presupposed by Fish's account of practices: we have, finally, nothing but our own beliefs to go on in the world, and when we try to find something more, we are thrown back on the very contingency of self which we sought to deny. But they also argue that there is nothing fatal in the position for ethical and political argument; rather, their claim is that as we learn to locate our ethical and political beliefs within the contingent self, we will come to see that ethics and politics require nothing more. Accordingly, what I now want to explore is whether contingency theory's account of the subject can be successful in explaining how, in the absence of a public determination of ethical and political experience, we can still make claims about the shape our shared experience should take.

For Rorty, the heart of the problem here is how we should conceive the public demands upon an essentially private subject. Building upon his critique of foundationalism in his earlier work, Rorty argues that there is no possibility for supplying grounds for any of the claims we might want to make about social experience.[6] There can be, according to Rorty, no argument for, no theorizing about, a *public* subject, for such argument or theorizing would have to rely upon what are finally circular claims about what constitutes a good society:

> For liberal ironists, there is no answer to the question 'Why not be cruel?' no noncircular theoretical backup for the belief that cruelty is horrible. Nor is there any answer to the question 'How do you decide when to struggle against injustice and when to devote yourself to private projects of self-creation?' This question strikes liberal ironists as just as hopeless as the questions 'Is it right to deliver n innocents over to be tortured to save the lives of $m \times n$ other innocents? If so, what are the correct values of n and m?' or the question, 'When may one favor members of one's family, or one's community, over other, randomly chosen, human beings?' Anybody who thinks that there are well-grounded theoretical answers to this sort of question – algorithms for resolving moral dilemmas of this sort – is still, in his heart, a theologian or a metaphysician. He believes in an order beyond time and change which both determines the point of human existence and establishes a hierarchy of responsibilities. (1989: xv)

What we can see here is that for Rorty, theoretical argument grows out of an unwarranted demand for certainty, and what exposes such a demand as unwarranted is the inevitable circularity of its deepest claims. Rorty's 'liberal ironist' has the courage both to acknowledge such circularity, and yet continue to insist as well that 'cruelty is the worst thing that we do' (p. xv). Further, the recognition that there is indeed a 'worst thing that we do' has consequences for how one construes experience: 'Liberal ironists are people who include among their ungroundable desires their own hope that suffering will be diminished, that the humiliation of human beings by other human beings may cease' (p. xv).

In considering Rorty's defence of the 'liberal ironist', we should begin by noting his general claim that our enunciations of the public dimensions of experience should be severely limited since any conflict they would seem to produce between what is being enunciated and the subjects of that enunciation cannot be legitimately adjudicated. Rorty wants to insist that even contingent selves have public dimensions to their experience, but he wants also to argue that nothing about such a public dimension can interfere with, or conflict with, those private contingencies which finally determine who and what we are. We need, then, a public rhetoric of 'solidarity', but such rhetoric is grounded in nothing more than a contingently produced certainty that cruelty and humiliation should not be features of experience:

> The right way to take the slogan 'We have obligations to human beings simply as such' is as a means of reminding ourselves to keep trying to expand our sense of 'us' as far as we can. . . . The right way to construe the slogan is as urging us to *create* a more expansive sense of solidarity than we presently have. The wrong way is to think of it as urging us to *recognize* such a solidarity, as something that exists antecedently to our recognition of it. (p. 196)

We can see here that solidarity, for Rorty, is a sort of minimal universalism, which is defensible because its putative universal force is nothing more than an extension of what are demonstrably contingent interests, and the ethical position that 'cruelty is the worst thing that we do' is defensible because it offers the only plausible content of solidarity.

Crucially, then, the subject's relation to solidarity succeeds only so long as the demands of solidarity are themselves both transparent and minimal: the subject's construal of its relation to other subjects must result from a shared identity whose basis can only be a pre-reflective consensus about what is to count as cruelty. If solidarity emerges from any stronger sense of identity, any sense of identity, that is, which is determined by reflection, then the very 'self-creation' which Rorty wants to insist has no relation to public experience must become part of that which determines solidarity, since 'self-creation' has been defined by Rorty as that which allows a movement beyond the pre-reflective. The question, then, is whether it is possible to demand that theoretical reflection be limited to 'self-creation', while also arguing that we have an obligation to '*create* a more expansive sense of solidarity than we presently have' (Rorty, 1989: 196). The obvious problem is that the very demand that solidarity be *created* seems to blur the distinction between the public and the private upon which the appeal to solidarity is based. However, the distinction will indeed hold if what is being created is not the particular content which defines solidarity

– the avoidance of cruelty – but rather the extension of that particular content to a wider and wider range of experience. For here, what would be *created* is not any particular self, but rather the *relations* of selves defined by their avoidance of cruelty, and by nothing else.

What solidarity requires, accordingly, is a definition of our relation to cruelty which would allow a potentially universal description of the relations we have to the subjects of that cruelty, but without any demand that those relations be determined by anything more than a shared understanding of what counts as cruelty. Solidarity, on Rorty's view, seems possible only if the extension of its content requires nothing more than a pre-reflective assent to that extension, for if something more than pre-reflective assent were demanded, then the distinction between the public and the private upon which solidarity is itself defined would collapse, since *reflection* has itself been defined by Rorty as private theorizing which has no public extension. Consider, then, two rather different examples of how we might respond to cruelty:

> I do not think that we liberals *can* now imagine a future of 'human dignity, freedom and peace'. . . . We have to take as a starting point the world Orwell showed us in 1948: a globe divided into a rich, free, democratic, selfish and greedy First World; an unchanging Second World run by an impregnable and ruthless Inner Party; and a starving, overpopulated, desperate Third World. . . . This inability to imagine how to get from here to there is a matter neither of loss or moral resolve nor of theoretical superficiality, self-deception, or self-betrayal. . . . It is just the way things happen to have fallen out. (1989: 182)

> Consider . . . the attitude of contemporary American liberals to the unending hopelessness and misery of the lives of the young blacks in American cities. Do we say these people may be helped because they are our fellow human beings? We may, but it is much more persuasive, morally as well as politically, to describe them as our fellow *Americans* – to insist that it is outrageous that an *American* should live without hope. The point . . . is that our sense of solidarity is strongest when those with whom solidarity is expressed are thought of as 'one of us', where 'us' means something smaller and more local than the human race. (1989: 191)

What seems most obvious from these examples is that the injunction to avoid cruelty is itself severely limited by the insistence that our *apprehension* of cruelty be linked to the possibility of a solidarity which is itself nothing more than a contingent feature of shared experience. Thus, while wide-scale oppression may seem a clear example of cruelty, because we have no possible sense of solidarity with such a wide array of possible subjects, other than the discredited claim that we share an essential identity with those subjects, we are limited to seeing such oppression as 'just the way things happen to have fallen out'. On the other hand, the cruelty of racism apparently does allow solidarity, and while Rorty doesn't explain why, the reason would seem to be that we have a capacity to *identify* with the victims of racism, to describe them in shared terms which would then make impossible the distinctions upon which racism is based. Further, such identity is possible because it has nothing to do with *private* experience; solidarity is possible because the relations which it describes are accessible independently of our private determinations of who we are. But this apparent distinction between forms of cruelty which allow an impersonal solidarity and those which do not falls apart as soon as we put pressure on what it means to *apprehend* the cruelty of racism itself. For the real distinction between, on the one hand, granting that pervasive cruelty is 'just the way things happen to have fallen out', and, on the other hand, insisting that we should regard victims of racism as 'one of us', is between differing ways of relating public determinations of identity to ethical claims about experience, and what distinguishes the two examples of cruelty is finally nothing more than whether a given context of putative cruelty (an instantiation, that is, of our deepest ethical beliefs) can be connected with a public description of identity. Thus, the issue is formulated wrongly if it is seen as a dispute over the extension of solidarity, for what is instead at issue is precisely whether solidarity itself best describes the public identity necessary for cruelty to be minimized. But if the issue is how public identity might be formulated, if solidarity ceases to function as an intuitively obvious given of shared identity, then the distinction between the public and private can no longer be sustained, since what we now need is precisely the capacity to *reflect* upon, to *theorize* about, the public and private dimensions of our identity, and the way the distinction was initially formulated left us powerless to do this. Further, if theory and reflection are now seen as necessarily a part of our apprehension of public identity, then we no longer have a pre-reflective way of distinguishing between those parts of our identity which are public and those which are private; rather, both public and private are forms of identity which can be understood only as we reflect upon the relations of those forms to the ethical and political shape we believe experience should take.

Thus, what I think we can conclude is that the minimal public self works for ethics only as long as the demands of ethics are themselves both minimal and transparent – but as soon as that transparency is denied, as soon as we work towards descriptions of our relations to the social contexts which we might describe as cruel but which seem not to have a transparent relation to our own identity, then we discover that it is precisely our identity which must be determined. The very apprehension of such contexts presupposes a conception of the subject as situated within mutually determining first person and third person descriptions of its identity such that neither a simple first person (irony/theory/autonomy) nor a simple third person (solidarity) description suffices. Rather, as Rorty's own examples indicate, our apprehension of cruelty will always presuppose the location of our identity within a complex mix of third person complicity and first person judgement, and the reason for this is that only such a mix allows both our ability to apprehend cruelty, and our certainty that what we are apprehending is something more than a projection of our own contingency.

I noted earlier that Rorty's derisive dismissal of what he calls 'algorithms for solving moral dilemmas' seemed to me to be a straw man, and what we have now seen is that what makes such a dismissal empty is that it is premised upon an opposition between an absolute grounding of our beliefs and an inescapably contingent private self which cannot be sustained as soon as we try to locate that self in the world. Indeed, Rorty's position is finally incoherent because he is unable to commit himself to the implications of believing that we have nothing more than our own contingency. Barbara Herrnstein Smith is, however, committed to precisely such a view, and I think we can see in her defence of that view both the absurdity on which it is based, and the emptiness to which it leads. For while Smith, like Fish and Rorty, denies that a consequence of her position is a private subject incapable of offering an explanation of its relations to the world, in fact her argument moves towards precisely such a view of the subject, and it does so because the very way in which the contingency of experience is characterized precludes any public description of the subject which is not finally reducible to privately determined interests, Indeed, what is perhaps most puzzling about Smith's argument is her denial that she views value as 'personally whimsical, locked into the consciousness of individual subjects' (1988: 11), for, as we shall see, it is precisely such a view of the subject as standing outside public description which produces the claim that all value is contingent.

Barbara Herrnstein Smith and the Contingent Subject

The centre of Smith's argument is the claim that traditional accounts of value and meaning have failed because of their reliance upon what she calls the 'axiological account of the phenomena of human preferences' (1988: 54), an account whose central feature is its reliance upon what she calls an '*asymmetrical explanation* of preferences' in which

> intrinsic qualities of objects plus universal, underlying principles of human nature are invoked to explain stability and convergence; historical accident and error and the defects and imperfections of individual subjects are invoked to explain their divergence and mutability – and also, thereby, to explain the failure of the universal principles to operate universally. (p. 61)

The idea here is that the 'axiological account' can be shown to be a failure by revealing its contradictory appeal to both universality and contingency; because the 'axiological argument' is forced to admit the very contingencies which its appeal to universals would deny, its own argument is 'ultimately self-canceling' (p. 54). Further, since the 'axiological account' is presumably the sole alternative to understanding value and identity as contingent, the critique of that account is also a compelling argument for contingency: in the absence of transcendent universals, what else is there?

While Smith's general account of traditional philosophy seems to me to be woefully simplistic,[7] I want for a moment to grant her argument about the failure of the 'axiological account', in order to see what a non-axiological explanation of value and identity would look like. For Smith, the central feature of such a contingent explanation would be its refusal to appeal to anything other than contingent interests in its explanation of what counts as value. Thus, while the 'axiological account' wants to insist that there are universal or transcendent principles governing our construal of value, Smith argues instead that 'all value is . . . the product of the dynamics of a system, specifically an *economic* system' (p. 30). While we might assume that what would follow from this is an analysis of the particular kind of economy which produces the values in which Smith is interested, instead the discussion immediately moves to what she calls the 'personal economy constituted by the subject's needs, interests and resources' (p. 30), and the general claim is that because 'a subject's experience of an entity is always a function of his or her personal economy' (p. 31), any assertion that a particular entity serves as a value must be limited to the particular personal economy in relation to which the entity is perceived as having value. There can be, from such a perspective, no public values whose origin is not a personal economy, and thus all value is contingent in the sense that its *public* force is a mere accidental consequence of private interests. For Smith, any attempt to characterize an impersonal or intersubjective realm which might have priority over private interests is deluded because it fails to see that the impersonal or the intersubjective are merely contingent extensions of personal economies; further, Smith argues that such extensions, insofar as they would seek to surmount or deny their economic underpinnings, are simply unnecessary for anything we might want from the world. Thus, she ridicules Habermas's notion of an ideal of free communication, arguing that such an ideal seeks unnecessarily to retreat from the very contingency which defines human experience:

> The image of a type of communication that excludes all strategy, instrumentality, (self-)interest, and, above all, the profit motive, reflects what appears to be a more general recurrent impulse to dream an escape from economy, to imagine some special type, realm, or mode of value that is beyond economic accounting, to create by invocation some place apart from the marketplace – a kingdom, garden, or island, perhaps, or a plane of consciousness, form of social relationship, or stage of human development – where the dynamics of economy are, or once were, or someday will be, altogether suspended, abolished, or reversed . . . it is understandable that the dream of an escape from economy should be so sweet and the longing for it so pervasive and recurrent. Since it does appear to be inescapable, however, the better (that is, more effective, more profitable) alternative would seem to be not to seek to go beyond economy but to do the best we can going *through* it. (p. 112)[8]

What we can see here is that for Smith, the subject defined by its contingent interests is not merely the 'inescapable' consequence of an omnipresent economic determination of identity, it is also sufficient for the pursuit of whatever we might want the world to be. While we might note how conveniently the two arguments support each other – my identity is contingent because it is determined economically, while I have only an economic conception of who I am because my identity is contingent – what seems more important is the question of whether it is genuinely the case that any impersonal identity is a fantasy.

We can begin to answer this question by considering whether our only way of characterizing the impersonal or the intersubjective is to appeal to transcendent universals which stand outside contingent experience. Smith, of course, insists on the impossibility of describing experience from anything other than personal contingency, and thus denies that we have any access to the impersonal or the intersubjective, but her own argument indicates the difficulty of maintaining this perspective. For example, she concludes a critique of the idea that 'shared objective standards' should form the basis of a community, arguing instead that

> the well-being of any community is also a function of other and indeed opposed conditions, including the extent of the *diversity* of the beliefs and practices of its members and thus their communal resourcefulness,

> and the *flexibility* of its norms and patterns and thus their responsiveness
> to changing and emerging circumstances. (p. 93)

While there is little to object to in such a view of the 'well-being of any community', what is inconceivable is that an argument for such well-being could emerge from any description of the private economies of individuals. Rather, what Smith has described is an *ideal* of shared identity which could be defended only by assuming that identity is itself socially determined.

To see this, consider what would define 'beliefs' as 'diverse' or 'norms and patterns' as 'flexible': in each case, what seems to be an appeal to a diverse array of private subjects can in fact be seen as an *assessment* of subjects in terms of their relation to a common good. For what would define a belief as instantiating a social good, diversity, is not the relation of that belief to a privately determined economy of contingent interests, but rather the degree to which the belief did or did not contribute to the good itself. Thus, the description of the 'well-being of any community' presupposes the possibility of the very social determination of identity which the description of a 'personal economy' was intended to deny, for what is now being granted is that while private subjects may well have beliefs which conflict with a community's well-being, in relation to that community such beliefs are not to be judged as evidence for privacy, but rather as preventing that which the community itself requires. The issue gets even more complicated when we try to imagine arguments for why certain beliefs which contribute to the community's well-being should be encouraged, while others which threaten that well-being should somehow be blocked. Such an argument could never even begin if the 'personal economy' model of beliefs were accepted, for that model simply precludes any description of the relation of a belief to a community good. But without such argument, we would be placed in the curious position of knowing what array of beliefs would count as the good of our community, without being able to argue *for* those beliefs because we regard any and all beliefs as simply contingent concerns of private subjects.

My argument has been that the contingent subject has no way of explaining its relation to the world, and I have further argued that such an explanation is necessary if we grant that our identities are in any sense tied to the world (say, by appealing to the 'well-being of any community'). With this in mind, consider Smith's own description of the community she imagines growing out of her account of contingency:

Since the relativist knows that the conjoined systems (biological, ideological, institutional, and so forth) of which her general conceptual taste and specific conceptualization of the world are a contingent function are probably not altogether unique, she expects some other people to conceptualize the world in more or less the same ways she does and, like her, to find objectivist conceptualizations more or less cognitively distasteful, unsatisfactory, and irritating along more or less similar lines. She may have found it worth her while to seek out such fellow relativists, to promote conditions that encourage their emergence, and where she has had the resources, to attempt to cultivate a few of them herself: 'worth her while' because, since she cannot herself live any other way, she's glad for a bit of company. (pp. 183–4)

I've already indicated what is wrong with believing that the 'world' has no more force over one's identity than as the raw material for one's contingent 'conceptualization', but I want now to point to the *smugness* of such a view of the world. Nothing about the 'world' poses any threat to the relativist, and no part of the relativist's identity has any determining contact with the 'world'. The relativist needs nothing more than a modest 'hope' that she will find what she seeks, not because her hopes are themselves so modest, but because her relation to the world is so comfortable. There is, of course, nothing inherently wrong about having a comfortable relation to the world, but what is puzzling is why such a transparently self-interested position has been offered as a prescription for the *public* interests of academics, for surely what Smith's position cannot explain is why the performance of such comfortable self-interest should be perceived as a public good. Indeed, Smith's arguments would seem to lead to the conclusion that contingency theory contributes only to the interests of those whose own identity (contingent or otherwise) is so comfortably situated that questions about the public status of that identity are somehow an act of bad taste.

Conclusion

Implicit in much of recent critical and cultural theory has been the belief that the defence of contingency can be tied to a more general articulation of the interests of the oppressed. In arguing against this belief, I have tried to show how contingency theory leads inevitably to a notion of the subject as *essentially* private, and I have tried to indicate that such privacy serves the interests only of those for whom the world functions largely as an extension of comfortable self-interest. What contingency theory precludes is any *public* description of the world, but such a description is presupposed by any critical or cultural theory which seeks to move beyond self-interest to a consideration of the political and social determinants of identity. As Nancy Fraser has argued, in showing how political and social argument might address a realm of 'needs' traditionally consigned to the merely private, 'the best need interpretations are those reached by means of communicative processes that most closely approximate ideals of democracy, equality, and fairness' (1989: 282). Implicit here is the cogency of Habermas's claim that the very possibility of communication presupposes the existence of norms which are the basis of a subject's articulation of its interests and needs. For Fraser, the interpretation of need is itself made possible by the existence of 'communicative processes' which are the frame from within which interests and needs can be seen as having public significance. Indeed, for Fraser, 'interpretation' is a process of argument, a form of contestation, about how putatively private interests or needs might command public attention, and 'communicative processes' are for her the intersubjective form which allows such argument or contestation to take place. Further, such a process of *contest* about how social experience might be changed to meet those needs which require public mediation can take place only in the context of ideals or norms – what gives 'democracy, equality, and fairness' their value is not their status as universals, but rather their function as norms which allow the public articulation of precisely those needs which, in the absence of such norms, are either denied or dismissed as merely private.

Where contingency theory argues that interpretations of the world devolve to the projections of an isolated subject, Fraser instead indicates how communicative processes constitute a public space which makes possible the articulation of an intersubjective world. As Donald Davidson has argued, the 'I' defined in relation to its own contingency has no access to such an articulation:

> If I were bolted to the earth I would have no way of determining the distance from me of many objects. . . . Not being bolted down, I am free to triangulate. Our sense of objectivity is the consequence of another sort of triangulation, one that requires two creatures. Each interacts with an object, but what gives each the concept of the way things are objectively is the base line formed between the creatures by language. The fact that they share a concept of truth alone makes sense of the claim that they have beliefs, that they are able to assign objects a place in the public world.[9] (1982: 327)

From this perspective, the contest over norms and needs described by Fraser is itself made possible by the role which language plays in allowing the pursuit of objectivity, the pursuit, that is, of a world that we can share. The denial that such a contest is possible (the insistence that all linguistically articulated norms devolve into private contingencies) is the denial that such a world can be had, but since the world will continue no matter what we do, the only issue is whether it is worth pursuing some knowledge of where we are, and where we might be. A central premise of recent literary theory has been that our theoretical accounts of literature, and finally of culture, help us to know where our values are located (and why they aren't located where we want them to be); contingency theory, if its arguments are examined closely, wants to deny that this is worth doing, and proposes instead that we simply accept things as they are. I have tried to show that the basis of this quiescence is the belief that our claims about the world are based upon nothing more than what Rorty calls an 'ungroundable desire', and I want to end by pointing out that there is no reason, *in theory*, for believing that this is true.

Notes

I would like to thank Daniel O'Hara for his suggestions on how to revise an earlier draft of this paper. This essay was written while I was on leave with a Fellowship for Recent Recipients of the PhD awarded by the American Council of Learned Societies, and I gratefully acknowledge their assistance.

  1. Thus Paul Smith, in a discussion of mail-order catalogues, argues that 'the heterogeneity of the discourses contained here produces a kind of swirling texture of differences among which it is hard to discover any overarching principle of discursive control. . . . What I am suggesting is that at the end of the kaleidoscopic tunnel of the postmodernist text (art-text or commodity text) there still sits the figure of that most traditional moral authority – the Author/Producer' (1988: 143, 145). The implication seems to be that we know who the enemy is – the 'Author/Producer', the 'moral authority', and so on – and the task of theory is thus what is finally a kind of broadly pragmatic *description* of the omnipresence of that enemy. It seems indicative of the banality of the politics derived from contingency theory that mail-order catalogues can be seen as a significant feature of the social form of oppression.
  2. Thus, Cornel West defends American pragmatism as 'less a philosophical tradition putting forward solutions to perennial problems in the Western philosophical conversation initiated by Plato and more a continuous cultural commentary or set of interpretations that attempt to explain America to itself at a particular historical moment' (1989: 5).
  3. It is worth noting that the problem here is *not* the appeal to 'settled' practices, but rather the impossibility of giving an account of how one knows what a practice is.
  4. In fact, Fish never mentions Kant so I am simply guessing what he would say about the distinction. However, it is significant that Fish writes as if issues about how knowledge might be grounded are reducible to a simplistic opposition between foundationalism and anti-foundationalism, while ignoring the more subtle formulations of these issues which can be found, among other places, in the debates within

German idealism about Kant's characterization of the transcendental. For a good discussion of this issue, see Beiser (1987).

5. Fish (1989: 371) argues that what is customarily called 'external scepticism' – the kind of scepticism which denies that we have *any* claims to knowledge – is itself a practice. However, this claim simply presupposes the ubiquity of practices which it was supposed to demonstrate. There are good explanations of why external scepticism is *not* reducible to our customary ways of knowing in Unger (1984: passim) and Stroud (1984: 83–128).

6. See Rorty (1979) for his critique of foundationalism.

7. To take only one example, she analyses Kant's description of universality as if he were offering an empirical description of cognition (1988: 67–71), although Kant states explicitly in the section of *The Critique of Judgment* that Smith discusses that he is *not* 'relying on psychological observations' (1951: 76).

8. Of course, what Smith offers here is little more than a parody of Habermas. For a defence of the cogency of Habermas's notion of undistorted communication, see Dews (1987: 220–4). The political problems raised by Habermas's appeal to ideals have been carefully set forth by Brenkman (1987: 49–56).

9. I use Davidson's work as the basis for a critique of how the subject is understood in contemporary theory in Cole (1993).

References

Beiser, F.C. (1987) *The Fate of Reason: German Philosophy from Kant to Fichte.* Cambridge, MA: Harvard University Press.

Brenkman, J. (1987) *Culture and Domination.* Ithaca, NY: Cornell University Press.

Cole, S.E. (1993) 'The scrutable subject: Davidson, literary theory, and the claims of knowledge', in R.W. Dasenbrock (ed.), *Literary Theory after Davidson.* University Park: Pennsylvania State University Press. pp. 59–91.

Davidson, D. (1982) 'Rational animals', *Dialectica,* 36 (1982): 317–27.

Dews, P. (1987) *Logics of Disintegration: Post-structuralist Thought and the Claims of Critical Theory.* London: Verso.

Fish, S. (1989) *Doing What Comes Naturally: Change, Rhetoric, and the Practice of Theory in Literary and Legal Studies.* Durham, NC: Duke University Press.

Fraser, N. (1989) *Unruly Practices: Power, Discourse and Gender in Contemporary Social Theory.* Minneapolis: University of Minnesota Press.

Kant, I. (1951) *The Critique of Judgement.* J.H. Barnard, trans. New York: Hafner Press.

Nagel, T. (1986) *The View from Nowhere.* Oxford: Oxford University Press.

Norris, C. (1985) *The Conflict of Faculties: Philosophy and Theory after Deconstruction.* London: Methuen.

Rorty, R. (1979) *Philosophy and the Mirror of Nature.* Princeton, NJ: Princeton University Press.

Rorty, R. (1989) *Contingency, Irony, and Solidarity.* Cambridge: Cambridge University Press.

Smith, B.H. (1988) *Contingencies of Value: Alternative Perspectives for Critical Theory.* Cambridge, MA: Harvard University Press.

Smith, P. (1988) 'Visiting the banana republic', in A. Ross (ed.), *Universal Abandon? The Politics of Postmodernism.* Minneapolis: University of Minnesota Press. pp. 128–48.

Stroud, B. (1984) *The Philosophical Significance of Scepticism*. Oxford: Oxford University Press.

Unger, P. (1984) *Philosophical Relativity*. Minneapolis: University of Minnesota Press.

West, C. (1989) *The American Evasion of Philosophy: a Genealogy of Pragmatism*. Madison: University of Wisconsin Press.

3

The Limits of Pure Critique

Kenneth J. Gergen

For the better part of the past twenty years I have been heavily engaged in critical and reconstructive work in the social sciences. Initial attacks were lodged against the established practices of behavioural research, along with associated forms of theory and their justificatory base in empiricist foundationalism. Volleys were variously directed against the traditional presumptions of cumulative knowledge, value-free theoretical formulations, unbiased observation, knowledge through hypothesis-testing, measurement of psychological processes, and more. Gradually I became aware of the extent to which this work was both preceded and accompanied by steadily expanding efforts within philosophy and across the social sciences, efforts that collectively form what we now see as a genre of *post-empiricist critique*. The works of Popper, Quine and a host of ordinary-language philosophers had wreaked havoc with assumptions of empiricist foundationalism, and the later works of Kuhn, Feyerabend and other historians of knowledge, along with a great number of sociologists of knowledge, began to offer alternatives to the traditional understanding of scientific activity. Over time, these voices were joined by increasing numbers within the social sciences – humanists, critical theorists, hermeneuticists, constructionists, feminists, phenomenologists, ethogenecists and many others. Empiricist foundationalism and its associated practices may continue to be dominant, but for a substantial number of scholars they lie essentially dead.

Both simultaneous and intertextual with the expansion of post-empiricist critique have been two other major forms of critical scholarship. On the one hand, with the gradual erosion of the empiricist account, intellectual space was increasingly opened for *ideology critique*. If theoretical accounts cannot be rendered authoritative by virtue of empirical data, and if these accounts enter social life as catalysts or suppressants, then science is opened to a form of evaluation scarcely voiced since the nineteenth century. Specifically, scientific theory can be evaluated in terms of its effects on the culture, the forms of social life which it facilitates and obliterates, or, in short, its ideological impact. Such critique was long championed by Marxists and critical theorists, but with the empiricist erosion the way was opened for a vital expansion of ideological critique. At present the range of such critique is ever broadening. Feminist critique has been honed to a razor finish; black, Native American, Asian, Hispanic, Arabic and gay scholars lend significant new dimensions to the withering attack. Even the erstwhile victims of such critique – typically the right-wing, male-dominated establishment – now respond with their own form of ideology critique: the argument against the tyranny of political correctness.

The weapons of attack within the domains of post-empiricist and ideology critique have been further strengthened by developments in *post-structuralist critique*. Reader-response theory undermines the presumption that texts carry inherent wisdom or profundity; texts contain only so much authority as interpretive communities are willing to grant. Deconstruction theory demonstrates the internal tensions of the text, the dependence of the said on the unsaid, and the eternal aporia of the foundational or grounding text. With deconstruction theory, not only does the object of the text disappear as a serious matter, but so does the mind of the author as an originary source. And, coupled with reader-response and deconstruction theory, rhetorical analysis further reveals the bag of tricks, ruses and hijinks essential to the intelligibility and persuasive appeal of any text. Under these conditions, all attempts by authorities to establish knowledge, convey wisdom or establish values are placed under suspicion.

We now stand with a mammoth arsenal of critical weaponry at our disposal. The power of such technology is unmatched by anything within the scholarly traditions of longstanding. There is virtually no hypothesis, body of evidence, ideological stance, literary canon, value commitment or logical edifice that cannot be dismantled, demolished or derided with the implements at hand. Only rank prejudice, force of habit or the anguished retaliation of deflated egos can muster a defence against the intellectual explosives within our grasp. Everywhere now in the academic world the capitalist exploiters, male chauvinist pigs, cultural imperialists, warmongers, WASP bigots, wimp liberals and scientistic dogmatists are on the run. Nor are these capacities for deflation and decapitation limited to the academic establishment. Post-empiricist critique finds ample targets throughout society. Presumptions of empiricism can be located within all domains of high-level decision-making – in government, business, the military, education and so on. Similarly, the targets of ideology critique are scarcely limited to the academy. Feminists, critical theorists and minority groups find oppression and bigotry at every turn – in film, art, architecture, clothing preferences and even the design of public toilets. And in the wake of post-structuralist critique, all that passed for trustworthy opinion – in the political sphere, the news media, the courts, the ministry – now teeters on the brink of blather. The revolution is on, heads are rolling everywhere, there is no limit to the potential destruction.

It is at this juncture, however, that my present inquiry begins. For I am not at all sanguine about our present condition and the future which it invites. It is not simply that we who share the arsenal do not always share turf, and these weapons may turn internecine. (Already, there are antagonisms among and within various post-empiricist enclaves, feminist camps, gay and lesbian groups, and post-structuralist clans.[1]) Rather, my chief concern is with the limits of critique – and most particularly the emerging body of critique – as a genre of scholarship. We find ourselves now in a position not unlike that of the French revolutionaries; we may simply choose the target and send the tumbrels forth. But is the result to be an ingurgitating bloodbath? Will there be no trustworthy or honoured views, only a dismantling that ultimately turns to destroy itself? Sober reflection seems essential on the forms of our interrogations – their intelligibility, coherence and societal effects.

In what follows I wish to identify five substantial problems that pervade the critical effort. The initial shortcomings are relevant across a wide body of existing critique; the latter two are specifically germane to lines of recently emerging critique. Attention will then turn to possible alternatives.

The Containment of Conversation

Critique acquires both its impetus and intelligibility from a preceding advocacy. An assertion (or network of assertions) must be put forward in order to stir and make intelligible the impulse towards negation. In this sense, critique is a symbiotic enterprise, typically requiring assertion as its inspiration. Yet, owing to this genesis, critique operates to establish a form of binary – a discursive structure in which *this is opposed to that*. Thus, the voice of the critic is defined in terms of its opposition; the terms of critique are limited to the binary ontology. If the assertion is that 'armed intervention is necessary', critique is limited to a linguistic domain in which the binary 'war–not war', serves as the critical defining agent. To respond to the advocacy of armed intervention with 'I shall have a cup of tea', or 'I am for the Greens', would not be to engage in critique (indeed, one might view such rejoinders as nonsensical insertions into the interchange). The status of such rejoinders as critique *could* be instantiated, but only if it could be shown that drinking tea or voting Green represents the negation of armed intervention (e.g. as a display of disdain in the case of drinking tea, or with reference to the anti-war stance of the Greens in the second).

At the outset, this symbiotic condition means that the critic's voice will operate so as to reify the terms of the binary. In effect, the critique renders support to the ontology implicit in the initial network of assertions, an ontology that might wither or dissolve without the critical impulse. Feminist theorists have been most sensitive to this issue. As many have pointed out, arguments against male dominance simultaneously reify a distinction between men and women; they operate to essentialize gender as a factual difference. Similarly, as various criticisms are couched in the language of racial conflict, the concept of essential differences between races is sustained; to speak against upper-class domination is to engender the reality of class differences. Once reality has been struck in terms of the binary, the contours of the world are fixed.

This problem is closely coupled with a second, namely that of a dissolving periphery. For as arguments proceed within terms of the binary, other realities, values and concerns are removed from view. It is the terms of the binary that furnish the interlocutors with both their identities and the basis of their relationship. In battling against the destruction of the environment, for example, issues of race and gender equality recede from view. Critiques of racial unfairness are insensitive to gender inequality; and gender battles are myopic with respect to issues of race. Of course, it is difficult to contend with all issues simultaneously. However, as interchange is polarized around a single continuum, there is a ferocious flattening of the world and a silencing of other voices. Each interlocutor, in the face of the other, loses dimension; all human characteristics, relationships, investments and viewpoints unrelated to the binary are suppressed. And the interlocutors themselves become deaf to all those voices – family, friends, the needy and so on – who do not share the reality which they create and sustain.

There are further ramifications of this condition. Once the arena of reifications has been established, members of opposing sides often come to depend on the image of the other for their continued sustenance. Each position remains intelligible and important only so long as the opposition is sustained within the discourse. Should the opposition be removed from view, the favoured position lapses into insignificance. Thus, for example, so long as a religion can sustain the category of 'the infidel', it retains both a distinctive quality and a reason for commitment. Under certain conditions, outside critique may even be welcomed by those in power because it sustains or strengthens their cause. Here the critic doesn't undermine the target, but enhances the strength of that which is abhorred. Those in political power, for example, may facilitate a certain amount of dissidence (limited, let's say, to the university setting) as it can inspire continued commitment to 'the cause'.

To illustrate, I offer an early experience in the Society for Experimental Social Psychology. The society was initially developed to promote a tough-minded, systematic approach to understanding social interaction. The term 'experimental' was adopted not so much out of a commitment to laboratory experimentation per se, but because experiments were the most sophisticated means of warranting statements about causal relations. Indeed, many participants in the association employed interview methods, questionnaires, field observation and other research techniques. Semiotically, the term 'experimental' was merely to function as a synonym for 'systematically scientific'. As the association rapidly grew stronger and more élitist, some of us became concerned that the choice of names was too exclusionary. It seemed the term 'experimental' was becoming synonymous with 'preferred methodology'. Other forms of research were being discouraged, and systematic theoretical and conceptual work was being abandoned. At this point I joined with several colleagues in a critique of the existing name and its problematic implications, and a search for a replacement. The succeeding debate led to a heated defence of experimental methodology (not itself under attack at the time), an attack on all other methods as inferior, and a renewed commitment to the existing organizational name. Further, the debate was confined to the issue of methodology; concerns with the more general function of the discipline, its potentials and limitations, were never voiced. Only its methodological activities were in question. Handbooks and textbooks in social psychology now repeat the defence of experimental methodology as a virtual litany. Periodically the second-status journals of the field will feature a contrary view, but the very appearance of such critiques in the peripheral journals serves only to strengthen the intelligibility of 'experimental purity' within the dominant establishment. In effect, the attempt at critique primarily served to delineate a binary, to stimulate its defence, to truncate the range of significant issues and to ensure that further criticism remained at the periphery of disciplinary consciousness.

Critique as Rhetorical Incitement

Throughout this analysis I have made frequent use of the common metaphor: argument is war. The choice was not accidental, by underscoring this common theme (see Lakoff and Johnson, 1980), we are better positioned to appreciate the strategic implications of critique. Consider the position of argumentation theorists van Eemeren and Grootendorst, 'a language user who has advanced a point of view in respect of an expressed opinion must be prepared to *defend* that standpoint and . . . a language user who has cast doubt upon the tenability of that standpoint must be prepared to *attack* it' (1983: 1; my emphasis). Given this formalization of a broadly shared conception of argumentation, the posture of one who is targeted for criticism can scarcely be other than defensive. And the dimensions of this defence are profound. In the Western tradition one's words serve as outward expressions of inner essence. They are presumed to reflect the operation of thought – the logos – the originary process that renders one individual superior to another, and humans superior to the brutes. Because of the close historical association between soul and rationality, one's words are subtle indicators of one's kinship with God. To criticize another's views is not, then, a mere linguistic exercise; it is to invalidate the originary essence of the self. Or, to extend the symbolic laminations, criticism transforms the target's attempt at self-expression to mere foolishness, knavery or idiocy. It is to rob one's words of authority; to reduce one's likeness to God, king, hero and father; and to return one to the status of errant child – now corrected by a knowing parent.

Given this provocative context, how is the target of criticism to respond? Scarcely, one can appreciate, with zest for open and impartial exploration – with eagerness to pursue the issues to a just and impartial conclusion. When one is subjected to forces of annihilation – of one's sense of self and one's dignity – there is little choice but to seek all means of vanquishing the threatening force. Nor is deliberation on these matters required in every instance. The conversational conventions inherited from the cultural past virtually require that one 'defend oneself' against another's 'critical attacks'. In the available dances of the culture, critique invites counter-critique. And, once the rejoinder is set in motion, it serves to re-incite the adjacency pair; in effect, we confront a relational scenario with little means of termination.

Should coherent argument and substantial evidence not bring such mutually annihilating interchanges to an eventual end? There are principled reasons to think not. In open dialogue one can continue indefinitely to remain secure in one's beliefs – unaffected by counter-argument – because the very structure of dialogue ensures this possibility. The principal reason for the interminability of debate stems from the essential undecidability of meaning. One may voice an argument, but whether these words are granted meaning, and the particular meaning they are allowed to possess, is not determined by oneself but by one's interlocutor. One's utterances stand as open texts, subject to appropriation from virtually any standpoint. And, just as one's arguments always stand vulnerable to the adversary's reconstitution, so are the adversary's utterances subject to a reciprocal appropriation. In effect, each interlocutor confronts a situation in which 'I cannot control your interpretation of what I say, but I am positioned so as to grant (or deny) intelligibility to your reply, or to bend your words to my interpretive designs.' Under these conditions of interdependent intelligibility, protagonists are free to block or transform all communiqués that might otherwise threaten their differing positions.[2] The means for destroying the other's intelligibility are vast and varied. Sentences may be lifted from context, concepts altered through recontextualization, arguments pressed to absurd extremes, examples transformed through parody, insidious intentions imputed and so on. The three critical movements described above – anti-empiricist, ideological and post-structural – add incrementally to the means of deflating opposition arguments and reclaiming them for oneself. There are, then, myriad means of ambiguating, complexifying, doggerelizing or transforming any utterance to imbecility. Resultingly, there is no principled end to argumentation – unless participants are subjected to outside requirements (as in a court of law), or severely restricted by rules of procedure (as in the case of mathematics). Each combatant retains control over the effective contents of the opponent's position.

Illustrative of the exacerbating potential of critique is Paul Feyerabend's exchange with philosophers of science. In his earlier writings, Feyerabend developed a series of vigorous attacks against foundationalist views of science, arguing that virtually all the rules of procedure used to 'advance knowledge' by traditional standards would indeed stifle attempts in this direction. Counter-critique was rapidly forthcoming – much of it detailed and perceptive. Ideally one might envision this as a context for an extended dialogue, guided by a telos of enhanced understanding. Consider in contrast, Feyerabend's reactions to his critics in *Science in a Free Society*:

> I thought I was confronted with individual incompetence: the learned gentlemen (and the one learned lady who joined the dance) were not too bright and rather badly informed and so they quite naturally made fools

of themselves. Since then I have realized that this is a rather superficial way of looking at things. For the mistakes I noticed and criticized do not merely occur in this or that review, they are fairly widespread. And their frequency is not merely an accident of history, a temporary loss of intellect, it shows a pattern. Speaking paradoxically we may say that incompetence, having been standardized, has now become an essential part of professional excellence. We have no longer incompetent professionals, we have professionalized incompetence. (1978: 183)

Dialogue between Feyerabend and his colleagues was essentially terminated at this point.

The Atomization of Community

This concern with the rhetorical impact of critique is scarcely limited to the relationship between interlocutors alone. More generally, language serves to sustain communal patterns of conduct. As communities reach ontological and valuational consensus, so do patterns of relationship stabilize. As people come to agree, for example, about the concept of work, just compensation, adequate benefits and so on, they lay the groundwork for a mutually acceptable way of life. Thus, to abandon one's assertions in the face of critique is not simply to give way in a contest of logic, evidence, principles and the like. Rather, it is to threaten one's forms of relationship. For 'pro-life' protesters to 'see where we are wrong', and capitulate to the arguments of 'pro-choice' advocates, would be not only a loss of argument, but also, more importantly, the demise of the relationships sustained by the language of protest.

In this light, consider a group of persons among whom communication is open, fluid and unproblematic. Each member of the group is acknowledged and accepted by the others, and efforts are made at common understandings. In effect, the body of available signifiers circulates with relative ease, making it possible for new combinations to develop, and for the language of understanding to evolve over time. Now consider the insertion of critical practice into the community. Critique first serves to generate common consciousness among those placed in question. A category is either created (e.g. 'male chauvinist') or foregrounded that might otherwise go unnoticed. The targets of critique are thus put on notice that all who share in the network of assertions (and associated practices) are discredited. Not only are their social identities in peril, but so too are the relationships in which they are embedded. Under these conditions, cultural history offers little in the way of an intelligible alternative to collective defence. Those under attack close ranks, re-affirm their relationships, articulate the value of their positions and locate myriad ways in which their attackers are unjust and misinformed. The banner of defence, along with its raison d'être, are all furnished by those who have raised significant question.

As the process of reaffirmation and justification takes place, the efforts of the critics are thwarted. Not only do their criticisms go unheeded, but the targets defend themselves with 'cheap ruses' (further masking their faults), and mount 'unjustified' counter-attacks. The culturally sensible response to such loutishness is to increase the intensity of the attacks, reaffirm solidarity within the ranks and proselytize for further strength. Should these efforts prove successful, they are likely to provoke similar investments within the target group. In effect, the result is a polarizing split within the community as a whole. Mutual acknowledgement and a common quest for understanding are destroyed (or, more precisely, reserved for relations within the restricted boundaries of each group). The coordinated actions necessary for generating common meaning deteriorate; and, as the language within each camp evolves, communication across boundaries becomes increasingly arduous. The interpretive communities come to share argots within that are unheard, unacknowledged or found opaque within the opposing community. Mutually exclusive realities ('incommensurable paradigms') solidify with little means for reconciliation.

Illustration is useful. My earliest critical work took place in the context of what was – in the mid-1970s – called 'the crisis in social psychology'. My attempt at that point (Gergen, 1973) was to undermine the presumption that social psychology was a cumulative science, moving steadily towards the establishment of historically decontextualized truths, and to replace such an orientation with a historically sensitive and valuationally embedded form of inquiry. In the years immediately following this critique, there was an enormous amount of debate within the field. I found my interests increasingly allied with those of other dissidents, and simultaneously the established journals slowly sealed themselves off from the controversies. Time and relationships have since moved on, and I now find myself deeply immersed within a large and heterogeneous community of anti-foundationalists. We now have our own journals, our own associations, lines of scholarship and agendas. Traditional social psychologists would understand little of what we talk about – so much jargon, mystification and real-world irrelevance to them. And if they did understand they would be appalled and offended at the picture our literature paints of them. At the same time, they continue business as usual; the crisis is settled. By the same token, were any of *us* to attend *their* meetings or read *their* articles, we would find their efforts archaic, naïve and politically shallow. The atomization of communities is virtually complete.

These three problems, the containment of conversation, rhetorical incitement and atomization of community, are all endemic to the process of critique itself – at least as it has functioned within the Western cultural tradition. I wish now, however, to touch on two additional problems derived from the context of contemporary critique. Much post-empiricist, ideological and post-structuralist critique is based on a particular set of shared values or assumptions. As critique is mounted from these quarters, we confront additional tensions of significance.

Critique and the Totalizing Impulse

Much contemporary critique is designed to undermine any form of totalizing discourse, that is, any set of descriptions, explanations, principles, criteria of acceptability, directives or meta-theories that delimit the discursive domain or systematically reduce the array of voices that can speak to any issue or state of affairs. This concern is evidenced, for example, in social constructionist critiques of empiricist meta-theory, feminist critiques of androcentric language, Marxist critiques of capitalist economic theory, deconstructionist critiques of cultural marginalization practices, and postmodern critiques of modernist foundationalism. Virtually all of these efforts place the liberalization of linguistic practices in the forefront; they opt for a broad democratization of intelligibilities.

Yet, in what degree does the critical impulse truly serve the function of democratization? As we have seen, the problems begin with the symbiotic nature of the critical form. Once an assertion is followed by a critical negation, there is a radical truncation in the range of relevant voices. The combination of assertion and counter-assertion establishes the grounds for subsequent discussion; any voice registered outside the binary is rendered irrelevant. If we are arguing over abortion rights, there is no room for an advocate of migrant workers' rights; psychologists debating over experimentation vs more humanistic alternatives are unprepared for entry of 'Praise the Lord' proselytizers. Once the binary has been struck, it is not any voice that can be heard, but only those that remain within the reified world of the debate as structured.

The case is more severe, however, when the target of criticism is placed under attack for totalization – for pressing a single truth and extinguishing all dissent. As males, heterosexuals, capitalists, communists, empiricists, moralists and others are vilified for the dominating effects of their discourse, the symbiotic structure of critique again plays a deleterious role. Specifically, the arrangement lends to the critical impulse a deadly demeanour: the target of attack becomes subject to annihilation. Thus, if successful, the critique will indeed open the door to further voices – feminist, homosexual, Latino, non-Western, and so on depending on the particular binary in play. However, the fully successful critique will also stifle those voices placed under attack. They are thrust to the margins for their hegemonic tendencies. Should the critic prove successful, the accomplishment is not thus the broadening of the discursive domain. It is the replacement of one form of totalization with its opposite number. It is an inversion of the binary, with results that are no less stifling.

Illustration is furnished by my own critique of the mental health professions (Gergen, 1990). It is my contention that as the languages of mental disease and deficit generated by the professions are disseminated to the public, they are used by people to understand themselves. By constructing themselves in illness terms, a need is further generated for the very profession that creates the language. And, as the profession is consulted and remunerated, so does it grow and prosper. With its prosperity there is further growth in deficit terminology. In effect, we are witnessing a spiralling growth of terms that enfeeble the population, and the chief focus of critique is the mental health professions. In present terms, the binary is thus established between the *production of mental deficit terms* and *non-production*, or, more specifically, the production of *alternative*, and more promising constructions. The latter would, in my view, increase the number of available perspectives, and thus broaden the range of cultural patternings. However, the critical form of argumentation operates in such a way that the intelligibility of the new alternative is established in terms of the opposition's demise. There is no space carved out for the mental health professional to continue disseminating the 'bad old language', for it is this language that operates against the alternatives. In effect, the symbiotic character of critique operates to silence the voice of the target; the other's totalizing discourse is obliterated in order that the opposition (favoured by me) may take its place.

The Problematics of Principle

Within the interlocking movements of post-empiricism, ideology critique and post-structuralism we find a deep distrust of existing edifices of knowledge, belief systems and ideologies. All that was secure, foundational and established is thrown into question. For many post-empiricists (and social constructionists in particular), this suspicion is based on the view that our taken for granted understandings are not required by 'the way things are', but are derived from social interchange. Existing beliefs in knowledge, logic, morality and the like have no transcendent foundations, but are culturally and historically situated. From this perspective, all that is held to be so could be otherwise; all existing constructions could be replaced by myriad alternatives. For those engaged in ideology critique, the pervasive distrust stems primarily from a concern with motivational base. Agreeing with the constructionists that our taken for granted understandings are not required by the way things are, they explore the ideological or self-serving interests at work in the dominant discourse. Whose interests are being served by existing understandings; who is dispossessed or marginalized? Post-structuralists add an additional lamination of doubt in their concern with the internal logic of representation itself. The array of signifiers is not required by the way things are, but by the conventions of signification itself. Once these semiotic and/or rhetorical devices have been located and dissected, representation ceases to tell us about the world; it merely displays its own rules at work.

As proposed, these various lines of argument also form a critical arsenal of devastating potential. The social constructionist furnishes a sophisticated discourse on the way assertions emerge from social interchange, the ideology critic demonstrates the value biases that lend vitality to such assertions, and post-structuralists reveal the many literary and rhetorical devices at work in making compelling sense. The effect of each variety of weaponry is to rob the opponent's assertions of any form of validity or rhetorical force. At best, the opponent's words are reduced to hearsay or personal prejudice; at worst they are deprived of meaning altogether. Yet, at this point the problem of *tu quoque* begins. For while it has become enormously effective in undermining the opposition, such critique simultaneously casts aspersions on its own production. Not only the grounds of its arguments, but all forms of counter-assertion stand subject to the same forms of self-immolation. And in opening themselves to such analysis, they also lose both validity and possible meaning. To demonstrate the social basis of scientific fact is to reduce this demonstration to mere conversation; to attack the class bias underlying a given policy is to transform the attack to a class bias; and to deconstruct the rhetoric of war is to transform talk of peace to rhetorical flourish.

To make the case more concretely, consider one of my attempts to undermine the use of empirical evidence to substantiate propositions about the relationship of mental processes to the surrounding world. In this case (Gergen, 1988), my argument was that empirical evidence cannot inform us about the relationships of stimuli (the environment) to mental states (e.g. cognition, emotion, etc.), or about the relationship between such states and resulting action. This is so, I asserted, because all intelligible propositions linking mind to world are derived from a forestructure of understandings already available within the culture (either generally or within the specific culture of psychology). Any proposition that is antithetical to this forestructure, or that falls outside its domain, is either absurd or incomprehensible. For example, it would be impossible to demonstrate that all elephants are perceived as rabbits, not because this is untrue, but because the dualism of the Western tradition presumes that the elephants in the material world stimulate elephant-like reflections in the mind. No amount of experimental evidence could dislodge the presumption. Yet, while the critical attempt is interesting and intelligible enough, in the end it falls of its own weight. For once I have deconstructed mind and world as evidential sites – and cast them instead as elements in language – so have I also thrown my critique into jeopardy. For where are we to locate the 'forestructure of understandings,' the 'culture', 'the propositions' and so on, all of which are essential elements in my argument? If they are not part of the world or of mind, now fragments of a castaway epistemology, to what world do they belong? Why should the use of such terms in my argument count against the position I am assailing. If 'real-world' existants are irrelevant to the propositional network under attack, then the rationale for my critique is also placed beyond real-world concern.

Critique: Is There a Future?

As I am proposing, the common form of argumentation, with assertion and critique serving as the adjacency pair of focal significance, is deeply problematic. Critique establishes a binary ontology, reifying the terms of disagreement, and removing other entries from the ledger. Further, critique as a rhetorical move has the effect of demeaning the opposition, generating animosity, atomizing the culture and blocking the way to resolution. Contemporary critique, informed by post-empiricist, critical and post-structuralist thought, carries with it the additional difficulties of favouring the very kinds of totalizing discourses against which it is set, and destroying the grounds of its own rationality. This is not at all to deny the many positive ends served by critique, nor does it necessarily argue for its abandonment (another totalizing move). Further, this is not to propose that all forms of critique, in all relational contexts, have such problematic consequences. When and why this is the case is indeed an issue of some interest. However, the present analysis does prompt serious questioning regarding the centrality of critique within the scholarly (and cultural) arena. Do the limitations on this cultural form not invite inquiry into alternatives? Are there other means for reaching the same ends to which critique has traditionally been directed? These are important questions, and a space must be opened for continuing discussion.

Within this space, it seems to me that a thorough exploration is needed of the rationale for critical deliberation. That is, reconsideration is needed of the means by which critical argumentation gains its intelligibility. At present, the critical impulse largely acquires its justification from a family of interrelated suppositions, including but not limited to the following: (a) adequate or adaptive behaviour is guided by processes of rationality within the individual mind; (b) in matters of rationality, certain states of mind (e.g. logical, objective) are more desirable (or adaptive) than others; (c) the process of critique is essential to reaching a state of optimal rationality; (d) critical thought enables the individual to resist humbug, tyranny and the pressures of the social group; and (e) critical thought at the individual level is a necessary ingredient of a democratic society.[3] Yet, there is not one of these suppositions that can withstand close scrutiny, not one that can viably sustain the critical impulse. Within the contemporary intellectual climate, the presumption of individual rationality, capable of reflecting on the world as it is, and fundamentally separated from the social context, is found wanting on both conceptual and ideological grounds. Were these the only reasons for critical deliberation, then we might wish for significant restraint.

At the same time, if we reconsider the aims of the critical venture, abandoning the goal of individual enlightenment, additional options may be opened. Rather than viewing rational process as occurring within the individual mind, such process can fruitfully be placed within discourse – and thus within the ongoing relations among persons. From this standpoint, there is no adaptively superior state of rationality, that is, no transcendental optimum in the constitution of human discourse. Further, by adopting this standpoint we are positioned to reconsider both the utility of critical deliberation, and possible means of modifying the process. For if language is not a means of achieving some form of optimal rationality, what social purposes does it achieve? And if these are desirable purposes from some point of view, is critical deliberation in its current form the best means of attainment? Or, in short, what do we wish to achieve in the social world through critical deliberation, and are there superior alternatives to contemporary critical practice?

Transforming the Critical Process

A relational view of language does not itself favour any particular process or goal of deliberation. However, it does invite interlocutors to consider more self-consciously what they wish to achieve through their interchange. Is argument being carried out so as to sharpen and elaborate opposing positions, yield victory to one side or another, locate areas of compromise, entertain, develop public support, or for other purposes? I have very little doubt that current forms of critique do achieve certain of these goals, and, as suggested earlier, I am not opting for an abandonment of the critical enterprise. However, by articulating the relational goals, interlocutors may wish to open alternatives to traditional practices of contentiousness. (How often has the traditional scenario succeeded in atomizing scholarly groups otherwise meeting to explore mutual interests?)

To explore the possibilities, let us consider but a single goal, the attempt to maximize participation in cultural decision-making. Many would agree that in general it is a better society when all of its participants are allowed entry into the arenas of decision-making – both grand and local – than when institutions, policies and projects are fixed by only a minority. Such a hope is not only part of our democratic heritage, but one might say that broadscale dialogue is essential to a reasonably harmonious way of life. Further, as commonly reasoned, the process of argumentation is one means of expanding the range of available voices. If assertions are never confronted by counter-assertions, all voices outside the range of assertion are rendered mute. The stage is thus set for tyranny, oppression and conflict. Critical practice, it may be proposed, is essential to broadening the array of voices. It is a process that enables alternative interests to be made known; in effect, it stands as a cultural resource for the expansion of voice.

Yet, given the desideratum of maximizing participation, the critical tradition is significantly flawed. As previously reasoned, critique operates on a fundamental axis of opposition – assertion and counter-assertion – with two debilitating results. First, as the binary is established, the grounds for entering the dialogue are constrained. It is war vs anti-war, the political left vs the right, pro-life vs pro-choice. The enormous complexities surrounding any decision, and the enormous array of possible constructions, are thus narrowed to a minimal set. It is not just any voice that may now be heard, but only those voices relevant to the dimension in question. And, as debate continues the terms of the binary become increasingly objectified, its putative referents increasingly palpable.

The possibility for alternative voices – those that speak to the conditions but not 'to the point' – are increasingly subdued. In effect, the polarization realized by contemporary forms of critical deliberation move only minimally to expand the spectrum of commentary. In addition, by contemporary standards, to criticize is to threaten annihilation and thus to alienate. Agreeable solutions seldom emerge from the process of assertion and critique; the more common outcome is the creation of self-sustaining and self-satisfying enclaves of antagonists. In effect, critique serves to insulate groups from the 'good reasons' of the other. Critical voices go either unheeded, or are bludgeoned because they are critical. The result is the same in either case: decision-making not by virtue of common deliberation – that is, by participation of all – but rather through a jockeying for power, inside position or private control of outcomes. The atomization of culture does not mean an increase in the range of voices that may be heard, but a constriction. The local realities comprehend only themselves.

Are there means of examining assertions and contraries without simultaneously constricting the range of deliberation? Here I have no 'quick fix' alternative, no ready technology that can be locked in place. Traditions cannot so easily be changed, and whatever changes do occur will require a good deal of relational coordination. However, to further the dialogue, let us consider several exploratory attempts to transform critique.

As discussed, critique is often ineffective because it takes place within a tradition emphasizing war and mutual annihilation, on the one hand, and arguments as expressions of one's core self, on the other. The question to be considered in the present context is whether key elements of the rhetorical form may be changed without damaging the possibility for exploring contentions and contraries. For example, in what ways could we remove from the field the emphasis on ego, the sense of authorial ownership of arguments and the threat of spoiled identities? Such components are scarcely essential to critical deliberation. As a preliminary exercise in decentring the ego, certain choices were made regarding features of the present offering. This essay is, after all, a critical assessment of critique itself. However, to explore the possibilities of breaking the tradition of attack and defence, I have frequently used myself as the target. I have placed my own foibles and failings on display. By damaging my own identity, the reader may sense that these are not attempts to 'launch a perfect gunboat', a vehicle that camouflages its weaknesses and resists all opposition. To damage oneself is also to suggest that one's identity in the case is less important than the arguments themselves. Of course, I simultaneously risk credibility – admitting 'weakness' – but the hope is that in doing so the reader is more likely to join in productive dialogue.

I wish in conclusion, however, to consider two more concerted attempts to alter the critical process. The first places a strong emphasis on *removing the self* from the interchange, and the second on *refiguring the self* within the relationship. In the former case, my colleagues and I are working on a procedure we call *argumentation from nowhere*. The attempt here is twofold, first to remove considerations of ego identity from the deliberative process, and, second, to generate a sense of rationality as a communal process. We attempt to remove the grounds either for claiming one's assertions to be 'one's own', or for viewing counter-assertions as challenges to one's dignity. In this context, to assert, opine or pronounce is simply to offer a card from the culture's deck of possible intelligibilities.

To elaborate, it is useful to imagine an enormous array of intelligible sentences that might accompany any given assertion. For example, if one advocates strong birth control measures in Third World countries, there is an immense range of argumentation that might, by contemporary convention, serve to strengthen this advocacy (dealing, for example, with issues of health, economy, education, modernization and so on). At the same time, for each assertion and its accompanying structure of argumentation, there is an enormous range of counter-argument (concerning, for example, Western exploitation, cultural values, spiritual issues, the ills of modernity, etc.). Further, each of the accompanying assertions will also harbour a justificatory base that can be articulated, leading to a further array of assertions and counter-assertions, in an outward expanding network. And, too, each element in the network is also subject to reflexive analysis in the terms offered by the critical movements outlined earlier – more specifically, social determinants, ideological biases and rhetorical construction. In effect, we can envision an enormous unpacking of intelligible assertions surrounding the issue of birth control in the Third World. To explore the network would be to approach the theoretical limits of all that could be meaningfully said about the issue in question.[4]

Because of their immersion in a variety of subcultures, most people carry with them an extensive repository of intelligible sayings about many issues. Most importantly, the work of Billig and his colleagues (1988) on ideological dilemmas suggests that most people have available many arguments on both sides of any issue. Thus, for example, although pro-life and pro-choice advocates may remain rooted in a single position (by virtue of their placement in social groups), if the conditions were inviting, they could produce many of the opposition arguments. With these views at hand, my colleagues and I invite individuals to contribute entries from their private repositories into a broader (and principally uncompletable) network of opinions surrounding a given issue. The entries are made privately, and with the aid of a personal computer. After logging into the system, each contributor may scan various entries, both favouring and opposing a given position, as well as those which rebut these entries, and those attempting to reformulate the problem, see the issue as secondary to other problems, etc. The contributor may then enter additional opinions in any of these categories, on either (or both) side(s) of the issue, at a tangent, or in a reflexive move. There is no demand in this process to prefix one's entries with 'I believe . . .', 'I think . . .', or 'I feel . . .', for such would render one either vulnerable to opposing assertions, or insensitive to the repertoire one may otherwise harbour.

As the sharing continues, so does the participant's vocabulary expand regarding the various rationalities bearing on the issue. The result of such a process is not a more 'rational' or 'objective' decision in the traditional sense. However, there does appear to be a substantial expansion in sensitivities, sophistication and what is considered the range of relevant argument. Further, as participants reflect on the process itself, they indicate a keen appreciation of the enormous complexity surrounding what appear to be the simplest of issues. One might object by pointing to the way such a process obscures and muddies the issues; yet, on what grounds could one vindicate the clear and simple formulation? The process also reduces tendencies toward strong commitment, but the heady romance with causes – so central to the cultural tradition – produces most of the ill effects outlined above. However, the project is still in progress, and its advantages, shortcomings and possible applications continue to emerge.

Consider a second endeavour, designed to enhance argumentation without the costs of atomization and silencing. The logic for this procedure derives from the preceding demonstration. Rather than defining the individual in terms of a unified, rational core – the owner of a coherent logos – we may view the person as *fundamentally multiplicitous*, populated by views and opinions absorbed from the social arena over many years and differing conditions.[5] Whether an individual claims one of these views to be 'my belief', 'my value', or 'essential' and 'true' is not the result of introspective discernment (e.g. 'I know it is my opinion because I can feel or see that it is'). Rather, the claim to possession is the result of social positioning, where the individual is placed at a given time vis-à-vis ongoing relationships.[6] For example, authors may claim their written opinions to be 'theirs', or abandon them as 'once my beliefs, but no longer'. One may heatedly defend a position in an argument, only later to admit, 'That was too extreme; I got carried away.' Or, the mother may say to the child, 'I was just saying that because it was for your good.' In effect, people's claims to their words – as expressions of individual identity – are socially contingent.[7]

In this case it should be possible to establish conditions favouring multiplicity, that is, a recognition of one's many diverse and competing standpoints. Richard Harvey Brown (1987), drawing from a long line of philosophic work, extending from Socrates to Kierkegaard, develops a case for what he terms 'dialectical irony'. Dialectical irony involves taking both a position and its contrary, not so much to negate oneself as to emancipate oneself from the demands of either alone. The dialectical ironist 'simultaneously asserts two or more logically contradictory meanings such that, in the silence between the two, the deeper meaning of both may emerge'. This 'deeper meaning', proposes Brown, 'is dialectical. It does not inhere in either the initial literal assertion or its negation; it is rather the tension and completion set off between them that constitutes dialectical ironic awareness' (1987: 173).

How and under what conditions a stance of dialectical irony can be evoked in daily life remains unclear. However, I have participated in a relevant process of such remarkable efficacy that recounting is merited. At the beginning of a three-day conference, the organizers arranged a confrontation pitting radical constructivism (as represented by Ernst von Glazersfeld) against social constructionism (which I was to profess). The subsequent critiques were unsparing, the defences unyielding, and as the audience was drawn into the debate polarization rapidly took place. Voices became agitated, critique turned ad hominem, anger and alienation mounted. As the moderator called a halt to the proceedings, I began to see the three days before me as an eternity. Sensing the impasse of the condition, a group of family therapists, led by Sue Levin and Karl Tomm, invited conference participants to a rump session. Here Tomm asked if von Glazersfeld and I would be willing to be publicly interviewed. Most important, would we be willing to do so *as the other*? Uneasily, we agreed. Consistent with the earlier reasoning, our exposure to each other did allow each of us to absorb aspects of the other – intellectual views, attitudes, values – which we now carried with us as potentials. The initial question was whether we were willing and able to give these potentials credible voice. Through an extended series of questions, carefully and sensitively addressed, Tomm was able to elicit 'the other within'. Playing the other's identity, we discussed issues of theory, views of the other, self-doubts, fears, personal relationships, feelings about the conference and so on.

The results of the procedure were striking. As both we and the audience learned, we could communicate intelligibly and sympathetically from within the other's framework. Each could give voice to the rationality of the other. Further, the binary was successfully broken. Rather than a showdown between competing epistemologies, the debate could be understood within the context of a long interpersonal history, imbricated friendships, private aspirations and doubts, the demands of public debate and so on. A new level of discussion ensued. The conference was thereafter marked by its civility of interchange; there was expression without domination, careful listening and sensitive reply. No, this did not mean a resolution of differences; the lines of difference remained clear. However, it did allow the exploration to move forward, and with the resulting emergence of new complexities, the old yearnings for victory and defeat – heroes and villains – receded from view.

Here, then, are but a handful of alternatives to critical argumentation in its traditional form. They, too, would benefit from broad examination. At the same time, they are scarcely inclusive; broad exploration would certainly yield a plethora of additional possibilities. Ideally such exploration should be extended beyond the arena of professional life. After all, people confront an enormous range of disagreeable assertions within a lifetime, and critical argumentation serves as but one class of activity set in motion in such cases (perhaps limited, as well, to certain educational and economic strata). Ethnographic inquiry into the range of grass-roots alternatives would seem a valuable undertaking at this juncture. Perhaps the scholar can profit more, in this context, by listening to the laity than professing.

Notes

1. For an illustration of the intensity of this conflict, as currently taking place in anthropology, see Nencel and Pels (1991).

2. For a more extended account of the relational creation of meaning, see Gergen (forthcoming).

3. Brian Fay (1987) traces the assumptive basis for critical analysis to Plato. Although Fay, as others (see, e.g., Berman, 1989), discerns a variety of different emphases and rationales for the critical enterprise over the centuries, the present assumptions are closest to what Fay calls 'the humanistic variant'. Fay, himself, uses this variant to form the basis for a critical social science. He seeks 'theory which is capable of interpreting in a cognitively respectable manner the social world in which

we live in such a way that this world's oppressiveness is apparent, and in such a way that it empowers its listeners to change their lives' (1987: 23).

4. It would be a mistake to view this as 'a limit' in any more than an idealized theoretical sense. Owing to the polysemous character of the various concepts at stake in an argument, and the theoretically unlimited possibility for generating associational linkages to a given set of propositions, the field of intelligibility is more properly viewed as protean. It may be frozen for inspection at any given point, but it would be a mistake to presume the stop-frame structure is either fully general or enduring.

5. For a more extended account of multiple selves, see Gergen (1991).

6. See especially the work of Davies and Harré (1990).

7. See also Foucault's (1979) widely cited essay, 'What is an author?'

References

Berman, R.A. (1989) *Modern Culture and Critical Theory*. Madison: University of Wisconsin Press.

Billig, M., Condor, S., Edwards, D., Gane, M., Middleton, D. and Radley, A.R. (1988) Ideological Dilemmas: *A Social Psychology of Everyday Thinking*. London: Sage.

Brown, R.H. (1987) *Society as Text: Essays on Rhetoric, Reason and Reality*. Chicago, IL: University of Chicago Press.

Davies, B. and Harré, R. (1990) 'Positioning and the discursive production of selves', *Journal for the Theory of Social Behaviour*, 20: 43–63.

Fay, B. (1987) *Critical Social Science: Liberation and Its Limits*. Ithaca, NY: Cornell University Press.

Feyerabend, P. (1978) *Science in a Free Society*. London: Verso.

Foucault, M. (1979) 'What is an author?' in J.V. Harari (ed.), *Textual Strategies: Perspectives in Post-structuralist Criticism*. Ithaca, NY: Cornell University Press. pp. 101–20.

Gergen, K.J. (1973) 'Social psychology as history', *Journal of Personality and Social Psychology*, 26, 309–20.

Gergen, K.J. (1988) 'Knowledge and social process', in D. Bar-Tal and A. Kruglanski (eds), *The Social Psychology of Knowledge*. Cambridge: Cambridge University Press. pp. 30–47.

Gergen, K.J. (1990) 'Therapeutic professions and the diffusion of deficit', *Journal for Mind and Behavior*, 11: 353–68.

Gergen, K.J. (1991) *The Saturated Self*. New York: Basic Books.

Gergen, K.J. (forthcoming) *Realities and Relationships, Soundings in Social Construction*. Cambridge, MA: Harvard University Press.

Lakoff, G. and Johnson, M. (1980) *Metaphors We Live By*. Chicago, IL: University of Chicago Press.

Nencel, L. and Pels, P. (eds) (1991) *Constructing Knowledge, Authority and Critique in Social Science*. London: Sage.

van Eemeren, F.H. and Grootendorst, R. (1983) *Speech Acts in Argumentative Discussions*. Dordrecht: Foris.

4

Inscription and Horizon:
a Postmodern Civilizing Effect?

Ian Angus

The contemporary postmodern moment of cultural studies runs the danger of rejecting the component of ethico-political evaluation that is essential to critical theory in favour of a cultural relativism that supposedly better recognizes the legitimacy of the plurality of cultures. To the extent that the evaluative component is regarded as entirely internal to cultural forms, and therefore as incapable of radically criticizing them, cultural studies is pushed towards a pluralism that is practically indistinct from relativism. This essay attempts to redesign the ethico-political evaluative component that can hook cultural studies into a critical theory of society. To do so, it sketches a tripartite historical periodization of the development of the concept of culture from the classic modern European into national-critical traditions and, finally, into contemporary postmodern international culture. The point of this history is to define with some precision two interrelated components of postmodern culture: the increasing emphasis on spatial, transversal relations over the historical formation of a tradition; and, the loss of an ethico-political standpoint for criticism within a given tradition in favour of a plurality of cultural forms that leads to an ethical relativism. It is argued in this chapter that, in the context of this new spatialized moment of global culture, the theoretical legitimation of critical theory can be reinvented through 'comparative media theory' (see Angus 1988, 1989, 1992a, 1993b, 1994, forthcoming). Such a focus on the 'materiality' of media of communication can root the interpretation of symbolic representations in the more fundamental issue of the constitution of social relations. Only in this way can the concept of 'critique' from literary criticism be based on 'critique' as social criticism and cultural studies be fused with the critical theory of society.

Contemporary postmodern cultural studies has emerged as an international discussion through the development and intersection of national traditions of cultural criticism. These national traditions themselves emerged as newly independent formations at an earlier historical moment through a critique of the ideological formation of classic modern European cultural theory. This classic modern tradition was articulated through an overriding and unifying conception of 'European civilization' which synthesized national and regional diversities. It is because of this lineage that postmodern cultural studies must rethink the concepts of 'modernity' and the 'West' (Amin, 1989; Laclau and Mouffe 1985; Angus 1992b, 1993a). Without such a rethinking cultural studies tends to back off into a mere abandonment of social criticism, rather than producing the renewed theorization that is demanded by the postmodern context.

The classic modern hierarchical architectonic gave form, purpose and unity to specific social and literary studies and their critical evaluation. Whereas classic modern cultural theory synthesized diverse cultural traditions with the conception of civilization in a hierarchical manner, the newly independent national traditions criticized this hierarchy as exploitative and exclusivist. Such criticism drew its inspiration from specific conditions of social and cultural life which were overlooked or distorted in the previous ideological formation – such as class, race, gender, nation, etc. The issue of whether such new national critical formations were compatible, or even capable of a new synthesis, was immediately raised. For example, Marx claimed to synthesize (the critiques of) German philosophy, British (mainly Scottish) political economy, and French socialism. But despite considerable cross-fertilization, such attempted syntheses failed to overcome the resurgence of national feeling associated with the First World War.

More recently, national traditions of cultural criticism, though engaging distinctive problematics and issues, have converged through new spatial, transversal relations. Yet this postmodern convergence does not amount to a 'synthesis' of classic proportions since the formation of criteria for evaluation and criticism are seen as internal to the traditions themselves – rather than posited as universal and transhistorical. This transversal relation of cultural studies, and also of the cultural theories that they depend upon and extend, undermines any fixed standard for criticism of the ideological function of cultural forms. Any such fixed standard would seem to be internal to a given discursive formation and could attempt to regulate the translations between cultural forms only by an unwarranted assertion of the universality of a specific cultural, and often national, tradition.

Such imperialistic claims are untenable within the postmodern global formation of cultural studies in which any evaluative standpoint must remain open to the criticism that it emerges from within a specific and limited cultural formation. The present formation can thus be called 'postmodern' in that the interaction of national traditions can be neither totalized nor kept isolated. The danger arises at this point that *all* claims to evaluation might be jettisoned along with the critique of ethnocentrism. A key contemporary issue for cultural studies is thus the reformulation of the critique of ideology in the postmodern condition. The critique of ideology, in both its Marxian and Nietzschean forms, was a critical current in polemical relation to the unified concept of European civilization. We must ask: Where is the interest in emancipation that can make contemporary cultural studies genuinely critical?

The present chapter explores the *historical lineage* between classic modern cultural theory with its hierarchical architectonic, through the national-critical formations, to the contemporary transversal 'translation' between cultural forms in order to locate and address the question of critique in contemporary cultural studies from the perspective of comparative media theory. In conclusion it focuses on the transversal relations between textual inscription and the cultural horizon in the postmodern cultural field in order to begin an exploration of metaphors of inscription that may illuminate such transversality.

The Historical Lineage

The new open postmodern field which contemporary cultural criticism must negotiate originated from the decay of the classic modern unified conception of high culture which, in the English-speaking world, is identified with the name of Matthew Arnold. Culture, in his view, could be defined as

> enabling ourselves, by getting to know, whether through reading, observing or thinking, the best that can at present be known in the world, to come as near as we can to the firm intelligible law of things, and thus to get a basis for a less confused action and a more complete perfection than we have at present. (1883: 150, see also pp. 13, 37, 52, 67–9)

In the focus on 'enabling' the assumed connection between writing, audience effect and criticism stands out. Literature and the arts were expected to establish an inwardly cultivated taste sanctioned by the authority of reason and culture and formed into a national tradition that could oppose critically the externality of the machine-world.

From our present viewpoint, it is the formation of culture into a totality encompassing individual works that is significant in this description – and the key role allotted to the reader's cultivation in this formation into a totality. It is the reader's 'best self', formed through culture, that stands above the mere self-interest of the ordinary self that is simply the internal reflection of the externality of the machine world. It is easy enough to call this a conservative, even reactionary, defence of state authority against the untutored masses – and one would not be wrong in doing so – but, in our present circumstances, it is worth recalling that this classic conception of the totality of culture enfolded individual works, their creators, their audience, and the debates of critics within an aesthetic, political and rational unity.

This conception of totality was by no means confined to the English-speaking world. On the continent the French word *civilisation* and the German word *Kultur* expressed a similar binding unity encompassing distinct parts. In both cases, the terms were originally used by the middle class intelligentsia to distinguish themselves from other classes. Later, with the rise of the bourgeoisie to a dominant position, they came to refer to the national self-image as a whole. As Norbert Elias has put it,

> Unlike the situation in which the concept was formed, from now on nations consider the *process* of civilization as completed within their own societies; they see themselves as bearers of an existing or finished civilization to others, as standard-bearers of expanding civilization. (1978: 50)

In the same way that specific creative works were enfolded within the unity of culture, the European nations were enfolded within the unity of 'the West' – which as we all know from the introductory lecture to almost any university course, can be traced back to a few Greek artists and thinkers, and forward to a telos of aesthetic and rational universality. This mutually implicatory unity of origin and goal overarches the differences between the conservatives who regarded the final state as already achieved, the liberals who thought it must be pushed further, and even many 'progressives' and socialists who thought in similar terms of unilinear development. There was, though, another, darker, socialist tradition for whom such a unity of origin and goal was deeply problematic – since they saw their ancestors in the workers and slaves upon whose backs this version of culture had been erected. Walter Benjamin (1973) is especially important for bringing this tradition into thought.

For this reason the First World War can be regarded as the definitive end of the classic stage of European culture. Not only was it clear that the European cultural formation could become warlike and barbarous, as it had been for some time in its relations with non-European peoples, but also the enfolding of nations into a unified European culture was highly problematic – since these destructive characteristics were turned toward other European countries who were supposed to be similar bearers of 'civilization'. Thus, the interpretation that 'we' were being dragged down to the level of savages by our interaction with 'them' was seriously undermined. The concept of an encompassing cultural unity, including both diverse traditions and 'the West' as a whole, could not survive the tearing apart of Europe from within. The failure of the labour and socialist parties of the Second International to prevent this internal destruction is one of the most tragic parts of this story (see Joll, 1966). A whole generation of intellectuals and artists, from every European nation, too numerous to mention individually, were forced to rethink their activity and their social role in a radical way. Let me just mention three that have been important for me, Wilfred Owen, Harold Innis and Edmund Husserl. Both Innis and Husserl were forced out of their rather specialized concerns to undertake investigations into the origin, meaning and telos of civilization. Those of us on the other side of this watershed have had to learn to tell stories of disunity and discontinuity, and the very possibility of a single narrative has become the most problematic thing of all.

From this internal rending of Europe, bourgeois civilization could not survive intact. For both better and worse, internal class antagonisms re-emerged and intensified so that cultural productions and evaluations were required to take sides in the conflict. Moreover, further internal antagonisms articulated around sex, race, nature, and so forth have emerged alongside those of class. Both the capitalist and communist forms of mass society that have emerged in the twentieth century have integrated the cultural industries as either commodity-producing or state-sponsored agencies whose utility in the dominant order has become so self-evident that it no longer seems to require critical justification (Adorno and Horkheimer, 1972; Haraszti, 1987). In an age of cultural industries and cultural police, culture comes to reinforce the barbarism of state capitalist power. But, while culture can no longer be simply separated from barbarism, the concept of 'barbarism' seems to lead nowhere at all – whereas 'culture', for all its problems, still has some promise for renewing the ethico-political component of social critique.

In a parallel and potentially critical vein, various new intellectual formations in different nations have developed approaches to cultural studies that combine the focus on literature and the arts, now understood in the widest possible way to include mass cultural production, with a sociological and ethnographic focus on culture as a way of life. These new 'national' formations of cultural studies are different from the diverse modern traditions (sometimes 'national') in the classic Arnoldian sense, since they emerge from the rending of unified European 'civilization' developed by a triumphant bourgeoisie. For national-critical developments of cultural studies, the unity of the nation and its relation to other nations has been itself a key problem. No longer the guardians of an unbroken tradition of high culture stemming from the Greeks, contemporary national traditions are constituted by discontinuous histories of subordination, immigration, revolt and repression where even the idea of national culture itself must be suspected to be a repressive formation with respect to internal cultural differences. Indeed, the very invention of the idea of an unbroken linear history of cultural advance that is central to the classic modern conception of civilization must now be understood as ideological, as the assertion of temporal continuity over 'external' spatial influences (Amin, 1989). For this reason, the critique of Eurocentric bias in the formulation of the idea of civilization is fundamental for contemporary cultural studies. It can come as no surprise that attempts to formulate a guiding telos in this situation are deeply problematic. I will argue, however, that no matter how radically this task must be rethought, it must not be abandoned. Without such an ethico-political component, the critical edge of cultural studies is irreparably blunted.

In order to theorize such a discontinuous and multiple spatial and temporal formation, the sociological and anthropological concept of culture as a way of life is as important as the literary-artistic one. The field of contemporary cultural studies is opened up by the convergence of these two conceptions of culture: on the one hand, the 'high culture' of literary and artistic studies and, on the other, the sociological and ethnographic concept of culture as a practical form of life. From these derive two concepts of criticism: an activity of discernment of the value of individual works of art based on the general cultivation of the taste of the critic; and, denunciation of particular injustices in the light of their function in the social form as a whole. It would be easy enough in the present context to dismiss the first as the activity of self-appointed cultural policemen and the second as a delusion of the social theorist's phony concept of totality, if it were not for the danger of abandoning the critical task altogether. For better or worse, we must struggle to transform and preserve this dual legacy of critical thought. For all the assertions of discontinuity, there remains a 'certain continuity' of the *problem* of understanding culture as a civilizing project – it is really the radical reformulation of continuity and discontinuity that must be our contemporary theme.

It is certainly important to show, in the words of Walter Benjamin, that 'There is no document of civilization which is not at the same time a document of barbarism' (1973: 256). Indeed, this must be a large part of the work of cultural criticism. But, when the issue of the reflexive justification of the standpoint of criticism is raised it can't be simply pushed aside. Not that the critic's standpoint can ever be guaranteed 100 per cent barbarism-free, but rather that its only justification comes from that, perhaps small, percentage in which it is something else than domination. At this point in the activity of contemporary cultural studies, epistemological and ethical reflexivity converge on a notion of 'critique' which is the contemporary inheritor of the classic modern concept of a 'civilizing project' – a notion that remains deeply problematic, but also unavoidable. For criticism annuls itself if it can claim nothing more than to recycle equally valid, or invalid, perspectives. One can undertake no criticism, even of the greatest horrors, under the banner of barbarism. And, having recognized this, we may also extend the same understanding to earlier, limited formulations of the civilizing project – without abandoning the right, even duty, of denunciation. The field of contemporary cultural studies opens up the interplay between everyday life and cultural articulation. Every determination of this interplay is itself a political intervention in the cultural field tied at once to denunciation and the precarious vision of something better.[1]

Differences in the way in which this field was opened up in various national-critical formations can illuminate both the field of cultural studies itself and the type of intervention that it may make possible in the national culture. Very briefly, we may recall that the German tradition, in particular as it is represented by the Frankfurt School, was profoundly shaken by the failure of German high culture in the face of Nazi victories in popular culture. In France, cultural studies was opened up primarily by critics and philosophers influenced by avant-garde literature. In Britain, it was formed by Marxists who wanted to wrest the national tradition away from Arnold and his ilk. In the United States, cultural studies was a continuation of the pragmatist tradition, with its emphasis on philosophy as social intervention. In Canada, cultural studies was opened up primarily from two directions: by Harold Innis, whose historical studies of communication emphasized the relationship between colonial dependency and social identity; and, by government reports, notably the Massey Commission in the 1950s, which investigated the universities and, later, the cultural industries. Contemporary Canadian communication and cultural studies is situated primarily in this uneasy alliance, and sometimes tension between government policy and national dependency that confers both a historical and a prospective dimension on the theoretical vocation. The perspective of comparative media theory advocated here is an extension of Innis's work and, in general, the 'technology and culture' problematic rooted in Canadian history and theory.[2]

These national formations do not exist in placid isolation – an unlikely event in an age of increasing international trade and competition. All of these components – reactionary elements in popular culture, the disturbances produced by artistic interventions, the class formations in national culture, social engineering and intervention, social identity and dependency and many more – are part of the postmodern field of cultural studies, which has become both global in scope and international in its formation of the project of cultural criticism. The point here is that the very condition for the emergence of these 'national' formations of critical cultural studies – and thus the subsequent postmodern globalization – is the impossibility of a conception of culture like the classic modern one that can unify these discontinuous and diverse components into 'civilization'. We are confronted, in the first place, with an untotalizable spatial plurality and, consequently, the suspicion that the arts, the cultural industries, and cultural studies itself are entirely without any larger justification. If we want to link specific studies to a wider aesthetic, political or rational project, this link seems entirely idiosyncratic and arbitrary. This loss of the link between specific cultural productions and a unifying totality is characteristic of the postmodern cultural field. It is a loss of what Hegel called the *Aufhebung* – the internal connecting and encompassing link between both particular and universal, and origin and goal.

But the point here is not primarily one of loss, but rather of using this historical reflection for a positive characterization of the postmodern cultural field. The central feature of the classic modern unified conception was the *encompassing* of specific works, through the mediation of the author, *into* the totality of culture that could educate the taste of the audience to promote a reasonable authority that could guide (conservative) politics. It is neither the individual works nor the totality itself that is central here, but the 'passing-over', or *Aufhebung*, the moment of passage of the work toward totality that connects particular to universal and origin to goal. With the decay of this totality, the whole field of cultural production and consumption stands simply as a 'horizon' behind each specific work – neither as an enfolding totality, nor merely as a disaggregated empirical sum. Husserl used the term 'horizon' to describe a 'constant halo around the field of actual perception' in which what is determinately perceived is 'penetrated and surrounded by an *obscurely intended to horizon of indeterminate actuality*' (1982: 52, emphasis in original). He developed this metaphor in the context of describing how, while objects in the world are perceived directly, there is a co-present awareness of the whole world itself as a horizon 'behind' the objects. In using this metaphor of horizon in the present theoretical context of cultural studies, I am suggesting that the relation between the specific object of cultural critique and the whole historical and social context is the key issue for a critical theory of society. It is in the *relation between* a specific inscription and its unthematized background horizon where the question of the possibility of a postmodern concept of critique resides. It is argued in the section below that this relation is established by the medium of communication and becomes 'critical' through comparative media theory.

Hermeneutic Taming

In the rest of this chapter, I want to sketch an approach that connects specific cultural studies and interventions to a reformulated postmodern conception of ideology critique that continues the classic modern notion of a civilizing effect. This approach centres on the specific characteristics of each 'medium of communication' and argues that the horizon of the historical epoch can be named through the transversal intersection of a plurality of media. It is the contribution of each specific cultural production to the naming of this horizon that constitutes its capacity for ideology critique.

This analysis of the medium of communication can begin with a phenomenology of the distinction between speech and writing based primarily on the work of Paul Ricoeur and Hans-Georg Gadamer, though, as I will argue later, this phenomenology is later revoked by hermeneutic philosophy in a manner that confines it within the classic modern cultural theory sketched above, and therefore must be recovered and extended by comparative media theory.

Ricoeur defines a text as 'any discourse fixed by writing'. This fixture is an 'intentional exteriorization' which transforms both the event of speech and its meaning. We need to distinguish here between the written transcription of an oral speech event and a writing 'occurring at the point where the speech could have emerged' (Ricoeur, 1981d: 146; see also 1976: 25). In the case of transcription, such as the written transcription of speech in a courtroom, the writing clearly refers back to an anterior speech act which it preserves but does not replace, and therefore can be regarded as an extension of that original act. In contrast, the specificity of writing as a medium of communication only emerges when there is no prior speech act, when the meaning is written, one may say, 'instead' of being spoken. If we regard this as a mere replacement, as simply a different location for an identical meaning, we altogether miss the *productive and forming characteristics of the medium of communication*. But by focusing on the characteristics of direct inscription in writing we open up the possibility that the materiality of a communication medium is not merely an external coat that can be sloughed off at will, but constitutive of both the event and the meaning of the communication itself.

In an oral speech event, speaker and audience are present to one another in a common situation in the here and now. The positions of speaker and hearer can be exchanged repeatedly and, consequently, difficulties in understanding can be removed by clarification of the speaker's intention through further discussion. Reference in such an encounter is primarily ostensive and speech is above all an engaged presentation, rather than an imaginative representation of the world. Speaking is immediately rhetorical and agonistic since there is little space for a separation of knower and known (Ong, 1982: 31ff.; Ricoeur, 1976: 34ff.; 1981b: 176ff.; 1981d: 148ff.). In the absence of other media of communication, these characteristics have important implications for both artistic form and the social order, though we can leave these aside at present since our focus is comparative within the contemporary cultural field (Goody, 1977; Ong, 1982: 31–7).

The inscription of a written text shatters this reciprocity of speaker and hearer in a common situation and disperses the analogous relations in both space and time. Writer and reader probably never meet except through the text. Their roles are not reversible. Rather than addressing the present situation, writing addresses, in principle, all who can read. It is not an immediate act presenting an intervention in a situation, but a delayed representation. Thus, it manifests a distinction between an event and the meaning of that event. It is only the meaning that is fixed in inscription, not the event of communicating, nor the act of inscribing itself.

Consequently, the reference of a text is not directly to the world of the author but to a world opened up within the text, which must then be mediated by the reader's interpretation to his or her world. Historical consciousness derives from the experience of the tension between the horizon of the text in the past and the horizon of the present reader. By this 'fusing of horizons', in Gadamer's phrase, the text mediates across space and time.

> The projecting of the historical horizon, then, is only a phase in the process of understanding, and does not become solidified into the

self-alienation of a past consciousness, but is overtaken by our own present horizon of understanding. In the process of understanding there takes place a real fusing of horizons, which means that as the historical horizon is projected, it is simultaneously removed. (Gadamer, 1975: 273)

Thus, the possibility of distance between the reader and the meaning in the text calls for an active interpretation that constitutes the unity of a tradition in history. The distinction between the saying and the said is a distantiation that calls forth the subsequent activity of interpretation that aims to close the distance and create continuity. Consequently, Ricoeur claims that writing requires the act of 'application' which can 'fulfil the text in present speech' (Ricoeur, 1981d: 158; see also Gadamer, 1975: 274–8; Ricoeur, 1976: 25; 1981a: 134ff.; 1981c: 199, 205). In short, inscription creates distance, therefore the possibility of misunderstanding, and consequently the eventual possibility of a hermeneutic re-establishment of a 'conversation' that produces a much more extensive continuity over the dispersal.

The hermeneutic distinction between speech and writing thus concludes by postulating a two-fold mutual relation that encloses them within the same hermeneutic circle of tradition. It is this presupposed *relation between* speech and writing that returns the hermeneutic comparison of media of communication to classic modern cultural theory. First, the separation of event and meaning by writing is said to clarify what is only a 'virtual', or occluded, distinction that is nevertheless operative in speech (Ricoeur, 1976: 25, 91; 1981d: 152). Even in speech, event and meaning are not identical – though we might never have seen this without writing. Thus, writing brings forth the concealed possibilities of speech. In Gadamer's words,

[T]hat language is capable of being written down is by no means incidental to its nature. Rather, this capacity of being written down is based on the fact that speech itself shares in the pure ideality of meaning that communicates itself in it. In writing this meaning of what is spoken exists purely for itself, completely detached from all emotional elements of expression and communication. (1975: 354)

This hermeneutic centring on the ideal meaning-content of expression is a key assumption of classic modern cultural theory essential to its conception of totality. It is by centring on a meaning-content (supposedly) independent of the materiality of inscription that the plurality of media of communication can be totalized. It is for this reason that, for Ricoeur and Gadamer, as for all hermeneutic philosophy, the model of the text is in principle applicable to the entirety of human action, and therefore is the most complete method for the human sciences (Gadamer, 1975: 153–344, 1977; Geertz, 1973; Ricoeur, 1981c). Even in the case of history, where event and meaning seem to be identical (like in the case of orality) this separation is taken to be an emergent one, rather than an external imposition.

Second, hermeneutic philosophy argues that the distance instituted by writing must be hermeneutically 'fulfilled' in the present speech of the interpreter. 'All writing is . . . a kind of alienated speech, and its signs need to be transformed back into speech and meaning' since 'language has its true being only in conversation, in the exercise of understanding between people' (Gadamer, 1975: 354, 404). Thus, the ideality of the meaning-content is replaced within social relations such that expression can matter in the conduct of human life. This completes the hermeneutic circle, which could not span the plural materialities of media of communication without assuming an underlying identical site of expression. In this way, the assumptions of the ideality of meaning-content and the singularity of the site of expression reinforce each other. Hermeneutic philosophy, though it opens up a discourse of 'comparative media theory', nevertheless simultaneously closes down the implications of the different materialities of media of communication through these two assumptions.

With the assertion of this double hermeneutical relation of 'virtuality' and 'fulfilment', the initial distinction between different characteristics of speech and writing due to the materiality of their inscription in different media of communication is tamed and shelved. Tradition can be a hermeneutic unity because the plurality of media is transcended by an account of meaning that suspends the plurality. To put it succinctly, if writing occurs at the *site* where speech 'could have emerged', the hermeneutic taming occurs through the assumption that this site is, in principle, identical for both speech and writing. Speech and writing are enfolded within a unity of 'language' as the virtuality and fulfilment of the expression of meaning, and meaning is assumed to be the one and only site of human being.

Hermeneutic philosophy is in this sense characteristic of Eurocentric tradition, which attempts to encompass the spatially dispersed, radically Other within the tamed otherness of an alter ego. The radically Other would unsettle the duality of self and other itself and, thereby, undermine the universality of the typical European alienation-story which already prefigures its comforting hermeneutic return to itself.[3] In contrast to this Eurocentric closure, the point of departure for comparative media theory is a spatial dispersion, rather than a temporal alienation-and-return, which incorporates a less comforting, discontinuous, version of time than that which 'tradition' can offer. From this perspective, it is not the speech/writing distinction that is Eurocentric (though indeed the comparative forms in which it emerges is an important aspect of the distinction) but only the hermeneutic taming of the distinction in order to impose a singular historical tradition that represses spatial dispersal.

This hermeneutic taming is another instance of the classic modern aesthetic and social theory in which particular distinctions are overcome in the *Aufhebung* of a universal unity constituted in the temporal unfolding of civilization. In hermeneutic philosophy, the distinction between media of communication becomes, in the final instance, a secondary variable dependent on meaning-content. We are now in a position to follow up comparative media theory with a full sense of the radical attention to the materiality of discourse that it requires in order to come to grips with postmodern culture and not be re-inscribed within a classic modern totality. In short, we are confronted not simply with a plurality of discourses, but a plurality of sites of discourse and a critique of meaning.

Translation and Horizon

While the plurality of sites of discourse cannot be totalized in the classic modern sense through a temporal recovery, neither are the sites simply external to each other. The sites of discourse interact transversally with each other in a spatial dispersion, or, as we may also say, media *translate* other media. While there is, in principle, no closure to possible translations, neither are they all actually accomplished in any given social formation. Thus it is the specific character of the existing translations that defines a prevailing social form. Or, to reverse the proposition, a given social form is defined by those translations that are 'impossible'. Consequently, a specific media comparison, such as that between speech and writing, occurs against a background environment that is itself constituted by translation between all other media of communication. Media theory is, then, not a secondary analysis based upon a more primary, foundational reality – such as the mode of production. Though neither is the 'totality' within which a specific comparison occurs simply ignored – as it is in both mainstream media analysis and much 'postmodern' social theory (Angus, 1992b). Rather, the mode of production itself is understood as an environment constituted through the totality of media translations, against which specific media forms, and comparisons, stand out. It is the impossibility of totalizing all translations that constitutes the 'postmodern' aspect of this comparative media theory, not a supposed absence of totality as such. In short, totality is understood as a media *environment* rather than a self-referring *system* (Angus, 1990b, 1993a).

Understood in this way, *media constitute forms of social interaction and related modes of representation*. Media are not secondary to an externally-defined social form; rather, a specific medium occurs against the background constituted by the present state of media translations. Thus, the phenomenology of media of communication, sketched through the contrast of speech and writing above, is not simply concerned with comparisons of internal characteristics of media, but also with the institutional weight and perceptual engagement that they embody. In this respect, the perspective of comparative media theory incorporates the issues of long-term historical perspective and institutional stability that Harold Innis sought to address through communication theory.

Media of communication are thus most fundamentally *constitutive* of social relations but, based on the plurality of media constitutions, also produce *representations* of the world. Let us state more generally the hypothesis that the materiality of media of communication informs both the event and 'ideal' meaning-content of discourse. The performance of a communication act in a medium of communication constitutes both a distinct set of social relations and also a characteristic type of reference to, or representation of, the world – though the 'world' in this formulation cannot be understood as prior to that constituted by media, but as a *horizon* formed through the interactions between media constitutions (Angus, 1992a). In shifting the focus from the 'inside', or meaning-content, of discourse to its 'outside', or materiality of inscription, the world – as the totality of what can be experienced in whatever manner – is not merely represented within media but is formed through them. The world is thus understood as the horizon of the constitutive function of a given medium, and thus capable of being represented within that medium, and, also, as itself given its prevailing form by the mutual translations between media of communication. There are a plurality of sites of discursive acts which constitute distinct sets of social relations; the representational aspect of a given medium is possible because these sites are not simply external, but interact with each other. The world, as the horizon of these interactions, is the largest context of a given discursive act. Thus, the specific form that a given cultural world takes is constituted by the actual extent of media 'translations' between sites – and the limit of a cultural form is defined by the impossible translations.

In another place I would be interested in following up the institutional and perceptual dimensions of media of communication, or of their role in historical change, or of specific translations in the contemporary cultural field. In this context, I want to address the basic theme for a critical theory of society: the possibility of a civilizing effect of cultural productions in a postmodern cultural field. From the perspective of comparative media theory outlined above, it is in the relation between the site of a given inscription and the horizon of the world that we can locate the issue of a civilizing effect of culture in the postmodern cultural field.

The most basic philosophical issue here can be generalized from the transformation introduced by writing into the consciousness formed within an oral culture: by making marks, the limitations of unaided memory are overcome. By persisting in an external materiality, which can therefore be reactivated at will, human culture gains the ability to extend itself in time and space. As Jacques Derrida has put it, 'the durable institution of a sign' is 'the only irreducible kernel of the concept of writing' (1976: 44). Once the connection between the hermeneutic focus on internal meaning-content and the occlusion of the forming influence of the 'materiality' of media in hermeneutics is apparent, attention must shift to the 'externality' of meaning in the marks that institute the durability, or 'delay', of human culture in space and time.

Delay in communication is produced by a mark that produces a 'trace' of the act of inscription. This trace indicates a meaning that can be reactivated. Inscription is thus most fundamentally the inscribing of a trace that allows a later repetition. The plurality of sites of discourse suggests a plurality of modes of traces. If each medium is a fixing of discourse in a specific mode of inscription, then comparative media theory must investigate a plurality of modes of tracing. Culture is constituted by the mutual translation of these modes of tracing and delay.

Then we must say: it is the horizon that determines the effect of the specific inscription on the cultural field as a whole. Every specific inscription is constituted by its horizon through its medium. The horizon determines what can be expressed within the medium and that which remains outside. In the case of writing, the horizon of existing translations determines the unwritten. The cultural horizon similarly determines the unsaid, the unradiod, the un-videoed, and so forth. And since each medium is a formation of the senses, the horizon determines the unseen, the unheard, the unfelt, the unthought – in every case, the limit of contemporary expression.

This limit of the cultural formation is no longer a single limit. It is a plurality of limits. Every medium of communication has its own limit. In translating from one medium to another, there will always be something that does not translate. A residue, or silence, is produced by the act of translation (Angus, 1993a). Translation does not produce an identical meaning-content in another medium. Otherwise, it would not be translation into a *different* medium. In translation, something drops out. A medium is constituted not only by its own characteristics, but also by its horizon, which determines that which drops out in translation.

Thus, we may say retrospectively that in classic modern cultural theory the edge of culture could be thought of as nature – as that which is outside all cultural forms – because of the exclusive concern with meaning-content. But once we focus on the forming of expression by media of communication, which implies a plurality of media of communication, there will be a plurality of limits, of edges. Culture is like a polygon which we are inside, and which refracts a plurality of internal silences. These limits are what is excluded by the present cultural formation.

Each medium has its own inner horizon, in the sense that the horizon of the world determines that which cannot be translated into the medium in question. Each medium thus has an outside in relationship to the cultural environment. The function of translating from one medium of communication to another is precisely to take that outside and bring it inside, but this will, in the same moment, constitute something else that is pushed outside. The outside is not eternally outside. Limits, edges, appear through the activity of translating between media of communication. In translation, the edge of another medium of communication can appear.

There is a piece of music by Laurie Anderson called 'Talking About Music Is Like Dancing About Architecture', which raises some important questions in this regard. In the first place, consider the unspoken assumption of music criticism that we can get to the truth of music by translating it into words. Such criticism is really translation into another medium, but we tend to think that there is more truth there. Why? The answer will have to do with the horizon of music for self-understanding in relation to our commitment to a verbal or written model of self-understanding. The eye dominates the ear. We tend to suppose that dancing about architecture doesn't make much sense, whereas talking about music does.

In the second place, maybe dancing about architecture makes just as much sense as talking about music. What is the function of a prohibition against translation at this point? To the contrary, more translations are possible than we normally think; and it is only through such 'impossible' translations that the limits of our present cultural formation can appear. From this point of view, the impossible and ridiculous translations are the most valuable ones.

The limit of a cultural form will appear natural and immovable unless we do all translations. But, of course, we could never do all translations, so we will always think of something as immovable. Any state of human culture can thus be circumscribed. All our perception has limits, but these limits can be expressed. The limits come into human experience not by remaining forever outside it but by being brought in by some other medium whose limit is different. In this respect, it is important to note reflexively that the present argument has been developed only from the comparison of speech and writing and that other comparisons might uncover different aspects of comparative media theory.

To sum up: classic modern cultural theory is centred on the expression of a meaning-content. By eliding the question of media of communication, it could assume that cultural products can be synthesized into a totality encompassing each one. The focus on media of communication emerges through the decay of this assumption, when the horizontal context of culture comes into awareness. Hermeneutic theory occupies a transitional position in this respect, since it opens up the discussion of comparative media theory only to close it down by using it as a method of recuperating meaning-content. In the postmodern cultural field, no such recuperation can be successful. Thus, the question of whether there can be a civilizing effect to cultural productions arises with a vengeance. The previous analysis suggests that the idea of such a civilizing effect need not be abandoned and that it can be rediscovered at the moment of translation between media of communication. Whereas modernist cultural practice consisted in designing productions that reflected on their own constitution in a medium, in the postmodern field the critical point has shifted toward translation. Artists and critics who engage in translations that point cultural productions to their horizonal context can uncover limits within the cultural field. Expressing these limits begins to engage a civilizing effect. In a similar fashion, we can define reactionary cultural practice as the attempt to seal borders and prohibit translations.

This chapter has suggested that there are three key components to a cultural production: meaning-content, medium of communication, and the cultural horizon. Classic modern cultural theory expressed its civilizing mission by focusing on the first of these and presupposing that in the passage to totality nothing of significance was left out. (Hegel dismissed this left-out residue as 'lazy existence'.) Postmodern cultural theory can retain the civilizing component to the extent that it focuses on the *method of passage* from a specific production towards the cultural field as a whole. The emphasis thus shifts to the forming influence of the 'materiality' of the medium of communication, to the 'outside' of meaning, and the durability that it institutes (see also Angus, 1994, forthcoming). Consequently, the totality of cultural productions must be reconceived through the notions of translation and horizon.

There can then be no simple cumulation of cultural products into a civilizing effect. What drops out through the constitution of the horizon is of the greatest significance. These limits of the cultural form – plural and internal, though capable of expression – form the site of creative cultural intervention today. Really, there is not a single site, but a switching between sites in a radical homelessness, or placelessness. This homelessness can be named by focusing on the 'drop-outs', on an existence that may be lazy in the sense that 'it doesn't work' for the present system. It is yet to be seen whether this homelessness can itself switch through the focus on the civilizing moment, resist the submission of local sites to global system-engineering, and design borders within which those at home can dwell without fearing the outside. At least until then, it is the task of the critic to peer over the edge.

New World-Metaphors

Hermeneutic cultural theory begins from the metaphors of near/far and internal/external in order to develop a notion of 'depth' meaning as opposed to merely 'surface' readings that are stuck at the level of historical difference and discontinuity. The far is brought near; the external becomes internal; horizons are fused; the going-out of alienation is retrieved by the snugness of coming-back home. Thus, criticism is figured as 'distance'; understanding as coming home. The whole of culture becomes one story of this loss and recovery of home.

In our time these metaphors have become deeply problematic; they seem to elide that which presses itself to be thought – difference, discontinuity, dispersal. But we cannot think that which presses upon us by simply reversing the dualities, nor even by abandoning them. To speak of 'loss' is to suppose a prior belonging and anticipate a return; to speak of 'fragmentation' is to presume the loss and recovery of totality; to speak of discontinuity supposes a break with a prior continuity and cannot help but place itself at the next-to-last position – anticipating, whether spoken or not, a final return. To attempt simply to speak differently is more attractive, but no less seductive. One is likely to recreate traditional root metaphors in other guises: the alienation-story of Ulysses or the Bible may be discovered as if brand new in the wilderness of the

New World. What better way to re-assert their universality – when the straightforward assertion of cultural superiority would no longer be allowed? The attempt at direct difference tends to rebound in a way that reproduces the Same.

I can recommend no faithful maps in this too recently trodden wilderness. Surely, it is different for those who trod in the New World before the Europeans imagined it as theirs and peopled it with the stories they have always known. But, we, who have come to be who we are through these stories, must find another way. In order to step on and beyond these stories, we need to step back and into them; allow them to arise again, as if they were new, but with a sharp eye out for the incomplete fit. And take this incompletion as our clue, our incentive for bending, breaking, metaphors and, perhaps, eventually discovering new stories. We work with the same material, but begin to work in a new way. There is indeed danger here, but there is no movement toward the horizon without danger. It is always possible to discipline oneself to the trodden pathways, where no wild animals dare to interfere with the most dangerous of all.

So we must risk terms like the 'New World', and 'civilization', which go deep into the European imaginary and – because of this, not despite it – allow us to prepare to enter another world, one we have inhabited for a long time without knowing it (see, for an example of this approach, Angus, 1987). Ex-Europeans in the New World have been postmodern for too long without knowing it. In using the metaphor of the horizon, this chapter has attempted to problematize the internal/external, ideal/material, near/far, depth/surface metaphors of hermeneutic cultural theory – which are central to the Eurocentric notion of a linear, temporally-developing tradition. Like much of contemporary cultural theory, it has exploited the reversal of dominant terms, privileging (at least for a moment of discovery) externality, materiality, spatiality, discontinuity and dispersal. Though, as the central concern with a 'civilizing moment' makes clear, this reversal – even as a strategic entry into a difference beyond the opposition – cannot be ultimate. Deeply, even essentially, problematic as it is, without some such concept, critical cultural studies is impossible.

In a time of warranted suspicion of internal development, it is necessary to explore the metaphor of inside and outside – though not as enclosed vessels as in the traditional concept of empathy, which thereby poses the insoluble problem of how a mental internality can ever gain access through external marks to another internality and thus motivates a *denial* of externality. Rather, inside/outside need to be posed as a *problem*: how can an open cultural field become demarcated into separate regions? Or, what is the productive activity involved in establishing a *border* between inside or outside? (Angus, 1990a). Through this replacement of metaphors, we can replace the hermeneutical conception of an 'expansion' of culture, and by culture, which establishes continuity over time and space, and instead begin to chart a territory in which the nearest and the farthest do not traverse a distance that needs mediation (Adorno and Horkheimer, 1972: 42). Rather, distance itself becomes the most problematic of all in a culture at once both global and local. Inscribing a border makes a difference and thus a distance. When inscription begins to incite our wonder, when the marking of a pristine space becomes the site of our questioning, we are beyond the settled boundaries of Europe and begin to face the near-distance of remembered history in the New World. Still, no longer simply accepting this history, but opening it into a critique of Eurocentrism. When the very idea of 'original settlement' becomes a source of wonder, the New World confronts its own origins as a European marking of its imagined pristine space. In the confident New World, time was eliminated in the rush to settlement. But in our own time this rush is forced to describe itself. It must wonder not only at its own settlement, but at the inscriptions that were already settled when Europeans arrived. Inscriptions that marked without defacing, in which inscribing and surrounding were not thrust at a distance from each other. Our task is not to rescue tradition, but to embrace the horizon. We are not so distant from origins that we can forget the love of the unbounded.

Notes

This chapter is a revised version of a keynote lecture given at the Australian Cultural Studies Conference at the University of Western Sydney, Nepean, December 3–5, 1990.

1. This is a key point at which the perspective of this chapter differs from deconstructivism. It is both a small point, in a specific and remote location, and one with far-reaching and crucial implications. Consider the 'formula' for deconstructing hierarchical oppositions of, first, *reversing* the dominant and dominated terms in order to unsettle their hierarchical relation and, second, proposing a tentative *exit* from the conceptual duality. This strategy would suggest that the formation of the term 'culture' within relations of both conceptual and political power renders it useless and in need of deconstruction through the term 'barbarism'. This seems to me not only a dead end but a genuinely dangerous strategy. There is still plenty of real barbarism about. There are some socio-intellectual formations that one would not wish to deconstruct, in the face of available alternatives. Of course, deconstruction 'recognizes' this . . . My intervention begins from the *dominant* term in the civilization/barbarism dualism – which is indeed metaphysical – and is thus 'higher', more 'true', 'valuable', and so forth. I am not denying here that there is a moment

when one can deny this, a moment in which torture and opera are 'equivalent', only that such a moment is not, and cannot be, constitutive of cultural studies. This chapter begins from within the dominant term in order to reform and extend it and is, in this sense, more akin to old-fashioned ideology critique than deconstructivism. It supposes that there is still more to be wrung from the term 'culture'. This is a fundamental philosophical point underlying contemporary cultural criticism and I cannot follow it any further at this point. Nonetheless, this short mention of the difference should serve to allude to philosophical differences of a more extended sort.

2. The formation of Canadian cultural studies, and intellectual life generally, by European theory recognized in these remarks must now be extended to include critiques that can turn the Eurocentric tradition into a merely European one – such as the Latin American discussion of 'identidad', for example, or the Indian historiography of the 'subaltern'. The situation of Canada as a postcolonial, dependent country establishes the basis for this new dialogue – which must be through the indigenous perspective of 'technology and culture' represented by Harold Innis (see Angus, 1993b).

3. I am utilizing Emmannuel Levinas's distinction between 'autre' and 'autrui' here, rendering it in English as 'other' and 'Other', in order to distinguish the other as tamed within the solipsistic frame from the Other whose face shakes the 'foundations' of self-knowledge and assertion (Levinas, 1969: 24, translator's footnote). The connection that I am setting up here between Levinas and Amin's (1989) conception of Eurocentrism connects the critique of metaphysics to the critique of imperialism and unequal development. This connection is extremely important for contemporary cultural studies, though I cannot follow it up further here.

References

Adorno, T. and Horkheimer, M. (1972) *Dialectic of Enlightenment*, J. Cumming, trans. New York: Herder and Herder.

Amin, S. (1989) *Eurocentrism*. New York: Monthly Review Press.

Angus, I. (1987) *George Grant's Platonic Rejoinder to Heidegger: Contemporary Political Philosophy and the Question of Technology*. Lewiston and Queenston: Edwin Mellen.

Angus, I. (1988) 'Oral tradition as resistance', in M. Lupul (ed.), *Continuity and Change: the Cultural Life of Alberta's First Ukrainians*. Edmonton: Canadian Institute of Ukrainian Studies.

Angus, I. (1989) 'Media beyond representation', in I. Angus and S. Jhally (eds), *Cultural Politics in Contemporary America*. New York: Routledge.

Angus, I. (1990a) 'Crossing the border', *The Massachusetts Review*, XXXI (1–2): 32–47.

Angus, I. (1990b) 'Habermas confronts the deconstructionist challenge: on *The Philosophical Discourse of Modernity*', *Canadian Journal of Political and Social Theory*, 14 (1–2 & 3): 21–33.

Angus, I. (1992a) 'Mediation and new social movements', *Communication Theory*, 2: 71–83.

Angus, I. (1992b) 'The politics of common sense: articulation theory and critical communication studies', in S. Deetz (ed.), *Communication Yearbook 15*. Newbury Park: Sage. pp. 536–71.

Angus, I. (1993a) 'Learning to stop: a critique of general rhetoric', in I. Angus and L. Langsdorf (eds), *The Critical Turn: Rhetoric and Philosophy in Postmodern Discourse*. Carbonale: Southern Illinois University Press.

Angus, I. (1993b) 'Orality in the twilight of humanism: a critique of the communication theory of Harold Innis', *Continuum: An Australian Journal of the Media*, 7(1).

Angus, I. (1994) 'Democracy and the constitution of audiences', in J. Cruz and J. Lewis (eds), *Reconceptualizing Audiences*. Boulder, CO: Westview Press.

Angus, I. (forthcoming) 'From ideology-critique to epochal criticism', *Argumentation*.

Arnold, M. (1883) *Culture and Anarchy*. New York: Macmillan and Co.

Benjamin, W. (1973) 'Theses on the Philosophy of History', in H. Arendt, (ed.), *Illuminations*. New York: Schocken Books.

Derrida, J. (1976) *Of Grammatology*. G. Spivak, trans. Baltimore: Johns Hopkins University Press.

Elias, E. (1978) *The Civilizing Process, Vol. 1, The History of Manners*. E. Jephcott, trans. New York: Pantheon Books.

Gadamer, H-G. (1975) *Truth and Method*. New York: Crossroad.

Gadamer, H-G. (1977) 'On the scope and function of hermeneutical reflection', in *Philosophical Hermeneutics*. D. Linge, trans. Berkeley: University of California Press.

Geertz, C. (1973) *The Interpretation of Cultures*. New York: Basic Books.

Goody, J. (1977) *The Domestication of the Savage Mind*. Cambridge: Cambridge University Press.

Haraszti, M. (1987) *The Velvet Prison: Artists Under State Socialism*. New York: Basic Books.

Husserl, E. (1982) *Ideas Pertaining to a Pure Phenomenology and to a Phenomenological Philosophy, First Book: General Introduction to a Pure Phenomenology*. F. Kersten, trans. The Hague: Martinus Nijhoff.

Joll, J. (1966) *The Second International*. New York: Harper and Row.

Laclau, E. and Mouffe, C. (1985) *Hegemony and Socialist Strategy*. London: Verso.

Levinas, E. (1969). *Totality and Infinity*, A. Lingis, trans. Pittsburgh: Dusquesne University Press.

Ong, W. (1982) *Orality and Literacy*. London and New York: Methuen.

Ricoeur, P. (1976) *Interpretation Theory: Discourse and the Surplus of Meaning*. Fort Worth: The Texas Christian University Press.

Ricoeur, P. (1981a) 'The hermeneutical function of distantiation', in *Hermeneutics and the Human Sciences*. J. Thompson, ed. and trans. Cambridge: Cambridge University Press.

Ricoeur, P. (1981b) 'Metaphor and the problem of hermeneutics', in *Hermeneutics and the Human Sciences*. J. Thompson, ed. and trans. Cambridge: Cambridge University Press.

Ricoeur, P. (1981c) 'The model of the text: meaningful action considered as a text', in *Hermeneutics and the Human Sciences*. J. Thompson, ed. and trans. Cambridge: Cambridge University Press.

Ricoeur, P. (1981d) 'What is a text? Explanation and understanding', in *Hermeneutics and the Human Sciences*. J. Thompson, ed. and trans. Cambridge: Cambridge University Press.

5

Staying Dumb?
Feminist Research and Pedagogy
With/in the Postmodern

Patti Lather

> To understand just one life, you have to swallow the world. I told you that. (Rushdie, 1982: 126)

> What is known is always in excess of knowledge. Knowledge is never adequate to its object. (Spivak with Rooney, 1989: 133)

My project in this chapter is to explore the implications of deconstruction for those of us who do our research and teaching in the name of liberation. Positioning research and pedagogy as fruitful arenas for the development of emancipatory practices in a post-foundational era, I attempt to *enact* rather than simply *state* the upheavals produced as deconstruction circulates across recent critical social theory. In the 'performative' part of what follows, the part of this essay that attempts to 'do data differently', my primary focus is the issue of narrative strategies in the writing of social science. In an effort to evoke the politics of varied and competing conventions of analysis and writing, the structuring impulse I have settled on is to craft four narrative vignettes, to tell four different 'stories' about my data. After this use of the site of pedagogy to elaborate the parameters of deconstructive inquiry, I then tell a pedagogical tale that uses the site of research to address the implications of deconstruction for pedagogy. I conclude with some attention to the issues raised by the problematic intersection of postmodernism and the emancipatory projects.

In the intense competition for critical authority and intellectual legitimacy in academic feminist theory,[1] my position on 'the postmodern' can be summed up as follows: because postmodernism is an 'unavoidable ensemble of new cultural practices and know-ledges', it is more than an academic fashion rooted in white French male intellectuality (Ebert, 1991: 24; Fraser, 1989). As the code-name for the crisis of confidence in Western conceptual systems, postmodernism is borne out of the uprising of the marginalized, the revolution in communication technology, the fissures of a global multinational hyper-capitalism, and our sense of the limits of Enlightenment rationality, all creating a conjunction that shifts our sense of who we are and what is possible. Changing the frames of knowledge and politics by disrupting the founding concepts of patriarchy and overturning the necessary grounds of feminism, postmodernism is 'unavoidable' for feminists (Ebert, 1991). What-ever one does with the elision of both power and agency and the kind of 'white boy angst' that mark much of postmodern theory, postmodernism's 'dilemmas of difference' challenge all totalities as reductive fictions, including those at work across the various feminisms. Hence, I join Ebert's recent call for a 'resistance postmodernism'[2] that refuses to abandon the project of emancipa-tion and, indeed, positions feminism as much of the impetus for the articulation of a postmodernism that both problematizes and advances emancipatory work. This chapter is an attempt to enact a 'resistance postmodernism' in the arenas of feminist research and pedagogy.

My database in this effort is interviews, research reports, journal entries and my own insights/musings collected over the course of a three-year inquiry into student resistance to liberatory curricula in an introductory women's studies course, 1985–8. These data were collected by a team that shifted from year to year as students took the Feminist Scholarship class with me. Begun in 1985, the study took place over a long enough period of time that my theoretical vantage point kept reshaping. I began by situating this empirical work within neo-Marxist studies of resistance (Giroux, 1983) and feminist efforts to explore empowering research approaches (Lather, 1988). I have since grown increasingly intrigued with all the talk about 'the crisis of representation' and 'postmodern writing strategies', such as 'multi-voicedness' and texts which interrupt themselves and foreground their own constructedness. Hence, my goal in this essay is to move outside the domain of conventional textual practices, outside the restricted repertoire of rhetorical devices usually attendant upon 'scientific" writing (Bazerman, 1987). In that space of the conventional writing of science, empirical work is concerned with portraying findings as factual and well-founded in ways that are, often, in Van Maanen's characterization, 'as if to satisfy some fetish of documentation or legitimation' (1983: 23).

Instead, I want to attend to the textual operations of my own production and organization of meaning, to write in a way that foregrounds the performativity of language. Especially, I want to attend to the textual production of a certain appearance of transparency where a found world is assumed, communicable in a 'clear' style in which there is no intrusion by language or an embodied researcher. I want to problematize conceptions of 'the non-discursive "real" or empirically discoverable world' (Sheridan, 1988, p. 2), without falling into languacentricity, the collapse of the real into language. The ground I explore is that of a relentlessly heterogeneous reality, the irreducible particularies of which do not take well to dualistic categories. Such exploration is based in a politics that wants other than to marginalize that which does not fit categorical unities that order and classify. Additionally, rather than the erasure under which the 'researcher' typically operates, I assume myself to be a social subject in relation with others. My specificity, not least my own particular interests in the discourses of emancipation and the methodologies of the human sciences, is assumed to shape profoundly the process and product of inquiry.

As I wrestle with what it means to 'do' critical, emancipatory science in a post-foundational context, the following questions become key. What is the special status of scientific knowledge? What work do we want inquiry to do? To what extent does method privilege findings? What is the place of procedures in the claim to validity? What does it mean to recognize the limits of exactitude and certainty, but still have respect for the empirical world and its relation to how we formulate and assess theory?

Foucault's method of archaeology looks at discarded systems of linguistic and institutional artifacts left behind by successive generations as each took up anew the task of creating categories to explain its perception of the human condition. Such a method foregrounds that to put into categories is an act of power. The category systems we devise to 'explain' empirical 'findings' are re-inscribed by post-structuralism as strategies of legitimation where exactitude and certainty deny the unthought in any thought, the shadow, supplement, alterity, the structuring absence inherent in any concept. By conceiving useful categorical schemes as provisional constructions rather than as systematic formulations, our focus shifts from how to impose a specific direction of meaning on the unfolding of the narrative to how data escape, exceed and complicate. We stand poised in some movement into an altogether different approach to empirical inquiry. From the use of interview data to construct a prose poem (Patai, 1988) to the 'dada data' invoked by Clifford (1988: 149), new practices are emerging which reshape our sense of the possibilities for what we do in the name of the human sciences.

This chapter explores not only what to do with 'data' but also how to see one's own teaching as a situated discourse. With all of this in mind, I turn to pedagogy.

A Pedagogy for Transcending Our Limits[3]

> Pedagogy must itself be a text. (Ulmer, 1985: 52)

> Pedagogy should be construed less as an interesting application of theory and more as a means for reconstructing the arena for intellectual debate. (Hariman, 1989: 226)

By pedagogy, I mean that which addresses the transformation of consciousness that takes place in the intersection of the teacher, the learner and the knowledge they together produce. Pedagogy refuses to instrumentalize these relations, diminish their inactivity or value one over another. It, furthermore, denies the teacher as neutral transmitter, the student as passive, and knowledge as immutable material to impart. Instead, the concept of pedagogy focuses attention on the conditions and means through which knowledge is produced. Arguing for the centrality of pedagogy in both cultural production and the popularization of critical analyses, Lusted (1986: 3) sees the neglect of pedagogy, its 'desperately undertheorized' nature, as at the root of the failure of emancipatory objectives. His argument underscores a recent turn to pedagogy in cultural studies (e.g. Henricksen and Morgan, 1990), a turn Spivak attributes to teaching as 'the only place where we actually get any experience in strategy, although we talk a lot about it' (1989: 146).[4]

All pedagogies are situated – specific and contingent to the cultural fields within which they operate. Critical pedagogies are those which attend to practices of teaching/learning that interrupt particular historical, situated systems of oppression. Such pedagogies go by many names: Freirian, feminist, anti-racist, empowering, liberation theology. With both overlaps and specificities within and between, each is constructed out of a combination that includes Frankfurt School critical theory, Gramscian counter-hegemonic practice and Freirian conscientization (Luke, 1992).

Too often, however, tied to their version of truth and interpreting resistance as 'false consciousness', liberatory pedagogies fail to probe the degree to which 'empowerment' becomes something done 'by' liberated pedagogues 'to' or 'for' the as-yet-unliberated, the 'Other', the object upon which is directed the 'emancipatory' actions (Ellsworth, 1989). Positioning such pedagogies as one of many conflicting voices in a context of semiotic bombardment, it is precisely this question that postmodernism frames: How do our very efforts to liberate perpetuate the relations of dominance?

Pedagogy is fruitful ground to help us address such a question at the micro-level of local resistances. As Atkins and Johnson note (1985), however, the powerful resources of deconstruction are not much focused on pedagogy.[5] While much of the small body of literature that does exist is abstract theorizing, a few more situated presentations have emerged. Zavarzadeh and Morton (1991), for example, situate themselves within the debates about humanities curriculum reform. Ellsworth (1989) deconstructs the prescriptions of critical pedagogy within the context of her teaching of a university anti-racism course.[6] In this emerging tradition of situated, embodied deconstructive discourse on pedagogy, I want to focus on the situated pedagogy with which I am most familiar, the introductory women's studies class.

Each of the four tales I shall spin will be grounded in words generated via journals and interviews from students across varied sections of an introductory women's studies class. Borrowing loosely from Van Maanen (1988), I call these a realist tale, a critical tale, a deconstructivist tale and a reflexive tale. By *realist*, I mean those stories which assume a found world, an empirical world knowable through adequate method and theory. By *critical*, I mean those stories which assume underlying determining structures for how power shapes the social world. Such structures are posited as largely invisible to common-sense ways of making meaning but visible to those who probe below hegemonic meaning systems to produce counter-hegemonic knowledge, knowledge intended to challenge dominant meaning systems. By *deconstructivist*, I mean stories that foreground the unsaid in our saying, 'the elisions, blind-spots, loci of the *unsayable* within texts' (Grosz, 1989: 184). Deconstruction moves against stories that appear to tell themselves. It creates stories that disclose their constructed nature. And, finally, by *reflexive*, I mean those stories which bring the teller of the tale back into the narrative, embodied, desiring, invested in a variety of often contradictory privileges and struggles. After telling these four 'data' stories which explore the textual implications of deconstruction for empirical inquiry, I then delineate its implications for emancipatory pedagogy.

A Realist Tale

Mankato State University in Minnesota enrols approximately six hundred students a year in an introductory women's studies class. Multiple sections of the class are limited to thirty-five and taught by teams of faculty and teaching assistants, upper-level undergraduates and master's students who have taken a course in feminist pedagogy. The course is an elective (i.e. an option) that counts for general education credit, one reason for the swelling numbers which result in most sections of the class closing early in the registration process.

Based on a survey of 546 students who took the course in 1987, students are primarily entry-level undergraduates ranging in age from 18 to 70. Seventy-four per cent are under 23. Twenty-six per cent are 23 or over. The latter is due largely to the course being a popular draw for the university's Friday College Program which is aimed at 'the returning woman student'. Approximately 5 per cent of those who take the course are male. Most of the students are first-generation college-goers. Most are working part-time. Many of those in the evening classes work full-time and are raising families. Three per cent of the students at the university are minority, mostly Asian and African-American; 12 per cent of the students in the introductory women's studies class are minority. The university's Alternative Lifestyles office recommends the course to lesbian and gay students; many of the community's feminist therapists do likewise. Scholarship programmes are set up to enable women from the battered women's shelter, organizations working with impoverished women, and minority students to take the class. Students enter the course from a variety of backgrounds in terms of feminism. No few regard it as 'lesbian man-hating'. No few have mothers who self-describe as feminists. Some few self-describe as feminists (19 per cent from 1987 data), but many do not, with most being 'uncertain' as to whether they are feminists (50 per cent).

While each teaching team designs its own course, curricular coordination occurs via staff meetings and departmental curriculum guidelines. A review of the syllabi used from 1985 to 1988 reveals an issues approach to the course, with topics ranging across cultural images of women, violence against women and feminist responses, women in history, literature and the arts, the social construction of gender and sexuality, and the feminist movement, with the focus on the making of women-centred culture. While each teaching team decides whether or not to use exams or a contract grading system, all use the weekly journal as a primary means of course evaluation.

During the fall of 1985, I composed a research team (n = 11) out of the graduate and undergraduate students in my Feminist Scholarship class to do a sequential interview study of 10 per cent of the 200 students who take the introductory women's studies course each quarter. Additionally, one of the students collected interview and survey data for her thesis from six returning women students regarding their experiences of and attitudes towards women's studies (Anderson, 1986). In the fall of 1986, a second research team (n = 12) collected data from 50 per cent of the introductory students regarding their reactions to required reading for the course by using a participatory research design where students interviewed their peers. Throughout part of 1986 and all of 1987, pre/post-survey data were collected regarding student empowerment, critical thinking skills, and attitudes toward feminism (n = 890; Lee, 1988). The survey grew out of dialogue with students enrolled in the course and is, hence, couched in their own language and understanding of key experiences in taking an introductory women's studies course. As such, it exemplifies a *grounded* (Glaser and Strauss, 1967) approach to survey construction. In the fall of 1987, a third research team (n = 10) interviewed students who had taken the course between one and three years in the past (n = 19).

Over this time span, a pool of qualitative and quantitative data was amassed. Its richness was recently underscored for me as four doctoral students worked with parts of the journal data and found it 'compelling', 'engulfing', 'so mesmerizing' that it was 'difficult to maintain a clear perspective'.[7] What follows is a first-level analysis of that journal data, a section of a larger preliminary report that was written up and mailed out by the research team as a 'member check' to the twenty-two students in the introductory course who had been interviewed and worked with us on the construction of the survey. The entire November 1985 preliminary report is nineteen pages long and includes data summaries from three rounds of interviews, journals, field test of pre-post survey, and telephone interviews with ten students who had taken the course in the past. Part of that larger report, the journal data summary which follows was written across six sections of an introductory women's studies course, WOST 210: Women: Self and Others.

Journal Data: Extract from Preliminary Report
From our extremely erratic database – journal entries selected by instructors – it is difficult to make any broad generalizations. Although our information is largely decontextualized, some strong threads run through even the rather haphazard collection of journal pages to which we have had access.

One question we asked the journal writings was 'What topics

opened students up to a more critical perspective on society?' Almost every topic covered was mentioned as being especially thought-provoking to someone: economic realities for women, the human cost of sex role socialization and stereotyping, anorexia, sexism in language, the history of both misogyny and the 'struggles, hardships and suppressed lives of early women that were not in my history books – how long the struggle has been'. Two noted the realization of 'the way everything is connected, e.g. the oppression of Third World women affects everyone'. The use of women in advertising 'caused my first feeling of being discriminated against'. The subject that elicited the most mixed feelings was that of welfare. For example, 'I didn't realize how little these people get.' But later in the same entry: 'I think there are a lot of hidden issues that weren't discussed. We took the person's side but all the others were left out.'

One pattern was the realization of naïveté and being 'saddened by my ignorance'. With the anti-pornography material: 'I feel like my stomach is still tied in knots'. 'The subjects we discuss are very interesting and controversial and shocking due to the fact they exist without us even realizing it or how severe they are in society . . . the topics arouse my inner thoughts.' 'I'm really struck by the subtle ways women are discounted. It's no wonder I've felt disregarded a lot of my life.'

A second pattern was contrasting new knowledge presented in the class with what had been previously learned. In regards to the standard portrayal of the Temperence Movement, 'I never thought to question it.' One student noted the huge difference in the way genital mutilation was presented in a psychology course versus her women's studies course.

A final pattern was a sense of exposure to topics which encourages further learning and action. After dealing with lesbian issues: 'There is so much searching to do in this.' 'Some of the issues get me so riled up inside I can hardly stand it. But being so riled gives me the ambition to want to work harder for what I want.'

A second question we asked the journals was 'What effect does the class have on the day-to-day lives of students?' Some students tell stories of taking action in some way regarding issues raised in class:

> ___ was down watching a 'skin flick' with some other guys. I asked him if he liked that kind of stuff. He said – I don't know – it's alright. I told him that I can't really stand it.
> I have no way of stopping the sexism in these textbooks but my mother is an elementary school teacher and I will talk to her about this problem.
> In class today was the first time I had told straight people and people

that I don't know very well that I'm a homosexual. I said, 'Are you surprised?' . . . All of the women in our group gave me support.
I asked him how he would feel if he lived in a culture where every single day of your life someone is telling you how worthless you are. He told me I was exaggerating. Then I pointed out that practically every TV commercial is saying that. Simple, subtle put downs.

Some write of re-seeing past experience:

One of my brothers was particularly mean. If we didn't do as he said, we were in trouble. When I look back at this, I see it as battering and abuse.
I remember that___ and I went to the Adult Book Store . . . I know that now that I realize what happens in that building, I will never return, not even for a joke.
It is never good for one's 'image' to be seen with someone of another race or lower class. That is sad and I need to work hard to refrain from being so discriminatory.

And some write of the effects of taking the course on the lives of those around them:

Because of worrying that someone will think I'm gay for taking this class, my boyfriend told me not to tell anyone that I'm taking this class.

A third question we asked the journals was, 'Where is there evidence of student struggles with the course?' Reasons that emerged for having a difficult time with particular material presented in class ranged from conflict with religious beliefs, to a feeling that material was presented in a one-sided manner, to a feeling that the perspective presented in class invalidates one's own life: 'I am happy, proud and fulfilled to be a wife and mother.' Anti-feminist beliefs were challenged: 'I was taught to think that feminists went too far. I am disoriented because I have begun to agree with so many of the points I disagreed with for so long. I never wanted the ERA to pass and women's libbers were always "stupid radicals".' A final pattern in terms of student struggles with the class was a not wanting to know: 'This class has been hard for me, as I'm sure it has for others. If we don't see it, hear it and feel it, we won't know it exists.' 'This class makes me angry. I don't like to feel this way and avoid it whenever possible.' 'I don't want to believe the terrible things I am learning.' 'What good is knowing about this if I can't do anything about it?'

A final question we asked the journal was, 'What made students feel empowered?' It became evident that there is a painful first step which we call 'reality shock'. Students enter the classroom at varying stages of feminist awareness and those from the most sheltered lives seem to suffer the most 'reality shock'. 'At this time I feel disoriented, alienated, hopeless and angry. I feel somewhat like the floor has been pulled out from underneath me.' These feelings were often expressed in a two-part journal entry which began on a 'hopeless' note but ended with strength. For instance:

> I am glad I took this class even though it has caused me confusion, alienation and fights with my boyfriend and I wish it was a requirement for everyone.
> In this women's studies course I have gone from ignorance to being educated. I've felt the oppositional knowledge; indeed there are some days I wish I didn't have to deal with women's issues – but the wonderful hours come when I feel liberated, not angry, but full of love for sisterhood.

Many of the entries expressed simply an appreciation of the course and feelings of new-found power. 'I feel informed when I stand up for my rights.' 'I've had tremendous growth in my awareness of women's issues in the past three months. So many things make sense to me now.' 'I want to be a conscious woman growing stronger and more confident in my mind, body and spirit.' 'This course keeps me aware of my options, supports me in directions I want to explore and provides me with information and experiences I don't always have first-hand.' 'I'm not the same person that went into this class. I've grown and become better from it.' 'We came away richer, having learned from one another.'

One entry summed up what most students feel about the 210 class: 'I will never be the same. What else can I say? This class makes me feel angry, happy, sad, numb, sick, wonderful, intelligent, dumb, responsible and most of all *aware!*'

* * *

After students had a chance to read the preliminary report, group meetings of four to six students were held to discuss their reaction to it. Members of the research team asked students to assess our efforts in the report to represent adequately both their experience and the diversity of student experiences of the class and the usefulness to them of participating in such a study. The nineteen who took part in this 'member check' wanted few changes and expressed an enhancement of their experience of the class due to participation in the research process, a position summed up with 'Made 210 more meaningful to me' (Joycechild, 1987a).

In writing of the realist tale, Van Maanan notes the convention of interpretive omniscience, the imperialism of rendering the 'object' passive, the orchestration of quotes and footnotes, and the banishing of self-criticism and doubt on the part of an author who 'disappears into the described world after a brief, perfunctory, but mandatory appearance in a method footnote tucked away from the text' (1988: 64). In 'Doing realism' (p. 67), '[a]uthority rests largely on the unexplicated experience of the author' (p. 64) who is 'The Distant One' (p. 67) guided by the 'Doctrine of Immaculate Perception' (p. 73).

In contrast to Van Maanen's articulation of realist conventions, this study was from the beginning not situated in claims of omniscience and desires to foster passivity. Its desire is otherwise, situated as it is in a space of 'research as praxis' (Lather, 1986). Self-criticism is evident in the opening focus on a 'decontextualized', 'erratic', 'haphazard' database. Authority comes not from adherence to 'objective' method, but from engagement and the willingness to be self-reflexive. For example, the question 'Where is there evidence of student struggles with the course?' began, 'Where do you find resistance?' It was changed by a member of the research team. She writes,

> 'Reasons for resistance' implied that we are right and had an élitist, dogmatic ring to it. 'Sources for struggle' is also more descriptive of a process I found throughout in which students began with one line of thinking, but by the end of the journal entry or by the next entry seem to have come full circle or at least to have done some questioning of currently held beliefs. (Kim Luedke, October 1985, Feminist Scholarship class)

Performatively, the text demonstrates how a solidity of specification contributes to the 'reality effect'. For example, quotes are used to authorize, both in the sense of 'I, the researcher was there, in the field', and to say, 'Someone really said this exactly this way and this can be documented.' But quotes are also used to provide a profuse and diverse specificity, a kind of 'dialogical dynamism' beyond mere heterogeneity where 'voices are juxtaposed and counterposed so as to generate something beyond themselves' (Stam, 1988: 129). Additionally, framing itself via 'the questions we asked of the journals', the structuring elements of the text work to disperse the authority of specific embodied knowers by foregrounding the ambiguity inherent in constructed versus found worlds.

As such, this text works to deflate rather than inflate 'the enormous pretensions of the realist enterprise' (Van Maanen, 1988: 57). As a realist text, it assumes there is a world out there, that some things are knowable and that 'we know that we know them' (Simons, 1989: 8). Nevertheless, its elements of legislation and prescription are few; its policing of the boundaries of legitimate practice moves against an alternative canon characterized by totality, closure and coherence. Rather, its move is toward the ambivalence and open-endedness characteristic of non-dominating, non-coercive knowledges which are located, partial, embodied (Haraway, 1988).

A Critical Tale/A Deconstructivist Tale

My exploration of what it means to tell both critical and deconstructivist tales will be grounded in the following words from an extended journal entry submitted early in the quarter by a 21-year-old African-American woman who was the first in her family to attend college:

> The film, *Killing Us Softly*, and the discussion were interesting and informational to me. They brought out many of the abusive behaviors and gestures that some commercials direct towards women.
>
> The movie was at first really funny to me and I didn't think much about the ads except that they were funny and somewhat entertaining. Then when we started to discuss the topic in class, I realized not everyone thought as I did. I was thinking what's wrong with what the movie was saying? It's always been that way, hasn't it? But listening to other students' reactions started me to thinking more closely about it. As I did, I became more and more upset. The movie actually showed me how TV exploits women. Sex is used so much in commercials and television programs. I never really thought about how the commercials and television programs portrayed us women. It really makes us look like slabs of meat and sluts.
>
> As the discussion proceeded on, students were talking of guilt, anger and shame. I was surprised. I didn't feel this way at all. I thought the commercials were naturally always like that.
>
> I left the class last Monday wondering why certain people got all upset over some commercials when they have always been that way, it was a fact of life.
>
> During the week as I watched television, I started to pay more attention to commercials and television programs. I started not to like what I saw. Everything was exploiting women with sex. I started to categorize programs from good to bad. I ended up not finding too many good programs that depicted women as intelligent individuals. By the middle of the week, I was highly upset at myself for not giving more thought to the discussion on Monday. I felt angry and ashamed. Angry at the people who make the commercials and television programs and ashamed at all the people including myself who don't even think about it and let it go on.
>
> The movie and discussion now make more sense to me. They have made me more aware of how women are misused and treated by society. I find myself now wondering what can I do to make a difference, if anything. Things will probably always be the same.

How might one make meaning out of this journal entry as 'data'? I first present one possible reading, using hegemony theory. After this 'performance' of a critical story, I then interrogate the critical reading by juxtaposing it with a second reading of the same data, this time using the framework of deconstructiv: it theory. What is at work here is a performative logic in the form of interrogation by juxtaposition. I then contrast the codes of the two readings, setting up a tension between deconstruction and the emancipatory projects to which I return towards the end of this chapter.

Reading 1   The student has watched a film that is essentially a feminist ideology critique of the advertising industry. She positions herself as initially outside of what she constructs as the rest of the class's movement of sympathy, even illumination by the movie. Her journal entry presents a picture of every critical pedagogue's dream-come-true: the mystified student who undergoes 'a sea change in received interpretations' (Cocks, 1989: 191). Her common-sense conceptions are shaken up via a cognitive process of classroom exposure to and week-long wrestling with methods of analysis which enable her to see her real situation as woman in a patriarchal world. Additionally, her identification early in the course of the agency/paralysis issue, as read in the four times repeated 'but it's always been that way', and her marginalization by race and class as well as sex, position her as outside of and, hence, perhaps open to radicalization and activism. Her reaction to the film demonstrates both the value of 'radical information' in changing attitudes and hope in the maturation of people's consciousness and commitment to social activism.

Reading 2   A deconstructive reading attempts to use this student's words differently. Rather than positioning her to read against the ideology of the advertisements, their effort to produce a particular kind of consciousness, deconstruction makes her production of meaning the object of the curriculum. The complexity of her response to both the movie and the analytical methods introduced by the teacher, methods positioned as not neutral but as 'methods of analysis designed to reveal and to command assent to these answers' (Buckingham, 1986: 93), encourage her to formulate her responses and then rethink her formulations.

Such an approach asks, as she watches the television that week, does she define herself against the advertisements as ideologically suspicious texts, or does she probe the complexity of the contradictory meanings and pleasures she derives from the media? As a movie, *Killing Us Softly* does not validate or investigate the production of differential readings. It produces, engineers a consensus reading. Its task is to make ideology visible, to reveal the suppressed ideological function of advertisements, to unmask and expose underlying values. It positions itself as demystifying and reduces the complexities of ideology and subjectivity to false consciousness which correct information can overcome, information disseminated in classrooms such as this one by a vanguard which leads, shapes, urges (Buckingham, 1986). What is her reaction to methods of analysis designed to reveal and to command assent to those revelations?

Not necessarily consciously, although the game of producing what the teacher wants to hear cannot be overlooked, students in women's studies classrooms learn to produce 'correct' answers, to follow a kind of 'group-think' that repositions them within a 'sisterhood' of oppressed women unified in their newly discovered outrage at 'the patriarchy'. There is pleasure in this way of transcending the competitive individualism that permeates Western culture.[8] But there is, also, a suspiciously blanket rejection of popular forms here (Buckingham, 1986). She says a lot of ideologically correct things, with no foregrounding of the advertisements themselves as either contradictory or eliciting contradictory responses from her, pleasure as well as outrage.

Juxtaposing these two readings foregrounds the very different assumptions at work. The hegemony model assumes élites who, through the agency of ideological state apparatuses, impose their meanings and agendas on subordinate groups, in this case, the film's construction of a patriarchal conspiracy regarding advertising images of women. The 'oppressed', unaware of alternatives, consent to the élites' definitions, despite the contradictions such definitions pose to their own experiences. The hegemonic relation ' "locks" the consciousness of the oppressed into interpreting their experiences in the categories, terms and values of the dominant ideology' (Winter, 1989: 6), acquiescing to an encoding of the social world which acts against their own interests. Caught in false consciousness and mistaken about the real nature of the relations and ideas shaping their world, subjects are theorized via what Kipnis calls, 'discursively tying the people into a radical political logic' (1988: 151) where they are assumed to be invested in grasping a reality of domination, subordination and resistance, once they are engaged by 'critical pedagogues'.

The deconstructive model is more interested in a 'suspicious' reading which probes the desire of 'liberatory pedagogues' and foregrounds what there is here that is explicit heterogeneous and discontinuous, what escapes, is Other and opaque, what refuses to be totalized. Ideology critique positions teachers and researchers with liberatory intentions as 'The "we" who know better (who have somehow got science and can write the theory of their naïve narratives) . . . where "we" are the privileged subjects of knowledge and science' (Bennington, 1987: 24) Ideology critique views ideology as a property of the text, a cognitive lack/distortion, rather than as a process of production between text and audience. In contrast, post-structuralism positions ideology critique as a product of a binary logic in its moral denunciation of some 'Other' and argues that '"There are no social positions exempt from becoming oppressive to others . . . any group – any position – can move into the oppressor role" . . . "everyone is someone else's 'Other'"' (Minh-ha and Gentile, respectively, quoted in Ellsworth, 1989: 322).

Additionally, hegemony theories assume that once the subjugated grasp the 'true' nature of social reality, via the theoretical tools of the critical intellectual, they will then be free to remake the world in their own likeness. From a deconstructive position, while such theories have much to teach about how structural forces work, they assume an excessive faith in the powers of the reasoning mind on the part of subjects theorized as unified and capable of full consciousness, Furthermore, hegemony theories position the 'oppressed' as the unfortunately deluded, and critical pedagogues as 'transformative intellectuals' (Aronowitz and Giroux, 1985) with privileged knowledge free of false logic and beliefs. Such a bald statement points out the profound dangers in attempting to speak for others, to say what others want or need, of performing as the Grand Theorist, the 'master of truth and justice' (Foucault, 1977: 12).

From the position of hegemony theory, deconstruction contains its own dangers. Chief among these is the corrosive scepticism of Baudrillardian rhetorical excesses and intensifications which collapse 'the real' into its simulation, thereby erasing any ground for a unified political struggle towards some measure of emancipation. While 'the real' is mediated through language, it has not disappeared. Cornel West terms this the reality that one who has lived it *'cannot not know'* (see Stephanson, 1988: 277; original emphasis). Such structures of power exceed and complicate the collapse of 'the real' into language, the construction of an aesthetic radicalism as a substitute for a moral one (Connor, 1989).

Readings 1 and 2 are efforts to enact the limits and possibilities of reading data through the respective prisms of theories of hegemony and deconstruction. In creating a multi-voiced text, I have attempted a creative collision of incommensurable voices that do not map on to one another. My effort is towards a text that is multiple without being pluralistic, double without being paralysed. Decentring the use of empirical work to demystify and catalyse, I foreground how deconstruction encourages ambivalence, ambiguity and multiplicity by exploring what is most densely invested, what is usually muted, repressed, unheard in our discourses on liberatory pedagogy. This is far different from a reading informed by hegemony theory where one's narrative tracks are covered in the construction of an analysis designed to oppose a 'correct' reading against a 'mystified' one.

A Reflexive Tale: the Knowers and the Known

The following is a 'playlet' constructed out of the words of four doctoral students who worked with parts of the journal data on an assignment for a class in analysing qualitative data in the spring of 1989. Their words come from their class writings and a tape-recording of a meeting where the four of them compared and contrasted their approaches to analysing the data.

> *Michel*: I got my data from Patti today . . . I'm really excited about these journals and interested in seeing how much of them I can relate to. I've been so nervous and depressed lately that I'm looking forward to reading about movement in people's thinking, and the many feminist encounters of my life, while frustrating at times, have always lifted my spirits and moved me from my stance as a logical negativist!
> [. . .]
> I have been working on the data for Patti's women's studies journals and I must say that this has been fascinating. This is my first attempt at actual coding . . . for qualitative analysis. I LOVE it, hard as it is. I feel like I am in this data . . . in my coding but also in these women's stories and reflections. The data is so rich . . . and the opportunities for direction are seemingly endless.

> *Dan*: I became totally just engulfed, immersed in the entries . . . the stories were so compelling. It's our own personal perspective that came into play with the data. Even though we were doing it as 'Patti's data', we were also looking at it as data that had personal meaning for us: one of us focused on social issues raised in the class, one on anger, one on labels people put on one another, one on what I as a curriculum leader in a school system can do to get more focus on women in the curriculum.

> *Myrna*: My personal notes physically interrupt the text. My own feelings that came up – this text is so powerful to me. When I first [started putting in my reactions] I was compelled to do it. I turned it into Patti, making no judgments about it. She encouraged me to continue this . . . I think this data has lots of stories to tell. It was personally validating for me to see women feeling free to express their feelings because mine had been suppressed for so long. So there was sort of an unconscious celebration of that, I think, that was very personal.

Ken: One interesting area was the instances of males being marginalized by this women's studies class. Being a white, Anglo-Saxon, Protestant, colonial, semi-thin, tall, upper-middle-class (I could go on) male, I have been aware of this marginalization within our class. It has not been in terms of deed, but in terms of this ever present list that seems to be in most every article of this sort. I am puzzled as to how to react to it. My first reaction is to say that it is OK because my accidental positionality has been privileged for so long that this marginalization is a small price for me to pay for my continuing privilege. My second reaction is to say this reverse discrimination is just as bad as the first and discrimination should not be tolerated by anyone. It should not be tolerated because it is *accidental* that I'm positioned within this group, and it is hard for me to support any act that distracts with people dealing with me as *me*, not just a member of some group. It is a rough dilemma.

Myrna: This stuff is so rich.
Michel: Oh, I thought so too.
Myrna: I just pray that my dissertation data is as rich; it'll be easy to do if it is. I just keep *wanting* to work on this.

Dan: The words, there was a jargon and allusions that I didn't understand. She had them thinking in a certain way.
Myrna: My experience with therapy and Michel's with taking an introductory women's studies course, a lot of these issues we've given voice to, so our experience [of the data] will be different.

Ken: Many students were kind of trying on voices. One was really mixed. She started talking about homosexuals and you heard the feminist or very liberal voice on how to treat homosexuals. Then all of a sudden she starts bringing the Bible in and the old stuff came back in. This was a very interesting passage and I think it may prove to be an interesting place to 'massage' [the data] more.
Michel: I like what you said, I like calling it trying on voices.
Myrna: Yeah, that's a neat idea. That would be a *really* interesting thing to use as a study with this material.

Michel: It doesn't sound like we're saying anything that different, which is validating for me.
Myrna: It's like layering our experiences with this data.

Patti's reflections: Having the doctoral student analyze this data grew in such unexpected directions. I didn't expect it to move my own work forward, to bring what I had come to call my 'dead data' alive. Begun as a last-minute effort to get data in their hands, it grew into another layer of this inquiry which shed much light on the 'black hole' of qualitative inquiry: data analysis. They came to the data without the theoretical baggage that I had. What struck me most was how much of themselves they brought to the analysis, how their wrestling to make sense of the data evoked their own investments of privilege and struggle, e.g. Ken's focus on 'the lists of the demonized/privileged Other' used by feminists: the litany of the white, middle-class, heterosexual male and how that silences/marginalizes/paralyzes.

> Listening to the tape especially put me in touch with how it feels to have your teaching and researching scrutinized – for example, their concern with whether I was imposing my own 'regime of truth' in terms of, 'She had them thinking a certain way.' More uncomfortable was their concern regarding confidentiality issues. While I made clear that students had signed permission slips regarding use of their journal entries in possible publications, in photocopying journal entries for the doctoral students to work with, I did not take off some names. The tape of their meeting included a discussion of the ethics of this.

In the 'reflexive tale', I use a narrative rationality as opposed to the kind of argumentative rationality demonstrated in the preceding tales. An argumentative rationality creates winners and losers while a narrative rationality works to 'illustrate rather than claim' (Van Maanen, 1988: 122). The text is used to display rather than to analyse. Data are used differently; rather than to support an analysis, they are used demonstrably, performatively. Data are used to condense, exemplify, evoke, rather than to embellish theoretical argument by collapsing data into an empirical instance where they are coded as a 'certificate of presence' (Barthes, quoted in Hutcheon, 1989: 91).

Summary Across the Tales

Across the tales, I have presented alternative, conflicting representations, juxtaposed disparate textual styles and foregrounded the unresolvable tensions between them in order to understand what is at stake in creating meaning out of 'data'. With the realist and critical tales, I inscribe the conventions, induce conditioned responses and then subvert those responses by bringing to the fore the politics of how these codes operate (Hutcheon, 1989). Such simultaneous inscription and subversion of the codes by which we make meaning creates the doubly coded narrative that characterizes postmodern textuality. The deconstructive tale aims not to govern a practice but to theorize it, deprive it of its innocence, disrupt the ideological effects by which it reproduces itself, pose as a problem what has been offered as a solution (Rooney, 1989: 54). With the reflexive tale, I use a performative logic to display a possible construction of the parameters of what I am calling deconstructive inquiry (Lather, 1991a, 1991b). There, knower and known are brought together in the representational form of a dramatic vignette that startles complacent comfort with older forms and conventional assumptions about language and representation. Collectively, all of the tales exemplify Bordo's words: 'We always "see" from points of view that are invested with our social, political and personal interests, inescapably "centric" in one way or another, even in the desire to do justice to heterogeneity' (1990: 140).

Spanos writes that the most useful work in the present crisis of representation 'is that which uses form to disrupt received forms and undermines an objective, disinterested stance' (1987: 271). Van Maanen urges movement toward unmasking fieldwork by breaking methodological silences and inventing forms of textual self-consciousness. While he cautions that such self-reflexivity can become 'vanity ethnography' (1988: 93), he welcomes the more experimental forms of ethnographic writing. The methodological self-reflection engendered by such experimental forms of textual construction is based on the realization that the so-called facts that one 'discovers' are already the product of many levels of interpretation. As Hutcheon notes, 'facts are events to which we have given meaning' (1989: 57).

To work towards what it means to do empirical work in a post-foundational context is to move into the space of deconstructing/deconstructive inquiry, to tell stories that end neither in comprehended knowledge nor in incapacitating textual undecidability. Disallowing claims to certainty, totality and Archimedean standpoints outside of flux and human interest, it is to tell 'a story that retrieves inquiry as a "way" that is always already beginning, always already "on the way"', a different story 'that makes a critical difference not only at the site of thought but also at the site of sociopolitical praxis' (Spanos, 1987: 275–6).

Deconstructing/Deconstructive Pedagogy

In this final section of the chapter, I return to the scene of pedagogy to focus on the ways an intendedly liberatory pedagogy might function as part of the technology of surveillance and normalization. In this pedagogical tale that moves across varied elements of the preceding ways of telling stories about 'data', three questions will be addressed: (1) How do we constitute the object of emancipatory pedagogy? (2) How do we attend to the social relations of the emancipatory classroom? (3) What practices might help us deconstruct authority in the liberatory classroom? My exploration of these questions will be grounded in the following words from students as elicited by interviews and journals:

> I feel like they were telling me I'm wrong to feel the way I feel.
> There are a lot of outside things trying to force us to become one way or another. Feminism should free us to become what we are. We need to be careful feminism doesn't become part of the problem.
> Take what you want and use it should be the message of the course.

[The] message I'm now getting: active involvement in feminism is being pushed. I don't want to become a radical . . . I want to go through the course and be able to decide what's good for me without anyone being judgmental.

I know I'm oppressed but I don't feel as oppressed/discriminated against as this class makes me feel I should feel.

My world is shaken up. I feel I am living in constant crisis. I can see that as each class goes by I am going to be less sure about things and more confused about what I probably should think and feel.

In response to the question, 'Who's to blame for our ignorance?': I think everyone is partly to blame for their own ignorance, yet I also think that society has an equal blame for making the lacked knowledge so meaningless to persons. [Written in response to being asked her views on the importance of herstory.]

I guess I'm a bit different from the majority of our class. My reason being is in this class everyone is always saying what's wrong with everything. I certainly realize that women only making 59 cents on the dollar is really unreal, but it's a lot better than 29 cents or 39 cents! I would love it if we made $1.00 on the dollar, but we don't. This class often dwells on the very negative side of every issue.

Each quote was selected from material elicited by a memo to course instructors (n = 7, myself included) asking for access to journal entries 'that capture the struggle involved in learning the "re-seeing the world" that is the hallmark of Women's Studies'. The students' words are presented in a deliberately fragmented, decontextualized manner in order to fight the desire 'to restoree transparency by means of a great deal of information' (Baudrillard, 1981: 201). Class, race, age, sexual orientation, etc. are unmarked, erased.

Constituting the Object of Emancipatory Pedagogy
The project of liberatory pedagogy requires a subject who is an object of our emancipatory desires. Who is this student? Rather than her demographics, let us focus on the desire that shapes her. My reading of the literature across the varied critical pedagogies foregrounds three primary characteristics of the object of emancipatory pedagogy: she is both victimized and capable of agency; while she has something approximating false consciousness, that consciousness is unified and capable of Freirian conscientization, knowing the world in order to set herself free from it. Finally, a basic assumption in the construction of this subject is that it is knowledge that will set her free. I will deconstruct each of these primary characteristics of the object of emancipatory pedagogy.

In foregrounding assumptions regarding agency, false consciousness and empowering knowledge, it is important to take into account Foucault's warning of 'the violence of a position that sides against those who are happy in their ignorance, against the effective illusions by which humanity protects itself' (1977: 162). How do we minimize such violence by focusing less on disturbing cultural self-satisfaction and more on enhancing existing penetrations and frustrations? How can we use the contradictory consciousness endemic to the proliferation of discourses that characterizes this era of electronic media and micro-electronic communication to minimize such violence? Lewis, for example, argues that many women

> both wish to appropriate and yet resist feminist theoretical and political positions. . . . We need to . . . consider the substance of why women may wish genuinely to turn away from the possibilities it offers. . . . We cannot continue to accept simple notions of false consciousness which buries the complexity of human choices in a too unproblematized notion of self-interest. . . . Rather than displace this young woman's terror into the safe ideological category of the falsely conscious . . . [we must take into account] the negotiations required to secure one's survival. (1989: 9–11)

To avoid the 'master's position' of formulating a totalizing discourse requires more self-consciousness about the particularity and provisionality of our sense-making efforts, more awareness of the multiplicity and fluidity of the objects of our knowing. An example of this is the evolution of the question mark in the title of this chapter. It was in the course of the inquiry and via the less neo-Marxist-saturated theoretical vantage points of the student co-researchers who worked with me that the concepts of false consciousness and resistance began to be problematized. Resistance became

> a word for the fear, dislike, hesitance most people have about turning their entire lives upside down and watching everything they have ever learned disintegrate into lies. 'Empowerment' may be liberating, but it is also a lot of hard work and new responsibility to sort through one's life and rebuild according to one's own values and choices. (Kathy Kea, Feminist Scholarship class, October 1985)

In terms of false consciousness, while a research memo written by myself makes clear that 'I want no predetermined definitions of consciousness. This will be emergent knowledge coming out of the research process' (19 January 1986), it also displays an unproblematic conception of the 'processes by which false consciousness is maintained'. By the following year, the question mark was added to the title of the study, marking movement in the research team's conceptions of the object of our inquiry. This is exemplified in Joycechild's (1988) movement 'from their resistance to mine' where the object of her inquiry shifted from student resistance to liberatory pedagogy to her own resistance to the assumption that 'their problem' was not buying into 'our' version of reality.

How do we use our position as teachers to breach the univocality of the 'message', to restore the ambivalence of meaning and demolish the agency of the code, to break the pattern of yet another controlling schema of interpretation, even if offered in the name of liberation (Buckingham, 1986: 179)? How can we position ourselves within our teaching less as masters of truth and justice and more as creators of a space where those directly involved can act and speak on their own behalf? How do we do so without romanticizing the subject and experience-based knowledge? Windschuttle, for example, writes:

> The idea . . . that working people are ignorant of the realities of the institution that most shapes their lives, the workplace, deserves to be rejected. Exploitation and inequality are widely recognized and injustices and contradictions are experienced every day. Indeed, major social institutions, including the trade unions and the labour parties, have been established by the working class to redress these very features of society. Any account of culture or ideology must start from this. (Quoted in Winter, 1989)

Yet many do remain ensnared in and constituting of disempowering frameworks of meaning. The best solution I have been able to come up with is to position intellectuals as other than the origin of what can be known and done, some positioning of ourselves elsewhere than where the 'Other' is the problem for which we are the solution. Such a 'solution' accepts the importance of specificity in critical practice. Situated in locatable, embodied critical cultural practices, it probes political conditions and circumstances in a way that refuses inside/outside dichotomies and the 'demonologies of the Other' common to ideology critique.

The object of emancipatory pedagogy might more usefully be conceptualized as the power-saturated discourses that monitor and normalize our sense of who we are and what is possible. Ellsworth writes, 'I am trying to unsettle received definitions of pedagogy by multiplying the ways in which I am able to act on and in the University both as the Inappropriate/d Other and as the privileged speaking/making subject trying to unlearn that privilege' (1989: 323). And pedagogy becomes a site *not* for working through more effective transmission strategies but for helping us learn to analyse the discourses available to us, which ones we are invested in, how we are inscribed by the dominant, how we are outside of, other than the dominant, consciously/unconsciously, always partially, contradictorily.

Attending to the Social Relations of the Emancipatory Classroom

In developing a deconstructive pedagogy, our search is not to designate an object or describe a content but to foreground a relation between knower and known, teacher and taught, from an embodied perspective. Giroux and Simon quote Hebdige's reporting from a young male member of a subculture he was studying: ' "You really hate an adult to understand you. That's the only thing you've got over them, the fact that you can mystify and worry them." Contemporary youth have cause to be wary of giving up their anonymity, of making their private and lived voices the object of public and pedagogical scrutiny' (1988: 20). To what extent is the pedagogy we construct in the name of liberation intrusive, invasive, pressured?

Many of these quotes speak of the kind of 'politically correct' thinking that can become operative in an intendedly liberatory classroom. Many speak of the 'shoulds' that add another coercive discourse to their lives, a discourse designed to shake up their worlds but which often loses touch with what that shaken-up experience feels like. The 29 cents quote presents a student who doesn't go along with such pressure, who resists both the 'group-think' in the classroom and the course's stress on women's negative social positioning, a stress designed to overcome the tendency of younger 'post-feminist' women to see feminism as a dinosaur, no longer necessary, the enabling fiction of another generation.

US feminism historically has valorized coercion as the truth of oppression (victimization theories) over *consent* as a political factor (Kipnis, 1988: 151). Yet, what I heard the students in this study wanting to know/tell had something to do with resisting victimization and passivity. How an individual sustains a society's givens (Patai, 1988: 143), how we are inscribed by dominant discourses (Haug, 1987), how we can come to understand our own collusion – this was the information they found most powerful. To begin to understand how we are caught up in power situations of which we are, ourselves, the bearers is to foreground the limits of our lives and what we can do within those boundaries. It is to begin to see the organization of knowledge and the production of ignorance in the curriculum, to probe what makes 'the lacked knowledge so meaningless to persons', in ways that valorize neither subjective agency nor objective determination.

The task is to construct classroom relations that engender fresh confrontation with value and meaning – not to demonstrate to students their ignorance in what Freire (1973) terms the 'banking concept of education' where authoritarian talk shuts down communication, even if done in the name of liberation (Berlak, 1986, 1989). To challenge the unequal distribution of power in the classroom is to ask, 'Who speaks? for what and to whom? who listens? who is confident and comfortable and who isn't?' (Orner and Brennan, 1989: 18). It is, also, to probe the many reasons for silence (Lewis, 1988; Lewis and Simon, 1986) and to heed Joycechild's (1987b) caution:

> The shoulds operating in the classroom, which students could feel after a few short weeks, need addressing. We need to learn more ways of hearing students' own voices, as we need to learn more ways of hearing one another's own voices, as different kinds of feminists in the movement. We need to unlearn political correctness, and move away from an oversimplified, monolithic, there's-one-best-way mode of presentation. We have a tendency to deny our own impositional 'stuff' in the name of liberation. I don't think the importance of this can be overestimated.

Deconstructing Authority

To deconstruct authority is not to do away with it but to learn to trace its effects, to see how authority is constituted and constituting. A pedagogy to take us beyond ourselves would privilege helping us become aware and critical of how the social forces of authority affect us as we form and re-form our thinking (Naidus, 1987). For example, in dealing with media-fed and video-schooled students, Ulmer recommends focusing on media studies, especially its enframing processes: 'It is not technology itself, but this blindness to its enframing, that must be confronted' (1985: 15). In doing so, teachers become providers of language codes of varying complexities as they create pedagogical spaces where students can enter a world of oppositional knowledges and negotiate definitions and ways of perceiving (Bowers, 1987). Our pedagogic responsibility then becomes to nurture this space where students can come to see ambivalence and differences not as an obstacle, but as the very richness of meaning-making and the hope of whatever justice we might work toward.

Instead of commenting on a text or practice in ways that define it, a deconstructive approach links our 'reading' to ourselves as socially situated spectators. It draws attention to the variety of readings, the partiality of any one view and our implications in historical social relations. This works against naturalizing, essentializing, and foregrounds positionalities. One example from my own teaching is Charlotte Perkins Gilman's *The Yellow Wallpaper* (1973) which serves as a strategic site for contestation of dominant ideological subject identities. By moving the text around provisionally, unfixedly, we begin by discussing how different audiences respond to the story, elicit student assessments as to whether the narrator goes crazy or not and then explore WHY we interpret this so differently, how our interpretations are rooted in our own positionalities.[9]

Deconstructive pedagogy encourages a multiplicity of readings by demonstrating how we cannot exhaust the meaning of the text, how a text can participate in multiple meanings without being reduced to any one, and how our different positionalities affect our reading of it. Johnson's questions can help us learn to link our comments to ourselves as socially situated spectators: Why am I reading *this* text? What kind of act was the writing of it? What question about it does it itself NOT raise? What am I participating in when I read it? (1987: 4) Fuss adds:

> What are the various positions a reading subject may occupy? How are these positions constructed? Are there possible distributions of subject-positions located in the text itself? Can a reader refuse to take up a subject-position the text constructs for him/her? Does the text construct the reading subject or does the reading subject construct the text? (1989: 86)

These questions can help us begin to interrogate critically our own unexamined techniques of sense-making. Hence, our reading of the text becomes the curriculum, a curriculum designed not so much to oppose a counter-hegemonic meaning system against a dominant one as to ask us to insert ourselves into the discourses that envelop us. Here, we deconstructively explore the relation between ourselves and how we negotiate the search for meaning in a world of contradictory information.

Such a pedagogy has no prescriptions:

> The terms in which I can and will assert and unsettle 'difference' and unlearn my positions of privilege in future classroom practices are wholly dependent on the Others/others whose presence – with their concrete experiences of privileges and oppressions, and subjugated or oppressive knowledges – I am responding to and acting with in any given classroom. My moving about between the positions of privileged speaking subject and Inappropriate/d Other cannot be predicted, prescribed, or understood beforehand by any theoretical framework or methodological practice. It is in this sense that a practice grounded in the unknowable is profoundly contextual (historical) and interdependent (social). (Ellsworth, 1989: 323)

Ellsworth's study of critical pedagogy within the context of her own teaching of a university level anti-racism course and my similar efforts in this essay turn away from a focus on dominant power to a focus on our own discourses of criticism and resistance. Such a deconstructive movement positions this time of foundational uncertainty as an opening for we who do our research and teaching in the name of liberation to make generative advances in the ways we conceptualize our purposes and practices. Collapsing the distinctions between research and pedagogy in order to use the present to construct that which works against the relations of dominance both creates complicating fragmentations and provides a richer understanding of the situations in which we do our oppositional work.[10]

'Resistance postmodernism' is full of contradictions and constantly emerging subjectivities, relational in its conceptual and political practices, full of post-Marxists and post-colonialists, and spawning terms like simulacra[11] and polyvocality. Against the inscription of 'resistance postmodernism' as most often couched in what Spivak (1990) calls 'Big Talk' or 'high theory', this essay's effort has been to render some sense of what 'the resistant postmodern' might be via a portrayal of emancipatory work which takes a deconstructive impulse into account.

Re-articulating deconstruction in use, I have enacted its inscription by those who want critically to preserve the emancipatory impulse within a framework sympathetic to postmodernism's resituating of that impulse (Peters, 1989). Moving to make the workings of our efforts towards feminist research and pedagogy more apparent, I have used deconstruction to open up structures of possibility in the hope of animating the elaboration of practices that might help us construct the material for struggle present in the stuff of our daily lives to which we all have access. In such a framework, women's studies has provided both critique and alternative practices, and served as a Gramscian 'historical laboratory' for developing oppositional theory and practice adequate to a post-foundational era.

Conclusion

Out of all the stories that could be told about the multiplicity of influences on an inquiry, this essay is a 'tale of the field' (Van Mannen, 1988), a self-reflexive pondering on the politics of our research and teaching practices. Rooted in the specificity of a particular, situated inquiry into the processes by which students may accept, integrate and/or reject oppositional knowledge, I have explored the parameters of deconstructivist empirical and pedagogical work. Those parameters blur genres, unsettle received definitions and create a space from which to do otherwise. With such parameters well-evoked in a stanza from A.R. Ammon's 'Corson's Inlet', it is with poetry that I leave you:

        I allow myself eddies of meaning:
yield to a direction of significance
running
like a stream through the geography of my work:
        you can find
in my sayings
        swerves of action
        like the inlet's cutting edge:
        there are dunes of motion,
organizations of grass, white sandy paths of remembrance
in the overall wandering of mirroring mind:
but the Overall is beyond me: is the sum of these events
I cannot draw, the ledger I cannot keep, the accounting
beyond the accounts

in nature there are few sharp lines: there are areas of
primrose
        more or less dispersed;
disorderly orders of bayberry; between the rows
of dunes,
irregular swamps of reeds,
though not reeds alone, but grass, bayberry, yarrow, all . . .
predominantly reeds.

I have reached no conclusions, have created no boundaries,
shutting out and shutting in separating inside
        from outside: I have
        drawn no line:
        as

        manifold events of sand
        change the dune's shape that will not be the same
          shape
        tomorrow,

        so I am willing to go along, to accept
        the becoming
        thought, to stake off no beginnings or ends

                     establish
        no walls . . .

                         (quoted in Spanos, 1987: 236–7)

Notes

This is a revision of a chapter in Lather (1991a). Early versions of this paper were presented at the annual conferences of the New Zealand Research in Education Association, Wellington, December 1989, the American Educational Research Association, Boston, April 1990, and the National Women's Studies Association, Akron, Ohio, 20–4 June, 1990. This version was first presented at 'Ideology Critique and Beyond,' Twelfth Annual Conference on Discourse Analysis, Temple University, Philadelphia, 18–20 April, 1991.

1. As my interest in this chapter is performative, the reader is referred to Lather (1989, 1991a, 1991b) for an elaboration of the conceptual issues involved in what it means to do critical, emancipatory work in a post-foundational context of postmodernism/post-structuralism/deconstruction. A recent example of the call for a feminist retreat from postmodern theory is Barry (1991). For a survey of the reception of postmodernism in the academy, see Lather (1991a, 1991b).

2. Calinescu warns against totalizing, creating false unities out of the heterogeneous elements of either modernity or postmodernity, as both are full of contradictory movements. He also points out how the tendency to construct 'a bad reactionary' postmodernism and 'a good, resistant, anticapitalist variety' reproduces the very binaries to which postmodernism is purportedly other than (1987: 292). That I persist in such a binary marks the difficulties of a position that seeks to use postmodernism to both problematize and advance emancipatory politics, issues perhaps best addressed in Nicholson (1990) and Spivak (1990).

3. This is a phrase from Ira Shor's comments at the Ninth Annual Curriculum Theorizing Conference, Dayton, Ohio, October 1987.

4. While the turn to pedagogy may be new to cultural studies, it has long characterized both feminist discourses and neo-Marxist discourses in educational studies. For bibliographies that include both feminist and neo-Marxist pedagogies, see Gore (1990), Kenway and Modra (1989), Lather (1991c), Shrewsbury (1987).

5. The centrality of pedagogy in postmodern discursive practices is paradoxically captured in a 1987 conference, 'Postmodernism: Text, Politics, Instruction' (sponsored by the University of Kansas and the International Association for Philosophy and Literature), where there was a complete lack of attention to issues of teaching and learning in the conference programme. The following attests to some change. From literary criticism and cultural studies: Atkins and Johnson (1985), Henricksen and Morgan (1990), Naidus (1987), Nelson (1986), Ulmer (1985), Zavarzadeh and Morton (1991). From educational studies: Bowers (1987), Brodkey (1987), Bromley (1989), Giroux (1988), Gore (1990), Lewis (1990), McLaren (1991), Miller (1990).

6. Elizabeth Ellsworth and I are pulling this emergent body of literature together as guest editors of an issue of *Theory into Practice* on 'Situated Pedagogies'.

7. Thanks to Dan DeMattis, Ken Hay, Myrna Packard and Michel Coconis. Each worked with parts of the data as an assignment for a course in the analysis of qualitative data that I taught at Ohio State University, Spring 1989. When I presented a version of this paper in Alison Jones's 1989 University of Auckland third-year course on women and education, students raised the paradox of whose names I use and whose I don't. The names of high-status theorists are recirculated and doctoral students are named (with their permission, of course), while undergraduates are positioned as unembodied, unnamed, unnoted 'data' sources. Much of this was done to protect confidentiality, but it bears thinking about.

8. A special thanks to Alison Jones, University of Auckland, for helping me work this through. Sue Middleton and Louise Johnson, University of Waikato, were also very involved in my rethinking of this essay.

9. A very powerful example of multiple readings of *The Yellow Wallpaper* is Lanser (1989), where she probes the absent presence of the politics of race in the story.

10. 'Lyotard has written that "oppositional thinking . . . is out of step with the most vital modes of postmodern knowledge"' (Schrift, 1990: 101). This raises questions about postmodernism and the discourses of emancipation, questions at the centre of Lather (1989, 1991a).

'Oppositional' is a problematic term on many levels, subscribing as it does to a logic of opposites. Nancy Fraser, however, has come up with a relational definition rather than a definition statically grounded in binaries. She defines oppositional as 'forms of needs talk, which arise when needs are politicized "from below"' (1989: 171).

11. Simulacra: copies without originals. Images of the Virgin Mary are the archetypal simulacra. Perhaps the contemporary simulacrum par excellence is the foetus as constructed by the New Right (Kroker, 1983). The Baudrillardian argument is that we have shifted from a culture of representation to one of simulacra. Simulacra function to mask the absence of referential finalities. Baudrillard's definition of simulacrum comes from Ecclesiastes, 'The simulacrum is never that which conceals the truth – it is the truth which conceals that there is none. The simulacrum is true' (Baudrillard, 1983: 1).

References

Anderson, S. (1986) 'A study of resistance to liberatory education and liberatory ideology in re-entry women'. Unpublished MS thesis, Mankato State University.

Aronowitz, S. and Giroux, H. (1985) 'Radical education and transformative intellectuals', *Canadian Journal of Political and Social Theory*, 9 (3): 43–63.

Atkins, G. and Johnson, M.L. (1985) *Writing and Reading Differently: Deconstruction and the Teaching of Composition and Literature*. Lawrence: University of Kansas Press.

Barry, K. (1991) 'Deconstructing deconstructionism (or, whatever happened to feminist studies?)', *Ms*, 1 (4): 83–5.

Baudrillard, J. (1981) *For a Critique of the Political Economy of the Sign*. C. Levin, trans. St Louis, MO: Telos Press.

Baudrillard, J. (1983) *Simulations*, P. Foss, P. Patton and P. Beitchman, trans. New York: Semiotext(e).

Bazerman, C. (1987) 'Codifying the social scientific style: the *APA Publication Manual* as a behaviorist rhetoric', in J. Nelson, A. Megill and D.N. McCloskey (eds), *The Rhetoric of the Human Sciences*. Madison: University of Wisconsin Press. pp. 125–44.

Bennington, G. (1987) 'Demanding history', in D. Altridge, G. Bennington and R. Young (eds), *Post-structuralism and the Question of History*. Cambridge: Cambridge University Press. pp. 15–29.

Berlak, A. (1986) 'Teaching for liberation and empowerment in the liberal arts: towards the development of a pedagogy that overcomes resistance'. Paper delivered at the eighth annual Curriculum Theorizing Conference, Dayton, OH, October.

Berlak, A. (1989) 'Teaching for outrage and empathy in the liberal arts', *Educational Foundations*, 3 (2) (April): 69–93.

Bordo, S. (1990) 'Feminism, postmodernism, and gender-scepticism', in L. Nicholson (ed.), *Feminism/Postmodernism*. New York and London: Routledge. pp. 133–56.

Bowers, C.A. (1987) *Elements of a Post-Liberal Theory of Education*. New York: Teachers' College Press.

Brodkey, L. (1987) 'Postmodern pedagogy for progressive educators: an essay review', *Journal of Education*, 196 (3): 138–43.

Bromley, H. (1989) 'Identity politics and critical pedagogy', *Educational Theory*, 39 (3): 207–23.

Buckingham, D. (1986) 'Against demystification: a response to *Teaching the Media*', *Screen*, 27: 80–95.

Calinescu, M. (1987) *Five Faces of Modernity: Modernism, Avant-garde, Decadence, Kitsch and Postmodernism*. Durham, NC: Duke University Press.

Clifford, J. (1988) *The Predicament of Culture: Twentieth-Century Ethnography, Literature, and Art*. Cambridge, MA: Harvard University Press.

Cocks, J. (1989) *The Oppositional Imagination: Feminism, Critique and Political Theory*. London and New York: Routledge.

Connor, S. (1989) *Postmodernist culture: an Introduction to Theories of the Contemporary*. Oxford: Basil Blackwell.

Ebert, T. (1991) 'Review of *Feminism/Postmodernism*, edited by Linda J. Nicholson', *Women's Review of Books*, 8 (4): 24–5.

Ellsworth, E. (1989) 'Why doesn't this feel empowering?' Working through the repressive myths of critical pedagogy', *Harvard Educational Review*, 59 (3): 297–324.

Foucault, M. (1977) 'The political function of the intellectual', *Radical Philosophy*, 17: 12–14.

Fraser, N. (1989) *Unruly Practices: Power, Discourse and Gender in Contemporary Social Theory*. Minneapolis: University of Minnesota Press.

Freire, P. (1973) *Pedagogy of the Oppressed*. New York: Seabury.

Fuss, D. (1989) 'Reading like a feminist', *differences*, 1 (2): 77–92.

Gilman, C.P. (1973) *The Yellow Wallpaper*. Old Westbury, NY: The Feminist Press. (Originally published in 1892.)

Giroux, H.A. (1988) 'Border pedagogy in the age of postmodernism', *Journal of Education*, 170 (3): 162–81.

Giroux, H. and Simon, R. (1988) 'Schooling popular culture, and a pedagogy of possibility', *Journal of Education*, 170 (1): 9–26.

Glaser, B. and Strauss, A. (1967) *The Discovery of Grounded Theory: Strategies for Qualitative Research*. Chicago, IL: Aldine.

Gore, J. (1990) 'What we can do for you! What can "we" do for "you"?: Struggling over empowerment in critical and feminist pedagogy', *Educational Foundations*, 4 (3): 5–26.

Grosz, E. (1989) *Sexual Subversions: Three French Feminists*. Sydney: Allen and Unwin.

Hariman, R. (1989) 'The rhetoric of inquiry and the professional scholar', in H. Simons (ed.), *Rhetoric in the Human Sciences*. London and Newbury Park, CA: Sage. pp. 211–32.

Haraway, D. (1988) 'Situated knowledges: the science question in feminism and the privilege of partial perspective', *Feminist Studies* 14 (3): 575–99.

Haug, F. (ed.) (1987) *Female Sexualization*. Erica Carter, trans. London: Verso.

Henricksen, B. and Morgan, T.E. (1990) *Reorientations: Critical Theories and Pedagogies*. Urbana: University of Illinois Press.

Hutcheon, L. (1989) *The Politics of Postmodernism*. London and New York: Routledge.

Johnson, B. (1987) *A World of Difference*. Baltimore, MD: Johns Hopkins University Press.

Joycechild, L.D. (1987a) 'Emergent highlights from the preliminary report'. Paper presented to women's studies faculty in-service, Mankato State University.

Joycechild, L.D. (1987b) Document prepared for the National Women's Studies Association annual convention as part of a panel presentation, 'Teaching and Doing Feminist Research', Atlanta, GA, June.

Joycechild, L.D. (1988) 'Presenting feminism: toward a reflexive pedagogy in the introductory women's studies course'. Unpublished MS thesis, Mankato State University.

Kenway, J. and Modra, H. (1992) 'Feminist pedagogy and emancipatory possibilities', in C. Luke and J. Gore (eds), *Feminisms and Critical Pedagogy*. New York: Routledge. pp. 138–66.

Kipnis, L. (1988) Feminism: the political conscience of postmodernism?' in A. Ross (ed.), *Universal Abandon? The Politics of Postmodernism*. Minneapolis: University of Minnesota Press. pp. 149–66.

Kroker, A. (1983) 'The disembodied eye: ideology and power in the age of nihilism', *Canadian Journal of Political and Social Theory*, 7 (1–2): 194–234.

Lanser, S. S. (1989) 'Feminist criticisms, "The Yellow Wallpaper", and the politics of color in America', *Feminist Studies*, 15 (3): 415–41.

Lather, P. (1986) 'Research as praxis', *Harvard Educational Review*, 56 (3): 257–77.

Lather, P. (1988) 'Feminist perspectives on empowering research methodologies', *Women's Studies International Forum*, 11 (6): 569–81.

Lather, P. (1989) 'Postmodernism and the politics of enlightenment', *Educational Foundations*, 3 (3): 7–28.

Lather, P. (1991a) *Getting Smart: Feminist Research and Pedagogy With/in the Postmodern*. New York and London: Routledge.

Lather, P. (1991b) 'Deconstructing/deconstructive inquiry: the politics of knowing and being known', *Educational Theory*, 41 (2): 153–73.

Lather, P. (1991c) 'Post-critical pedagogies: a feminist reading', *Education and Society*, 9 (2): 100–11.

Lee, J. (1988) 'The effects of feminist education on student values'. Paper delivered at the annual conference of the National Women's Studies Association, Minneapolis, MN, June.

Lewis, M. (1988) 'Without a word: sources and themes for a feminist pedagogy'. Unpublished PhD dissertation, University of Toronto.

Lewis, M. (1989) 'Problems of practice in radical teaching: a feminist perspective on the psycho/social/sexual dynamics in the mixed gender classroom'. Paper presented at the annual meeting of the American Educational Research Association, San Francisco, March.

Lewis, M. (1990) 'Framing: women and silence: disrupting the hierarchy of discursive practices'. Paper presented at the annual meeting of the American Educational Research Association, Boston, MA, April.

Lewis, M. and Simon, R. (1986) 'A discourse not intended for her: learning and teaching within patriarchy', *Harvard Educational Review*, 56 (4): 457–72.

Luke, C. (1992) 'Feminist politics in radical pedagogy', in C. Luke and J. Gore (eds), *Feminisms and Critical Pedagogy*. New York: Routledge. pp. 25–53.

Lusted, D. (1986) 'Why pedagogy?', *Screen*, 27 (5): 2–14.

McLaren, P. (1991) 'Post-colonial pedagogy, desire and decolonized community', *Education and Society*, 9 (2): 135–58.

Miller, J. (1990) *Creating Spaces and Finding Voices: Teachers Collaborating for Empowerment*. Albany: State University of New York Press.

Naidus, B. (1987) 'The Artist/Teacher as Decoder and Catalyst', *Radical Teacher*, Sept.: 17–20.

Nelson, C. (ed.) (1986) *Theory in the Classroom*. Urbana: University of Illinois Press.

Nicholson, L. (ed.) (1990) *Feminism/Postmodernism*. New York: Routledge.

Orner, M. and Brennan, M. (1989) 'Producing collectively: power, identity and teaching'. Paper presented at the annual meeting of the American Educational Research Association, San Francisco, March.

Patai, D. (1988) 'Constructing a self: a Brazilian life story', *Feminist Studies*, 14 (1): 143–66.

Peters, M. (1989) 'Techno-science, rationality, and the university: Lyotard on the "postmodern condition"', *Educational Theory*, 39 (2): 93–105.

Rooney, E. (1989) *Seductive Reasoning: Pluralism as the Problematic of Contemporary Literary Theory*. Ithaca, NY: Cornell University Press.

Rushdie, S. (1982) *Midnight's Children*. New York: Avon Books.

Schrift, A.D. (1990) 'The becoming-postmodern of philosophy', in G. Shapiro (ed.), *After the Future: Postmodern Times and Places*. Albany: State University of New York Press. pp. 99–113.

Sheridan, S. (1988) 'Introduction', in S. Sheridan (ed.), *Grafts: Feminist Cultural Criticism*. London and New York: Verso. pp. 1–9.

Shrewsbury, C. (1987) 'Feminist pedagogy: a bibliography', *Women's Studies Quarterly*, 15 (3–4): 116–24.

Simons, H.W. (1989) 'Introduction', in H. Simons (ed.), *Rhetoric in the Human Sciences*. London and Newbury Park, CA: Sage. pp. 1–9.

Spanos, W. (1987) *Repetitions: The Postmodern Occasion in Literature and Culture*. Baton Rouge: Louisiana State University Press.

Spivak, G. (1990) 'Gayatri Spivak on the politics of the subaltern: Interview by Howard Winant', *Socialist Review*, 20 (3): 81–97.

Spivak, G. with Rooney, E. (1989) 'In a word: interview', *differences*, 1 (2): 124–56.

Stam, R. (1988) 'Mikhail Bakhtin and left cultural critique', in E.A. Kaplan (ed.), *Postmodernism and Its Discontents: Theories, Practices*. London and New York: Verso. pp. 116–45.

Stephanson, A. (1988) 'Interview with Cornel West', in A. Ross (ed.), *Universal Abandon? The Politics of Postmodernism*. Minneapolis: University of Minnesota Press. pp. 269–86.

Ulmer, G. (1985) *Applied Grammatology: Post(e)-pedagogy from Jacques Derrida to Joseph Beuys*. Baltimore, MD: Johns Hopkins University Press.

Van Maanen, J. (1988) *Tales of the Field: on Writing Ethnography*. Chicago, IL, and London: University of Chicago Press.

Winter, P. (1989) Departmental seminar paper, Sociology Department, University of Waikato, Hamilton, New Zealand, 10 June.

Zavarzadeh, M. and Morton, D. (1991) 'Theory pedagogy politics: the crisis of "the subject" in the humanities', in D. Morton and M. Zavarzadeh (eds), *Texts for Change: Theory/Pedagogy/Politics*. Chicago: University of Chicago Press. pp. 1–32.

6
Teaching the Pedagogies:
a Dialectical Approach
to an Ideological Dilemma

Herbert W. Simons

The cultural left in the United States has been the recipient of intense criticism in recent years from conservatives (e.g. D'Souza, 1991; Kimball, 1990), civil libertarians (e.g. Woodward, 1991) and many in the news media (e.g. Adler, 1990; Henry, 1991) for allegedly requiring of students that they conform to the left's standards of 'political correctness'. Pedagogues on the left such as Henry Giroux (1988) respond that they are merely taking aim at racists, sexism, classism or other instances of oppression and exploitation that are kept in place by mainstream ideologies. Giroux argues that practices such as these are intrinsically objectionable, hence legitimate objects of ideology critique by the teacher. But even some on the left believe that current efforts at 'emancipating' and 'empowering' students often end up being oppressive or at least feeling coercive to the students.

Greatly complicating matters for the left are widespread commitments to egalitarianism in educational practice and to postmodern scepticism and multivocality. Thus, Lather (this volume) asks, 'How do our very efforts to liberate perpetuate the relations of dominance?' Lather's chapter projects her own unease over running a feminist 'liberatory' curriculum while at the same time hewing to postmodernist convictions 'that challenge all totalities as reductive fictions, including those at work across the various feminisms'. The problem is illustrated for Lather by a student's essay on the film documentary *Killing Us Softly* which presents a feminist critique of portrayals of women in television advertising. By a Gramscian critical reading, the student's essay is a marvel of liberation and empowerment, recounting as it does the student's initial resistance to the argument of the film and subsequent conversion. But from a deconstructive, postmodernist reading of the same essay, the student may only be saying what it is 'ideologically correct' to say in that learning environment.

Bizzell (1991) puts a somewhat different spin on the problem raised by Lather, reflecting perhaps her greater confidence in knowing what constitutes the 'common good'. How, she asks, can the left-oriented pedagogue exercise the power to do 'good' in the classroom while at the same time promoting a classroom culture that is non-hierarchical, exploratory, collaborative, dialogic, multi-voiced, heteroglossic and radically democratic? Despite her avowed commitment to egalitarianism in the classroom, Bizzell would have her students 'try to argue in a certain way, to enter into a particular audience's point of view, or to give credit to another writer's reasoning, even if these activities seem very uncongenial at the time' (1991: 58). She would attempt, in other words, to have her students say and write what they do not necessarily believe. Bizzell calls this a 'theoretical impasse':

> On the one hand, we wish to serve politically left-oriented liberatory goals in our teaching, while on the other, we do not see how we can do so without committing the theoretically totalizing and pedagogically oppressive sins we have inveighed against in the systems we want to resist. Another way to describe this impasse would be to say that we want to serve the common good with the power we possess by virtue of our power as teachers, and yet we are deeply suspicious of any exercise of power in the classroom. (1991: 54)

Between Lather's apparent self-doubt and Bizzell's expression of her 'theoretical impasse' we have a fair approximation of the type of dilemma to be discussed in this chapter, one whose precise shape in any given classroom situation will depend on such factors as the teacher's degree of commitment to the cause viewed against his or her moral and pragmatic commitments to pedagogical neutrality. While the focus of the essay is on issues currently being confronted by the cultural left, it should be emphasized that such questions as whether to promote one's views in the classroom, how far to promote, what to promote, how to promote, etc., are by no means new, nor exclusively confined to the left. Rather, the dilemma confronts educators of every political persuasion who, armed with conceptions of the good, the true or the beautiful, feel impelled to promote these same conceptions to their students, yet, who, for whatever reasons – lingering doubts about their position, an abhorrence of classroom indoctrination, a commitment to egalitarianism, a fear of legitimating parallel activities by those they oppose – are reluctant to use their classroom power. This was nicely illustrated for me at a conference on political communication at which the group – consisting mostly of academics like myself – was shown a video documentary produced by People for the American Way entitled *Life and Liberty for Those Who Obey*.

Life and Liberty is a hard-hitting critique of the politics of the religious right wing in the United States, complete with footage of demagogic harangues by leading right-wing ministers, indoctrination campaigns, censorship campaigns, a book-burning ceremony and a behind-the-scenes look at the machinations of political operatives seeking to promote the chances of conservative political candidates. I was much moved by this documentary critique, and I decided then and there that I would obtain a copy of the video to show my students. Still, I was troubled by the question of *how* to present it. One part of me wanted to use the video in support of an all-out critique of the religious right's anti-democratic character. At the very least, I wanted to register my opinions about the video in no uncertain terms. But another part of me wanted to hold back. Could I reconcile my desire to advance a strongly felt position with what many assume is the responsibility of the professor to steer a neutral course? I decided to pose these questions to my colleagues at the conference.

The questions unleashed a torrent of controversy. Opinions ranged from the position that 'A professor's job is to educate, not advocate' to the rallying cry: 'A professor's job is to profess.' Moreover, opinions in the latter group differed radically as to what my profession of belief should be. Thus, a conservative present insisted that it was the video I should be criticizing, not the religious right. 'While you're at it,' he said, 'do a hatchet job on People for the American Way for putting out such a propagandistic film.'

To be sure, *Life and Liberty* was one-sided. It certainly did not represent the religious right to a heterogeneous audience as the religious right would have represented itself. Visuals were no doubt selected for their denigrative effect. Thus, a televangelist was captured on camera having his make-up put on, and was later shown in close-up spitting into a microphone as he thundered at his audience. Word selection was similarly calculated to reflect ill on the religious right. For instance, major donors to the cause were described as 'Washington money men'. Were I of a mind to criticize the video, I might also have asked why actor Burt Lancaster was chosen to introduce the video. What, after all, did he know about the religious right?

How, then, should I have taught *Life and Liberty*? How, more generally, should academics deal with the dilemma I have posed? In what follows I comment critically on a number of pedagogical strategies, both those promotive of left-orientated positions and those that surrender to at least the appearance of pedagogic neutrality. I then propose a dialectical solution of sorts, which I call 'teaching the pedagogies'. This I admit is by no means an ideal solution, yet I argue that it best confronts the complexities of the problem.

Promotive Strategies: 'A Professor's Job is to Profess'

All Out Persuasion

This alternative embraces one horn of the dilemma, but it at least honours the other by attempting to refute its logic. Thus, Stanley Fish, in a spirited defence of 'professing', maintains that politics is simply the name for the condition of ideological difference, which society can never escape:

> Those who think they can choose politics are no less evading the fact of the political – the fact that point of view and perspectivity are irreducible features of consciousness and action – than those who think they can bracket politics. Politics can neither be avoided nor positively embraced: these impossible alternatives are superficially different ways of *grasping* the political, of holding it in one's hand, whereas properly understood, the political – the inescapability of partisan angled-seeing – is what always and already grasps us. (1992: 249)

Fish goes on to suggest that those who ridicule the cultural left for its brand of 'political correctness' are no less dogmatic but simply more envious, for the culural left is on the side of history – which, in the name of diversity, is making a place for a new generation of Americans.

Fish's first argument is hard to accept, for he would have us believe that there is no essential difference between a professor who professes a position on *Life and Liberty* (or *Killing Us Softly*, to cite an earlier example) and one who refrains from expressing his or her own views. The error here is one of failing to distinguish between having a view and promoting or even stating a view. Moreover, one wonders whether Fish's (uncharacteristically modernist) boast that his movement is on the side of history would sit as well with him if the same boast were uttered, say, by apologists for Muslim fundamentalism or for ethnic purity in Bosnia. Fish too quickly attempts to dissolve a dilemma that needs to be confronted directly, and he argues from a premise which, if taken seriously, could set a dangerous precedent. Beware of 'professing' in the classroom justified 'in the name of history'.

Interestingly, Fish's colleague at Duke University, Barbara Herrnstein Smith, also argues the inevitability of 'the political'.

> What is new about American education in this regard is not its political character as such; what is new is the wide range of interests and perspectives now in play, the increased sharpness of their divergence

from each other, and, consequently, the more numerous occasions for collisions among them. 'Politics', or 'ideology', is always part of education, but an invisible part so long as everyone agrees – or appears to. (1992: 10)

However, Smith qualifies her argument in two important ways, suggesting that perhaps there ought to be limits on the teacher's promotional efforts after all. First, she admits, the classroom can be politicized in greater or lesser degree. Second, she concedes that education can degenerate into 'indoctrination', and that it can become 'an abuse of authority'. Smith never says what she means by 'indoctrination' or 'abuse of authority', but it is to her credit that she raises the issues. Recognizing that these terms resist easy definition – indeed, that whatever judgements we offer in any given case will themselves be 'political' – we might nevertheless consider such questions as the following in relation to my teaching of *Life and Liberty*. (1) Would I be equally justified in defending the religious right's censorship efforts as in opposing them? (2) Am I obligated as persuader to defend what I profess with good reasons and good evidence, or can I simply rely upon my own 'expertise' as a teacher? (3) If the former, how, in an age of scepticism about value arguments of any kind, are these 'goods' to be vouchsafed? (4) Do I have a responsibility to be fair-minded in 'professing'? (5) If I oppose the religious right's political campaigning as an intrusion of Church into the affairs of State, must I be equally critical of such Church-sponsored civil rights efforts as those led by the Reverend Martin Luther King? (6) Am I ever justified in using the power of the grade to reward those who agree with me and punish those who disagree? From the very nature of these questions, it should be apparent why I have problems with all out persuasion as an unqualified principle of pedagogy.

Authority Buttressed by Persuasion

Let us return to Bizzell's (1991) article. On the assumption that she is indeed in possession of 'the good', Bizzell declares that she has three options available to her: coercion, persuasion and authority. Coercion is rejected as oppressive and not necessarily in the students' best interests. Persuasion is said to be insufficiently reliable as a pedagogical staple, but as essential at the beginning of a class in preparing the way for authority by enlisting support for its use. But on what grounds can Bizzell appeal to her students to surrender their will to her authority? Why, beyond the coercive power of a grade, should they agree to be 'liberated' by her from their racist, sexist, etc., ideologies? Because, says Bizzell, of links in historical circumstances between them and her. This is not spelled out, and it is hard to imagine how it could convince an entire class. Absent group conviction, Bizzell is thus left buttressing her authority with coercion, which she herself recognises as oppressive.

Restricted Dialogue

The alternatives Bizzell identifies may not be the only ones available to the left-oriented 'liberatory' educator. Giroux would have teachers enter into 'dialogue' with their students. However, he makes clear that student expressions which he takes to be racist, sexist or in other ways oppressive or exploitative should be considered out of bounds in the discussion. Thus, the issue of whether or not the Holocaust was justified would not, in Giroux's classroom be an allowable issue for discussion or debate. Permitting its consideration would suggest to students that supporting the Holocaust 'represented simply another point of view'. As to finding a place for dialogue in consideration of the Holocaust, Giroux proposes that

> different voices in the class could be engaged around questions of how the Holocaust developed, the nature of the ideology that informed it, why people supported and/or directly participated in it, what such an event tells us about the present, and how a similar logic might be manifested in different civil and cultural forms of contemporary daily life, and so on. (1988: 108)

Thus would Giroux restrict class discussion on the assumption that allowing the expression of repugnant ideas is tantamount to legitimating them as worthy of consideration.

At the same time, Giroux insists that teachers should not impose on or silence their students (p. 144) – an apparent contradiction. In a discussion of Rorty's case for extended conversation, Giroux asks the right questions. Who's in? Who's out? Who controls the choice of terms and definitions? Whose stories are distorted or marginalized? Why are some parts of the conversation played up or played down? How are choices made among visions of community life embodied in different strands of the dialogue (p. 64)?

But Giroux is not the egalitarian when it comes to his own ideological agenda. Significantly, he urges teachers to explore multiple voices in their discussions with students: the voices not only of student and teacher but also of the oppressive school system, bent on testing students rather than teaching them, on discouraging consideration of alternative visions, on regulating time, space, textuality, experience, knowledge, power and conflicting interests and histories (p. 159). But the one voice that Giroux does not encourage students and teachers to subject to critical discussion is his own. This is unfortunate, for Giroux speaks in a curious argot, well worth examination. In an effort to legitimate what he calls his 'critical pedagogy', Giroux routinely takes 'establishment' terms such as 'literacy', 'democracy' and 'citizenship' and assigns new meanings to them. For example, 'literacy' in Giroux's reframing is no longer simply the capacity to read and write. It is also the ability to perform ideology critiques of the sort proposed by Giroux himself.

Thus does Giroux attempt to resolve the dilemma, but one wonders whether he has not inadvertently provided further evidence of its intractability. As Elizabeth Ellsworth has observed, Giroux's critical pedagogy cloaks a strategy of subversion (of repressive school structures) with 'a posture of invisibility' (1989: 301).

Guided Discussion
A close cousin to restricted dialogue is guided discussion. This is actually a congeries of somewhat different approaches. At the University of Massachussetts in Amherst, students in beginning composition courses have been getting readings focusing exclusively on issues of racial and social diversity (Watkins, 1990). As reported in the *Chronicle of Higher Education*, the purpose of the programme is not to bring in specific content but to provide judiciously selected 'prompts' that encourage self-analysis of the students' experiences and prejudices while discouraging them from adhering to their prejudices. Rather than asking, for example, whether the beating of a black man by a white policeman was racist or not, and thus inviting a hardening of attitudes in the course of debate, now the students are asked, 'Have you been in a similar place? Can you imagine you are in the place of the policeman? Of the victim?' (p. A14)

Use of the term 'victim' by the teacher, rather than, say, 'suspect', is reminiscent of a centuries-old pedagogical technique which Billig et al. (1988) call 'cued elicitation'. In the early grades, Billig et al. report, 'teacher and pupils engage in an implicit collusion in which the solutions and answers appear to be elicited, while a close examination of what is happening reveals that the required information, suggestions, observations and conclusions are cued, selected or provided by the teacher' (p. 51). In this case, the questioner signals to the students that the 'beating' (itself a charged word) was unjustified. As an intended way out of the 'ideological' tensions in the classroom between authority and equality, argue Billig et al., cued elicitation is itself ideological.

Another approach to guided discussion is identified by Paula Rothenberg (1991). On the assumption that 'Society's institutions and practices perpetuate white, male privilege', Rothenberg invites her students to consider with her how this is so. But many among her typically white, working-class students strongly disagree. Rothenberg lends emotional support to their 'resistance', providing them with a 'safe space' for opposition (a favourite phrase among cultural left educators) while correcting their blatantly 'false' beliefs and encouraging students supportive of her views to have the last word. Unfortunately for Rothenberg, many of her wayward students manifest not only resistance but backlash. But Rothenberg never seriously considers the possibility that her students' objections may be justified. Indeed, a recurrent pattern in essays urging guided discussion is the pathologization of disagreement: the assumption that it is a reflection of denial, withdrawal, insecurity, unconscious hostility or some other defence against what the pedagogue takes to be an obvious truth (e.g. Giroux, 1988; Tatum, 1992). This leads to a curious combination of managed dialogue: part Socrates, part Freud. Meanwhile, the objecting student is double-bound: encouraged to talk openly, but then made an object of sympathy or derision.

Commentary
These, then, are among the promotive strategies available to the educator. While all are attractive in some ways, they by no means resolve the dilemma posed at the outset of this chapter. By contrast, the proposals to be considered next would deny the educator the right to advocate in the classroom, at least overtly, while posing yet another danger, that of persuasion smuggled in under the guise of pedagogical objectivity.

Neutralizing Strategies: 'Educate, Don't Advocate'

Accuracy and Even-handedness
One mark of 'educating, not advocating' is being accurate, free from distortion, true to the facts. But this presupposes a knowable standard against which we can determine 'the facts' and discover whether they have been fully or fairly represented (Hackett, 1984). It assumes, too, that langauge can be a clear window-pane upon reality (Gusfield, 1976). And it invites trust in reporting that may be misplaced. Better to 'profess openly', say the advocates of outright persuasion, than to smuggle in one's beliefs about People for the American Way or the religious right under the guise of providing a 'summary' of the film or a 'background' report.

But there is another avenue open to our non-advocating

educator, and that is to be even-handed, impartial, balanced, above the fray. This Mannheimian tack is taken by journalists and educators alike when matters are clearly controversial. For example, in reporting on the firing of a popular minister of state, as opposed to the reporting of a humdrum fire on Main Street, the journalist would be sure to present 'both sides' (Hackett, 1984). Likewise, I could say as many good things as bad to my students about the religious right, or an equal proportion of good things as bad about both the video and the religious right. Or, better yet, I could get my students to produce the appropriate balance by way of an even-handed discussion.

But that assumes that balanced teaching doesn't misrepresent an *imbalanced* state of affairs. One political party may in fact be running a clean campaign and the opposition party running a dirty one. As many good things may not be as sayable about apartheid as bad things. And, by this same reasoning, the religious right may be far more (or less) reprehensible than the video made by People for the American Way.

Unreckoned with by the principle of even-handedness is the possibility of a legitimate tilt in favour of one value judgement over another. Values, by the traditional objectivist view, are either consensual, in which case they can be described accurately ('At the fire on Main Street, one fireman who rescued a little girl displayed great *courage*.'), or controversial, in which case they must be treated even-handedly ('Some members of his party said the firing of the minister of state was *unjust*. But others thought it was *necessary*.'). Unfortunately, there is no rule that can tell us what should and should not be considered controversial; hence, what should be treated as a matter for accurate reporting, and what should be treated even-handedly.

Philosophical Pluralism

Philosophical pluralism is a close cousin to even-handedness, except that it presupposes the worthiness of multiple perspectives, looked at from a perspective above the fray (Booth, 1979). (In principle, one could be even-handedly denigrative of all perspectives; not so with pluralism.) Like the other forms of 'Educate, don't advocate', pluralism is subject to the charge of persuasion in the guise of objectivity. Like the others, its claim to a transcendent place above the fray is paradoxical. Note first that pluralists are themselves monists with respect to their very commitments to pluralism. Moreover, few among us are willing to allow all viewpoints into our pluralist classrooms, if for no other reason than that some are a clear waste of time (e.g. the proposition that liberal humanists should retaliate against the religious right by burning its books). Wittingly or unwittingly, moreover, we tend to privilege some views over others, even among those that we allow into the discussion (Booth, 1986; Rooney, 1986). W.J.T. Mitchell is particularly critical of pluralism's transcendent stance:

> The strategy is one of pure, unconscious appropriation of power. Pluralism takes the moral high ground by designating itself as the philosophy uniquely devoted to liberal generosity and tolerance; it takes the intellectual high ground by reducing all other philosophies to 'methods' that it contains and compares; and it takes the political high ground by appointing itself as a kind of supreme court of critical method, a power which derives from the paradoxical strategy of seeming to renounce all power. (1986: 500)

Teaching Critical Reasoning

One version of 'Educate, don't advocate' is expressed in another aphorism: 'Teach students how to think, not what to think.' But this principle is built on a questionable distinction. For, while everyone would agree that it is desirable for students to learn 'how to think', it is hard to imagine a choice of methods of reasoning – Eastern mystical thought, Western dialectics, 'closed-fisted' formal logics, 'open-palmed' informal logic, etc. (Billig, 1987) – that does not have implications for *what* people think. The general point made by Brown (1987), Jonsen and Toulmin (1988) and others is that reason (or should I say reasonings?) is rhetorical. If it does not teach a point of view, a given mode of reasoning at least invites us to have an angle of view and a scope of view – a way of seeing the issues in *Life and Liberty*, for example, as formally decidable or as matters of taste and judgement. (This takes us back to Fish's argument.) Thus, training in formal logic would more likely invite students to abstract from the particulars of *Life and Liberty* out of concern for its propositional content, and thus miss out on its nuances of shot selection and word selection. Training in informal logic might thus seem more applicable to *Life and Liberty*, but it is hard to imagine how anyone could teach informal logic without projecting personal beliefs and values in the selection and analysis of substantive examples. (For repeated instances of such projections by the editors of this volume, see Billig, 1987, and Simons, 1986.)

Devil's Advocacy

In *Life and Liberty* there is a scene showing a leading representative of the Moral Majority (a Christian right organization of the 1980s – since disbanded) contesting a court decision to deny custody to parents who had been found guilty of physically abusing their children. The representative, a minister, argues that corporal punishment – extending to turning a child's bottom blue – is legitimated by the Bible. His second line of defence is that the state hasn't the right to take the child from his or her natural parents, for only God has that right. Thus, what some call 'child abuse' is really biblical discipline. And what some assume is the state's obligation to end abuse is really an intrusion into a sacred relationship between God and the natural parents.

I deplore this point of view but I know how to support it. I could argue, reasonably, that 'child abuse' is a rather new idea in Western culture, a term invented as late as 1962 (Hacking, 1991), the product of a social movement made up of various secular types – e.g. social workers, radiologists, feminists (Pfohl, 1977) – who succeeded in ontologizing the term, leading most people to think of it as child abuse (without quotation marks) rather than 'child abuse' (Woolgar and Pawluch, 1985). I could point out that even today there is wide disagreement among the so-called 'experts' as to what ought to be counted as 'child abuse', to the point where, by one proposed definition, practically every parent is a child abuser, and by another proposed definition – offered by the same expert – practically no one is a child abuser (Hacking, 1991). I could argue that at an earlier and better time, before the meddling of the law courts and social workers, and, not incidentally, before the break-up of the American family, family members worked out their problems together, possibly with the aid of a minister or priest. What the representative of the Moral Majority was really calling for was the retrieval of the good we had lost.

Thus could I make the argument. But should I? There is a strong case for arguing the unpopular – and often wrong-headed – point of view with one's students. Doing so pushes them to formulate and defend counter-arguments that would not otherwise occur to them. Moreover, they may be led to glean valuable insights from otherwise flawed opposing positions.

The counter-side to devil's advocacy of the unpopular position is that it leads to an overly intellectualized approach to controversial issues. In arguing the Moral Majority representative's case, I model for my students the ease with which passions can be flipped back and forth like a pancake. How much better, then, to profess openly, especially on matters as sensitive and as consequential as child abuse.

A Dialectical Approach: Teaching the Pedagogies[1]

In his classic essay on the 'Four Master Tropes', Kenneth Burke

(1969) encourages us dialectically to transcend opposing perspectives by building upon their 'partial truths', rather than abandoning these perspectives completely or allowing our thinking to be framed entirely by any single perspective. Such is the ironic 'perspective on perspectives' that informs the proposal to be put forward in this essay.

From what has been said thus far, it seems a fair conclusion that there is no way of dealing with ideology in the classroom that does not in itself have ideological implications. That being the case, students should be thinking not only about issues like the liberalism of *Life and Liberty* or the conservatism of the religious right, but also about the politics of the pedagogies their teachers select for dealing with these and other issues. By my argument, even labelling something an ideology (e.g. objectivity, realism) is itself an ideological position. So, too, is *not* labelling it an ideology. Ideological commitments can be expressed not just by taking a liberal or conservative position on *Life and Liberty*, but also by taking no position: by encouraging students to provide a balanced discussion of the film, by teaching them one method of reasoning or another for thinking about the film, by playing the pluralist or playing devil's advocate.

Apart from the problems with each pedagogy which have already been discussed, there is a problem common to all of them: namely, that none provides a perspective on the pedagogies themselves. My dialectical alternative involves pedagogical talk about pedagogical talk of precisely the kind that was presented in the previous sections of this chapter. Rather than 'professing' exclusively, or 'educating but not advocating', I now am apt to ask my students how they would have me teach *Life and Liberty* (for example), given my own dilemma.[2] Predictably they come up with much the same list of promotive and neutralizing alternatives as were discussed above, and for much the same set of reasons. Yet the discussion is anything but routine, moving as it does among multiple levels of abstraction. In the process I both 'profess' *and* lead a class discussion, occasionally playing devil's advocate to stimulate further controversy, and occasionally pausing for philosophical analysis of the premises we have brought to bear upon the controversy. I generally conclude in Socratic fashion by answering my own question, proposing that the best answer to the question is the question itself. This inevitably prompts students to raise still other questions. Isn't this solution also a compromise of sorts, a cross between telling it like you think it is and discussing competing viewpoints? Yes, I admit, but it also invites your reflection on these alternatives, and that changes them and you. That is, they are no longer simply natural ways of teaching and learning. And you have to think about what you want from this class. But aren't you biasing the discussion by letting students know your own viewpoint? Mightn't students who take a different position be intimated by you, particularly since you also administer the grades in the course? Yes, I admit, that's a continuing problem. In the course of asking my question to various classes, I have also learned that it is not just the question that counts but the manner in which I do the questioning. When I probe, when I criticize, I have also got to be supportive of my students, especially those with whom I am inclined to disagree. The reward for supportive questioning is that these same students are more likely to risk themselves in subsequent interactions.[3]

'Teaching the pedagogies' has much in common with a proposal made popular recently by Gerald Graff (1992), one that he calls 'teaching the conflicts'. Graff is particularly interested in the conflict between educational conservatives – he calls them 'fundamentalists' – who would cling to the idea of preserving a common culture (as in the 'Great Books' tradition), and those on the cultural left who would subject the university's traditional premises of knowledge and taste to redefinition and revision. In Burkian fashion, Graff would build on the 'partial truths' offered by each, urging them to recognize that there are legitimate reasons for disagreement about what is to be taught in the university and how it is to be taught, and that rival positions cannot always be reduced to a clear distinction between trendy 'irrationalism and sound common sense' (1992: 67). For example, he says, educational conservatives are right in complaining that the cultural left's campaign for educational reform has led to a 'cafeteria-style' approach to education so incoherent as to constitute an obstacle to learning. The cultural left is on target in debunking the 'fundamentalists'' case for a common culture as a not-so-disguised plea for political conservatism.

But, while Graff has much to say about airing the conflicts between educational conservatives and the cultural left – for example, by encouraging representatives of the contending view-points to debate their differences in jointly taught classes, or by staging conferences on the conflicts for undergraduates – he has far less to say about what pedagogies professors should use, or talk about using, with their students in the isolation of their own, singly taught, classrooms. Indeed, Graff seems to offer a curious distinction between the pedagogical principles that should guide the construction of an entire curriculum and the 'professing' he would do in his own classroom:

> Speaking as a leftist, I too find it tempting to try to turn the curriculum into an instrument of social transformation. But I doubt whether the

curriculum (as opposed to my particular courses) can or should become an extension of the politics of the left. The question not addressed by proponents of the 'the pedagogy of the oppressed' such as Paulo Freire and Henry Giroux is what is to be done with those constituencies which do not happen to agree with them that social transformation is the primary goal of education. Such proposals seem to presuppose a school or department in which such dissenters do not exist. In so far as it is to provide a general model, no educational proposal is worth much that has no strategy for dealing with disagreement. No proposal will work that fails to make a place for those who will inevitably resist any single philosophy, leftist, rightist, or centrist. (1992: 70)

I agree with Graff as regards department-wide or school-wide curriculum-planning, but why not apply this same principle to one's particular courses? Is the difference simply one of whose resistance carries more weight: that of one's colleagues or of one's students? If so, then Graff's avowed commitment to egalitarianism in the classroom would seem to be something of a sham. In my classroom, I would preserve the dialectical tensions between promotive and neutralizing strategies, encouraging students to confront the tensions themselves. Were I Gerald Graff, I might tell my students early on that I am tempted to make my course an extension of the politics of the left, but that I also have reservations about doing so (for reasons discussed above). I would suggest, too, that every pedagogical choice was also an ideological choice – that there is no escaping considerations of ideology. I would then ask the students what I should do, and I would allow subsequent structuring of the course to be influenced by their answers.

A Final Comment

I began this chapter noting inconsistencies between the cultural left's inclinations towards ideology critique in the classroom and its flirtations with postmodernism. Insofar as my proposal involves self-reflexive talk-about-talk, it is very much in the postmodern spirit. This is not to suggest that *all* I do in my courses is ask students how they would have me teach them. Clearly, there is other work to be done that may lend itself to 'professing' at one moment, 'educating but not advocating' at another. The problems we have discussed notwithstanding, there is surely a place in the classroom for persuasion, authority, guided discussion and even, perhaps, restricted discussion. Similarly, there may be times when the best strategy will appear to be that of the fact-providing reporter, or of the even-handed discussion leader, the philosophical pluralist, the teacher of critical thinking or the devil's advocate.

Still, I believe it is important for my students to realize that these pedagogical strategies have ideological consequences, and for them to confront with me the dilemma I have as their teacher. Especially when dealing with politically sensitive issues, the dilemma can best be confronted by deepening our students' understanding of it, rather than simply choosing one or the other of its horns, or alternating between them. We can do this by 'teaching the pedagogies'.[4]

Notes

My thanks to Mick Billig, Patti Lather and Miles Orvell for their valuable comments on an earlier draft of this paper.

1. This is not to be confused with Graff's (1992) 'teaching the conflicts', to be discussed below.
2. For a somewhat comparable 'self-wounding' approach that problematizes the role of the teacher as 'the subject who is supposed to know', See Jay (1990: Ch. 5, 314).
3. None of this is meant to suggest that 'teaching the pedagogies' eliminates the instructor's self-privileging. When I pose the dilemma to my students, it is I who initiate the discussion, set its agenda, define its terms, generally have the last say. I am not by any means the consistent democrat, though this, too, is open for discussion.
4. The discerning reader of deconstructive bent will have noticed that this essay has been structured to this point by an absence of attention to its own constructedness. This inattention (which, at this point, might more aptly be called an erasure) might be expected from a conventional essayist, but here I am, in what I acknowledge to be a 'postmodern spirit', championing a self-reflexive pedagogy. In that same spirit, should I not have been foregrounding self-reflexively my writerly rhetoric?

   For example, just as Patti Lather, in her essay for this volume, offers a deconstructive reading of her own 'realist's tale', should not I have problematized the ease with which problems of considerable variety and complexity were reduced in this essay to a single dilemma, that dilemma structured into a simple binary, consisting, ever so symmetrically and 'even-handedly', of four pedagogies each? Should I not have subverted, or at least marked for attention, my tendency to link pedagogies with particular pedagogues (Fish, Bizzell, Giroux, Rothenberg); then, having taken issue with a particular pedagogue, let that critique stand as a synecdochal critique of the pedagogy considered generally? Should I not have foregrounded the elisions, allusions, shadings, shadowings and outright misrepresentations attendant upon my choice of linguistic representations – including, most especially, perhaps, that most mischievous of all labels, 'ideology' itself?

   Well, yes – and no. For, while I think that self-reflexive talk-about-talk can be useful, even essential, I fear that, as a foregrounding of one's own writing in the act of putting forth an argument, it can get in the way of old-fashioned clarity, leading to what Lather, in her essay, calls 'incapacitating textual undecidability'. Hence, by way of dealing with this essay's *writing* dilemma – paralleling the *teaching* dilemma that the essay is primarily about – I've elected to save my 'pomo-ing' for this final endnote.

As regards the structuring of a messy 'reality' into a relatively tidy statement and explication of 'the problem', simplification is the price one inevitably pays for the benefits of theorizing. Moreover, the reader was alerted to variations in the nature and severity of 'the problem', so the problem of over-simplification has at least been mitigated.

As for the use of synecdochal stand-ins for the various pedagogies that I sought to problematize, this may have deflected from consideration of the pedagogies considered in their own right. In my defence, the pedagogues I took issue with are not inestimable, and consideration of their positions gave concrete embodiment to each pedagogy. More worrisome to me is that the 'virtues' of all out persuasion, guided discussion, even-handed discussion and the like may have gotten short shrift in my construction of what was essentially a *negative* dialectic, one built on analyses of the problematics of each alternative. These, fortunately, can be open for discussion when one 'teaches the pedagogies'.

Finally, the problems of linguistic representation are legion, as deconstruction-ists are fond of pointing out, and they are certainly manifest in this essay. 'Ideology' is a logocentric relic of modernism which, in its Marxist rendering, assumed a scientific orientation towards ideology freed from the shackles of ideology. But acknowledging the error in Marx's self-satisfied ways does not require us to abandon 'ideology'. We need only be prepared to apply it to epistemologies, including our own, and not just to obviously political positions. This, as I understand it, is not inconsistent with deconstruction (Kenshur, 1988; Ryan, 1986)

But, as Kenshur (1988) cogently argues, deconstruction may itself be understood as an ideology, viewed here as a rationalized self-privileging, and I, for one, would not want it to have the final word. In personal correspondence (dated 6 May, 1993), Lather cites a philosopher friend of hers who claims 'we are all liberal humanists under a very thin veneer of our attraction to "the pomo". Learning to see the imperialism of our continued investments in teleology, "persuasion" toward consensus, some "real" outside of discursive renderings, etc., is neither easy nor fully possible.'

Well, yes, but this insight, too, contains its own form of blindness to the virtues of liberal humanism. Needed is a dialectical way out of that dilemma as well.

References

Adler, J. (1990) 'Taking offense: is this the new enlightenment on campus or the new McCarthyism?', *Newsweek*, 24 December: 48–54.

Billig, M. (1987) *Arguing and Thinking: a Rhetorical Approach to Social Psychology.* Cambridge: Cambridge University Press.

Billig, M., Condor, S., Edwards, D., Gane, M., Middleton, D. and Radley, A. (1988) *Ideological Dilemmas: a Social Psychology of Everyday Thinking.* London: Sage.

Bizzell, P. (1991) 'Power, authority, and critical pedagogy', *Journal of Basic Writing*, 10: 54–69.

Booth, W.C. (1979) *Critical Understanding: the Powers and Limits of Pluralism.* Chicago, IL: University of Chicago Press.

Booth, W.C. (1986) 'Pluralism in the classroom', *Critical Inquiry*, 12: 468–79.

Brown, R.H. (1987) *Society as Text: Essays on Rhetoric, Reason, and Reality.* Chicago, IL: University of Chicago Press.

Burke, K. (1969) *A Grammar of Motives*. Berkeley: University of California Press.

D'Souza, D. (1991) *Illiberal Education: the Politics of Race and Sex on Campus*. New York: Free Press.

Ellsworth, E. (1989) 'Why doesn't this feel empowering? Working through the repressive myths of critical pedagogy', *Harvard Educational Review*, 59 (3): 297–324.

Fish, S. (1992) 'The common touch, or, one size fits all', in D.J. Gless and B.H. Smith (eds), *The Politics of Liberal Education*. Durham, NC: Duke University Press. pp. 241–66.

Giroux, H.A. (1988) *Schooling and the Struggle for Public Life: Critical Pedagogy in the Modern Age*. Minneapolis: University of Minnesota Press.

Graff, G. (1992) 'Teach the conflicts', in D.J. Gless and B.H. Smith (eds), *The Politics of Liberal Education*. Durham, NC: Duke University Press. pp. 57–76.

Gusfield, J. (1976) 'The literary rhetoric of science: comedy and pathos in drinking driver research', *American Sociological Review*, 41: 16–33.

Hackett, R.A. (1984) 'Decline of a paradigm: bias and selectivity in news media studies', *Critical Studies in Mass Communication*, 1: 229–59.

Hacking, I. (1991) 'The making and molding of child abuse', *Critical Inquiry*, 17: 256–88.

Henry, W.A. (1991) 'Upside down in the groves of academe', *Time*, 1 April: 66–8.

Jay, G. (1990) *America the Scrivener: Deconstruction and the Subject of Literary History*. Ithaca, NY: Cornell University Press.

Jönsen, A.R. and Toulmin, S. (1988) *The Abuse of Casuistry: a History of Moral Reasoning*. Berkeley: University of California Press.

Kenshur, O. (1988) 'Demystifying the demystifiers: metaphysical snares of ideological criticism', *Critical Inquiry*, 14: 335–53.

Kimball, R. (1990) *Tenured Radicals*. New York: Harper & Row.

Mitchell, W.J.T. (1986) 'Pluralism as dogmatism', *Critical Inquiry*, 12: 494–502.

Pfohl, S.J. (1977) 'The "discovery" of child abuse', *Social Problems*, 24: 310–24.

Rooney, E. (1986) 'What's left out? A rose by any other name is still red; or, the politics of pluralism', *Critical Inquiry*, 12: 350–63.

Rothenberg, P. (1991) 'Teaching about racism and sexism: a case history'. Unpublished paper, William Patterson University.

Ryan, M. (1986) *Marxism and Deconstruction*. Baltimore, MD: Johns Hopkins University Press.

Simons, H.W. (1986) *Persuasion: Understanding, Practice, and Analysis*. New York: Random House.

Smith, B.H. (1992) 'Introduction: the public, the press, and the professors', in D.J. Gless and B.H. Smith (eds), *The Politics of Liberal Education*. Durham, NC: Duke University Press. pp. 1–12.

Tatum, B.D. (1992) 'Talking about race, learning about racism: the application of racial identity development theory in the classroom', *Harvard Educational Review*, 62: 1–24.

Watkins, B.T. (1990) 'Issues of racial and social diversity are the centerpiece of revamped freshman writing courses at U. of Mass.', *Chronicle of Higher Education*, 19 December: A13–A14.

Woodward, C.V. (1991) 'Freedom and the universities', *New York Review*, 18 July: 32–7.

Woolgar, S. and Pawluch, D. (1985) 'Ontological gerrymandering: the anatomy of social problems explanations', *Social Problems*, 32: 214–28.

7

Sod Baudrillard!
Or Ideology Critique in Disney World

Michael Billig

'A realized utopia is a paradoxical idea', writes Jean Baudrillard (1988: 79), suggesting that utopia has been achieved in the United States. The paradox is that social criticism is simultaneously implied and denied by the idea of a realized utopia. If utopia is realized in a specific place, then it no longer is utopia, which literally is a placeless dream of a perfect society. Hence, the idea of a realized utopia implicitly criticizes what is being realized. However, if reality is utopian, then it cannot be criticized from the perspective of higher, utopian standards: hence the impossibility of critique. Baudrillard's ironic language expresses the paradox. Santa Barbara is a paradise, he declares. So is Disneyland. The United States is paradise. Paradise is merely paradise: 'Mournful, monotonous, and superficial though it may be, it is paradise' (1988: 98).

The paradox draws attention to the difficulty of writing a critical analysis of a society which seems to be capable of realizing the dreams of its members. The dream of paradise was never intended to be mournful and monotonous. But how can the paradise of Disneyland be merely *paradise*? This paradise cannot be easily dismissed as a 'false paradise', as if there were other paradises with which it can be compared. Nor can the enjoyments of the masses, playing in their monotonous paradises, be easily overlooked. Baudrillard in *In the Shadow of the Silent Minorities* (1983a) declares that the masses may be indifferent to the philosophical projects of enlightenment; they may prefer spectacles over politics. However, their tastes are not to be contemptuously dismissed and high culture worshipped. But, then, does this leave the critic with nothing but the businesslike option of applauding the purveyors of the attained paradise?

No enjoyment is to be found on a more spectacular scale than the worlds of Disney, located in Florida, California, Tokyo and, now, also near to Paris. The success of these fun-parks is clear. Each year, thirty million people visit Walt Disney World in Orlando and thirteen million California's Disneyland. At such a rate, a mass roughly equalling the total population of the United States enters these Disney turnstiles every five years. Euro Disney, occupying a site a fifth the size of Paris, has proved to be a slight commercial disappointment. Nevertheless, over six million visitors are expected by the end of its first year (Hope, 1992). This is a phenomenon whose nature and proportions should not be ignored by those who wish to understand contemporary mass consciousness.

According to Baudrillard, Disneyland is 'a perfect model' of the entangled modern orders of simulation (1983b: 23): it is 'the microcosm of the West' (1988: 55). If, as Disney's own publicity stresses, the fun-parks are 'dreams-come-true', the contours of these successfully 'imagineered' fantasy-lands might reveal the structures of contemporary dreams. Or, rather, they might indicate the flattened structures of dreams, which have ceased to be dreams, and the emptiness of a utopia which, as a dream-come-true, has ceased to be a utopia.

Depopulating the Text

Any writer who wishes to criticize the Disney phenomenon has a problem: what sort of tone, and indeed literary form, should be adopted? If writers enter into the fun of things, they risk losing the critical edge: the resulting voice will be that of the contented customer. On the other hand, if critical writers stand back from the masses in their millions, then they risk sounding superior. Their voices may then resonate with disdain, as their prose looks down on the uncultured, unthinking masses, wallowing like pigs in the troughs of superficial pleasures. The voice of disdain is no stranger amongst the texts of ideology critique, even those written by writers claiming to be radically left wing. Adorno (1978), loftily dismissing the popular taste in music, and championing the cause of music too difficult for mass sensibility, is a case in point.

Critics who adopt the tone of cultural superiority put a distance between themselves and the very people who might have once been thought to be the agents of social change. Moreover, there is often something pitiless, even inhumane, about such writing. Much critical writing, in common with most orthodox social science, is *depopulated*. It is filled with abstract concepts, broad judgements and descriptions of general processes, but it is devoid of people (Billig, 1991, and forthcoming). Critical writings such as those by Adorno, and certainly those by Baudrillard, fall into the depopulated category. The consumers of those cultural and ideological products which are being critically examined do not appear as

individuals. The writers present no characters – no human individuals – to the reader. At best, there are only 'types'. The texts
indicate, by their depopulation, a distancing from common humanity – and thereby a distancing from the radical project of restoring
common humanity.

Writers who wish to describe critically the ideological pleasures of
today's social order, face this problem of finding a suitable textual
voice. If individuals are introduced into their texts, are they then to
be mocked as cultural illiterates, who gleefully accept trivial
pleasures? By contrast, critics who wish to reveal orders of misery
within the paradise do not have the same difficulty. Thus, feminist
writers, in experimenting with new ranges of expression to explore
the interstices of the public and the private, can populate their texts
with their own selves – and those of their mothers and their sisters.
By introducing readers to characters, they introduce readers to the
discontents of common lives (see, e.g., Smith, 1991; also Benmayor
et al., 1990). In contrast with most traditional writing of social
analysis, the self of the writer is located amongst the common
discontents. In consequence, the writer is not searching for a lofty
perspective. The intimate warmth of such writing contrasts with the
distancing chill of depopulated theorizing.

However, this intimate tone cannot be easily adopted by critical
analysts of mass society's contentments, rather than discontents.
Their topics are the obvious orders of pleasure, such as Disney,
rather than revelations of publicly hidden orders of oppression.
Without a certain resistance to these pleasures (or images of
pleasures) there can be little critique. The resistance must also
operate at the level of language, as analysts distance themselves
from the common discourses of pleasures, seeking not to repeat the
stereotyped discourses of the advertising brochure. From Walter
Benjamin to Jean Baudrillard, analysts of mass-produced pleasures
have called for experiments in writing. Critical writers have needed
to construct their own style, vocabulary and voice in order to
prevent their own passive incorporation into the mass language of
the twentieth century. To paraphrase Barthes, critical writing must
continually disavow the 'vulgate and its exhausting cortège of
motionless phrases' (1977: 53).

The analyst of Disney has no ready linguistic methodology, nor
tool set of concepts, which can be applied like power drills to the
surface of the 'imagineered' worlds. Or – to replace the gendered
stereotype lurking within the drilling metaphor – there is no
convenient, theoretical ironing board on which to fold and flatten
the world of Disney into fresh arrangement. Instead, the dilemmas
of critique – the dilemmas between incorporation and repetition,

distancing and depopulation – must be renewed. Forms of writing must be tested in order to find out whether they offer the possibility of a populated critique. Regrettably, critical writers engaging in this sort of enterprise will display a degree of linguistic self-consciousness – even an irritating preciousness – about their own words.

Disney and Ideological Revelation

In the earliest forms of ideology critique, writers tended to use the language of exposure. The assumption of *The German Ideology* was that sustained theorizing would be able to reveal 'the real'. Marx and Engels (1970) presented themselves as stripping away the concealing veils of illusion to disclose economic realities which ideologists and their capitalist masters would wish to keep hidden. Metaphors of depth lend themselves to this form of analysis. The base of capitalism is revealed beneath its misleading surfaces. This is a society of fatal depths, for the revelation of reality will hasten the collapse of the society. With its secrets exposed, capitalism will be negated by its own embodied negation, the proletariat.

However, this has not been the experience of the twentieth century. Ideological revelations of capitalism's negation have not threatened capitalism's existence. Instead, the revelation itself can be profitably incorporated as both education and leisure. Capitalist publishers, guided by market principles of profit, issue the works of Marx and Engels, along with those other ideology critics likely to sell in sufficient numbers. These texts can become 'compulsory reading' for students taking courses of sociology and philosophy at state-sponsored universities. The reading lists for such courses, despite occasional and politically motivated scares, do not cause the fly-wheels and rotor-blades of modern society to start juddering. Quite the contrary, success on such courses provides students with qualifications which are recognized by potential capitalist employers.

Baudrillard's analysis starts, as did Marcuse's in *One Dimensional Man* (1968), with the assumption that the incorporation of the negation is an operating principle of modern capitalism. The terrain is flattened with fewer depths to reveal. Baudrillard argues that images today, unlike the phantasms which Marx and Engels sought to expose, conceal no hidden truths. The age of counterfeit has given way to the age of simulacra, where images reproduce other images. The images, by which we live, are neither real nor false in the old sense of things – they are hyperreal. To quote from the prose of Don DeLillo, whose novels in many respect coincide with the vision of Baudrillard: 'One thinks of an image made in the image and likeness of images' (1990: 130).

Under these conditions, the revelatory style of ideology critique becomes redundant. No revelation of the 'real' is possible – except the revelation, made by Baudrillard, that the real does not 'really' exist any longer: 'We're in paradise. Illusion is no longer possible' (Baudrillard, 1990: 71). Thus, the day of ideological analysis has passed: 'It is always the aim of ideological analysis to restore the objective process; it is always a false problem to want to restore the truth beneath the simulacrum' (1983b: 48). If the age of ideological analysis is called the 'modern age', then now we are living in social conditions which have passed beyond modern times. Thus, Baudrillard is sometimes hailed as a postmodern theorist, a description which he personally rejects (see the interviews presented by Gane, 1993: esp. 21f.).

In *Simulations* (1983b), Baudrillard begins his short discussion of Disneyland by suggesting that the revelatory form of ideological analysis is now superficial. He takes the example of Louis Marin's essay on Disneyland in *Utopics: Spatial Play* (1984). Marin provides a structuralist reading of Disneyland, in order to represent the cultural playground as a 'narrative'. Baudrillard presents Marin as providing an ideological analysis which claims that American imperialist values lie beneath the narratives of Disney fantasy. 'To be sure', comments Baudrillard drily (1983b: 25). But, he suggests, the ideological revelation is beside the point – indeed, it conceals the point: the 'real' America is Disneyland, the paradise attained.

This argument can be taken further, in order to show the helplessness of the sort of ideology critique which Marin proposes. The revelations are not revealing, for they repeat what is openly proclaimed in Disney's own publicity material. As such, the narrative of critique limps along after the narrative of Disneyland itself. Far from concealing the American themes in its narratives, Disney advertises them: the image of America is part of its dream-come-true. Euro Disney has self-consciously reproduced the American tones. Frontierland and Main Street USA are there in France, as they are in Tokyo. This is not the result of an ideological plot to impose meanings upon empty consciousnesses. The strategies are dominated by market research – a process described by Baudrillard as the short-circuiting of reality. Moreover, this process itself can be advertised as part of the image of giving the customers what they dream. *Disney News* described in advance what the projected Entertainment Center for Euro Disney would be like: 'The theming of the Entertainment Center, like that of the Euro Disney hotels, is totally American' (spring 1991: 38). The

Development Manager is quoted: 'The American concept is extremely popular. That's the beauty of it – come to Paris to shop in America! At one time we were even thinking of calling it "America! America!"'

Perhaps the critic, instead of seeking to undermine the totality of the achieved utopia, might wish to reveal specific offences which mar the image of paradise. However, the revelations, far from subverting the utopia, can provide opportunities for the creation of yet more public images, which add to the image of success. In 1990 there were allegations that workers at Walt Disney World's Discovery Island were killing vultures (Moskowitz et al., 1990: 290). Adverse public images threatened the Disney Corporation. The response was not to deny the criticisms, but to incorporate them. A new corporate position was announced: Vice President of Environmental Policy. Disney was now declared a friend of the environment – a further plus for Negation Incorporated.

If the questionnaires of consumer satisfaction which the Corporation encourages visitors to complete and return to the 'Executive Vice President (Resorts)' were to reveal regular ideological dissatisfactions, there would be adjustments. Disney has no hidden ideological agenda: it is no mission school with curricula to instruct the natives in the true dogma. Instead, specific imagineered dreams can be sacrificed on the altar of consumer satisfaction. For instance, women visitors in their thousands might soon complain, via the questionnaires, about the Fantasyland display in which the audio-animatronic pirate chases the audio-animatronic wench. Perhaps, also, sufficient numbers of visitors from Nigeria or Zambia, let alone the States itself, might indicate dissatisfaction that no black African nation is to be found among the eleven which currently represent the world in the World Showcase. Professional calculations of profit and loss – consumer satisfaction and complaint – would then be computed. The world of the business market is, to quote Baudrillard, 'a circular operation of experimental modification, of incessant interference, like a nervous input tactile and refractile' (1983b: 121). Should the marketing graphs recommend change, there would be little to save today's racist or sexist images. They are expendable elements in the practical ideology of success.

Certainly, the fantasy fun cannot be disturbed by the revelation that a huge corporate enterprise (with an estimated annual profit of $729,000,000) stands behind the Disney playgrounds. Pleasure can always be mixed with business. Walt Disney World Conference Center seeks to attract corporate customers, and is pleased to announce that 30,000 square feet of convention space are reserved at the Contemporary Resort Hotel. Profits are not to be concealed, but are to be proudly proclaimed, for they provide confirmation that the Disney Corporation is the World's Number One. Profits, in this world, signify success, not exploitation; and success signifies hordes of satisfied customers. In their turn, these signify the promise of more success and of further realized dreams for corporation and customers alike. 'A lifetime of vacation dreams come true at Walt Disney World Resort', announces the opening sentence of the *Pictorial Souvenir of Walt Disney World*. The economics of corporate activity might have once been the hidden reality behind the image; now it is part of the public image, part of the dreams coming true.

Fiery Reflections and the Happy Ending

Baudrillard has credited Walter Benjamin with being the first critic to appreciate the deep changes in the modern world which have been brought about by the technical processes of reproduction. Such changes are decisive, for reproduction 'absorbs production changing its finalities and altering the status of product and producer' (Baudrillard, 1983b: 98). Benjamin recognized that the reproduction of images, occasioned the 'form and principle of a whole new generation of sense' (Baudrillard 1983b: 99). Nevertheless, Benjamin's writing still contained themes from earlier forms of ideology critique. There was still a landscape of depth in which clues of the utopian future were buried. Benjamin retained the echo of a hoped-for utopia, although now despair accompanied hope. However, in his prose he jettisoned the structure of traditional philosophy. As he wrote in *One-Way Street* (originally published in 1928), the day of criticism 'is long past' (1979: 89). Benjamin's critique had no hidden realities which would be disclosed as a conclusion triumphantly hey-prestoed, as it were, from the premises.

On Benjamin's street, down which he metaphorically strolled, the modern was juxtaposed with echoes of a disappearing past. This was not a Main Street USA, with its flattened, imagineered landscape of the attained utopia. This was a European city with its visible archaeology of past and present. Past the filling station, Goethe's house and the Polyclinic, Benjamin ends his walk on the final page of *One-Way Street* with messianic signs of hope – the stroller still looks to the future, for his journey must advance in one direction along the one-way street. Benjamin finds the signs of hope in the earliest of Disney ancestors: in the Lunaparks of Berlin. In a densely written finale, which simultaneously looks back to the horrors of the First World War and towards a utopian future,

Benjamin suggested that the Lunaparks were 'a prefiguration of sanitoria'. They convey the velocities and rhythms of the journey on which humankind was preparing to embark. Allusively, Benjamin held out hope that the journey would result in 'the paroxysm of genuine cosmic experience'. No causal factor is laid bare, but 'the power of the proletariat is the measure of its [humankind's] convalescence' (1979: 104).

Benjamin's street is curiously empty of characters; he walks alone, encountering no one. The proletariat, here, is hidden and anonymous. It is presented as the mysterious force for the future, rather than identified in terms of individuals who might then, or one day later, enter the world of theme-parks. The literary form of *One-Way Street* is the montage, producing, in the words of Ernst Bloch (1990), 'a philosophical revue'. The shards of hope revealed on its final page are neither the conclusions of a tightly organized argument, nor the results of empirical excavations. They are chanced-upon signs which abruptly terminate the journey. The days of criticism having passed, the hopes are oblique rather than confident. Older certainties – also, older counterfeits – have crumbled. In these times, suggests Benjamin, the advertisement speaks more directly than does metaphysics. What makes this so is 'not what the moving red neon sign says – but the fiery pool reflecting it in the asphalt' (1979: 90).

Benjamin's metaphor conveyed depth and distance: the advertisement was reflected downwards into something other than itself – into the street. Some depth, and, therefore, some vestige of revelation, was still possible. Yet, today, the image which Benjamin conveys has itself become a cinematic cliché. This image is contained within other images – the advertisement reflected into other advertisements, the forces of the street absorbed into the imagery of advertising. The contours are levelled to leave simulacra of other simulacra. And, today, could any critic seriously look to the fun-parks of Disney for indications of a future, cosmic ecstasy?

Indeed, the world of Disney incorporates its own images of the future – a Disney future which reflects without fire the Disney present. In Horizons, sponsored by General Electric at Walt Disney World, 'guests are whisked into a series of present-day dreams come true' (*Pictorial Souvenir*, p. 32). These dreams of the future are happily imagined as being realized by the machinery of the present: robots and microchips, gadgets and more gadgets. The Universe of Energy, presented by Exxon, transports visitors from scenes of 'primeval forests' into the world of twentieth-century science. Then there is a glimpse of the future – more machines and, alas, also the worry of an energy crisis. But the recorded voice reassures visitors:

Exxon helps to solve 'tomorrow's problems with science, govern-ment, industry and [*micro-pause for heightened meaning*] the people'. The forces of today are adequate for a future which reflects today. There are no depths, no fiery reflections, and no intimations of utopian ecstasy. The present images of the future have absorbed all these.

A Montage of Disney Revelations

Disney's celebration of the past and future is always a celebration of the present. 'Now is the best time of your life' repeats the theme tune of the Carousel of Progress. Audio-animatronic figures enact an American family at various times in the twentieth century. In each domestic scene, the figures praise the gadgets of their home. At first, there is irony as the turn-of-the-century scene fades into the chorused 'Now is the best time of your life'. Everyone knows more is to come – television, dishwashers, telephones, etc. How quaint to think that those times might have been thought to be the best time of our life! As the familiar gadgets are revealed in their turn, so the irony diminishes, but it does not disappear. 'Here we are in the frantic forties and the music is better than ever' announces one character. At last, there is the present, enacted in a happy Christmas Eve scene: 'We do have a lot to celebrate and it's not just things . . . it's the quality of our lives.' The theme song is repeated. There is still irony, but it is a cosy irony. Our children will find us old-fashioned in time: they will have even more machines and a better quality-of-life than us. We can imagine it now. It is being imagineered before our eyes.

Baudrillard writes that Disneyland performs one last function of concealment. Disneyland is 'meant to be an infantile world, in order to make us believe that the adults are elsewhere, in the "real" world, and to conceal the fact that real childishness is everywhere' (1983b: 25). It is as if there is a conspiracy to keep the two worlds separate, in order to confuse 'us'. However, the world of Disney might not be quite as straightforward as Baudrillard's ironic formula suggests. If dreams are said to have come true (and, thus, have been abolished), then the resulting world is one without concealment, or without ideology. The dream of the dream-come-true is a dream to fracture illusions – it is a dream of perfect realism, where even the dreams know themselves as mere dreams. This was the dream of ideology critique itself with its promise of a future utopia to be gained. As such, the Disney dream, as played out within its attained utopia, has absorbed into itself a pastiche of ideology critique.

Some theorists have recently been arguing that today's tourist has a playful sophistication: this tourist, or rather 'post-tourist', likes 'to explore back-stage regions' (Featherstone, 1991: 102; see also Urry, 1988). The world of Disney exemplifies this. It does not merely create fictions of a childish dream-world, but, in labelling the fictions as fictions, it also plays with appearances of reality. Constantly the visitor is invited to a 'backstage', which will offer revelations, or a pastiche of revelation. Like ideology critique, Disney promises to reveal the reality of 'our' commonplace day-dreams.

As visitors board the 'people-movers', to be carried around the imagineered wonders, so, also, it's 'all aboard for a montage of revelation!'

***

All aboard!

MGM Studios, Disney World, Florida. This is a 'real' studio, or, at least, the Disney sets are arranged to resemble 'real' studio sets, which create the false image of 'real' things. Visitors can wander down 'streets' of one-dimensional shop-frontages, which are just as they are in the studios: except that these flattened frontages are multi-dimensional. The backstage artificiality has been constructed to be viewed. Visitors are expected to notice that the 'shop' has no interior. It is a bright brick and mortar bill-board, with ladders and darkness behind. Visitors can see hoardings which, if they were filmed, would imitate the perspectives of skyscrapers. They can pose before these imitation imitations of buildings for their own personal studio shots.

Backstage Studio Tour: 'The best-kept secrets of the film industry are revealed on the Backstage Studio Tour.' This is a 'real working studio', visitors are told. A few dramas are filmed here, in order to make real the illusion of a reality, which really creates illusions.

You, too, can share in the experience. You are on the film-set, acting in your own film. As the guidebook says, 'your personal involvement in movie-making reaches thunderous new heights as earthquakes, flames and floods surround you.'

Everyone plays their part. 'Give yourself a hand, you ducked and screamed right on cue', says the guide, smiling. We are experiencing the backstage earthquake effects. We have ducked and screamed at a sudden explosion. We are living the illusion that we are backstage in the real dream-world of films. And we are smiling with the guide, whose job is to smile throughout the day. It's fun to pretend.

Indiana Jones Epic Stunt Spectacular. Several times a day, more backstage revelations of the film world. We can see how stunt-persons really do the dangerous business which everyone thinks the stars perform. We watch a scene from the movie *Indiana Jones and the Temple of Doom*. Or rather we watch an enacted scene, which pretends to reproduce a scene from *Indiana Jones* behind the scenes. We see the stuntmen and -women relaxing before their dangerous moment (stuntpersons playing the stuntpersons who played the stars playing their characters). We see directors and film-crews (or, rather, actors in these roles). A 'casting director' (or is it an actor playing at being a casting director?) asks for volunteers from the audience to take part in the enactment. We cheer the chosen few (another dream to come true). Mock cameramen film the scene, just like a real studio.

Tension mounts as the series of explosions, fires and falling-downs get underway. This is really dangerous, we are told. One of the volunteers is in trouble. Real danger.

We cheer when this volunteer is revealed to have been a real stuntperson after all. We enjoy being deceived, appreciating the art of the deception. At the finale, the stuntpersons, centre-stage on this backstage-stage, hug each other, as if having survived some-thing really dangerous. They do this several times a day – every day – in full public view.

We smile at the shifting montage of the real and the pretend. Reality is not elsewhere: it is here – somewhere. And so is play-pretend – also, somewhere. At the end, before leaving our seats in the open-air auditorium, we clap the show – we are the audience, responding on cue.

EPCOT Center. The initials suggest an institute of serious scientific research (NASA or MIT). The guidebooks do not explain what these letters represent, but the omission reveals the message: the letters represent the representing of other letters. Space Ship Earth, the Universe of Energy, The Wonders of Life, The World of Motion, Communicore, The Land, The Living Seas – it is all here. There are more scientific wonders than can possibly be viewed on a single tour. And there's 'imagineered fun' in science's variety parade: 'Listen to broccoli, cheese and yoghurt singing and playing musical instruments.'

EPCOT Center also offers the delights of behind-the-scenes

revelation. Visitors are 'invited "backstage" for a first-hand look at the electronic marvels which help to operate EPCOT Center and all of Walt Disney World.' This backstage, like those of the studios, is yet another carefully crafted front-stage show: 'In fact the computers steal the show in "Backstage magic,"' announces the *Souvenir* booklet.

The real show is 'behind-the-show'. We do not demand to know what is 'really' going on: why do we see a computer backstage of Disney? And not a boardroom? Nor a share-holder's meeting? Such things are not part of our fulfilled dreams. But they could be one day, if the Executive Vice President (Resorts) announces it so.

The lines of people waiting to see the popular attractions are folded back on themselves, compressing space in a display of compressing time. Sometimes extra attractions are provided for those in line, as an exordium before the main text.

Before 'The Great Movie Ride', there are several exhibits in glass cases, including 'the actual piano' used in *Casablanca*. It attracts hardly a glance, as the crowd waits for the 'people-mover' to take it round an extravaganza of 'fabulous sets, special effects and a lively cast of live and *audio-animatronic* stars'. The 'actual piano' isn't the 'real' one. How could it be? It's pink – unlike the 'real' piano projected on countless screens. Despite the museum-style casing, the pink piano exudes no 'aura', as the line passes on its way to the real show. An audio-animatronic, life-like Humphrey Bogart awaits them.

Disney has no final mystery to reveal. There is no central shrine to which homage must be paid. No attraction is permitted to outshine others in too obvious a way. There is an ultimate flatness, as wonder endlessly follows wonder, peak after peak.

Nevertheless, a hint of hierarchy is provided in Magic Kingdom. Figures dressed as cartoon characters wander about, signing autographs in the special autograph books on sale in the retail outlets. One figure is special: his ears represent the whole enterprise. Visitors have to wait in line to see the star – Mickey Mouse in Mickey's House.

After waiting, we are ushered in to meet the great figure (or someone, unseen, dressed in a Mickey uniform) 'backstage in Mickey's dressing-room'. The concept is dizzying, but not disorientating. Here we are in a dressing-room, with Mickey's stage clothes hanging on hooks. Or rather, it is an imitation dressing room, used by Mickey, not the person inside the uniform (whose dressing-room we do not enquire after). This is where this Mickey will change to appear in his great roles. But these roles were in cartoon films, made years ago. Our Mickey is pretending to be the real Mickey, the cartoon Mickey, just before he stepped on to the screen.

Backstage of the cartoons: we can go to see an animating studio. The secrets are turned into a show. There is a film about the making of cartoons, complete with self-referential jokes. A comic actor narrates on film and he meets the animators behind the Disney magic. To demonstrate their art, they turn the actor into a cartoon character – or so the story line goes. He (the filmed actor) complains that his (the cartoon-drawn actor's) bottom is too big. A cartoon brush (but no hand) sweeps across the screen to repaint the figure's behind. We do not see the brush behind the brush.

Each night (or, as the guidebook says, from 'Sunday to Saturday') at EPCOT there is a firework display above the World Showcase (an 'IllumiNation'). Backstage information reveals that twenty-five computers coordinate this display of six lasers, thirteen special-effects projectors and over seven hundred fireworks.
The sky is illuminated in time to a medley of recorded classics. Rousing bits from Handel, Rossini and Beethoven merge into one another. Visitors gasp as the '1812 Overture' moves to its climax. Never before have the cannons been so precisely matched by such cascading brilliance.
At the final explosion of light – at the final chord – we applaud. If a better display can be imagined, it will be there next year. Literally, this is a spectacular to end all spectaculars. Other firework displays will now appear paltry – whether they celebrate military victories, royal weddings or cosmic freedoms of the future.

This, the most glorious of all firework displays, celebrates no occasion except itself and the lives of the individual visitors: 'I saw the fireworks at Disney', they can now report. In this immaculate wonderland, the dream comes true nightly, vacuum-cleaning other dreams from the mind.

Abandoning the People

Only a consciousness at home with images of images could enjoy this collapsing of 'the real' and 'the unreal' as harmless fun – and applaud the tricks which expose the tricks, leaving everything more, not less, ambiguous. Similarly, the textual montage provides a second-hand Disney tour for the reader – some textual animatronics of the hyperreal. Neither the reader nor the Disney visitor is to be confused by the interplays of the display and the revelation. If the Disney tour leaves matters ambiguous, then so has the montage.

The montage seems to be written in a voice of critique. It appears to be alerting the reader against being the good, conforming tourist. Disney has an ideology, the text appears to warn: as Disney presents its dreams-come-true – and its self-referential exposés of their coming true – it expels dreams of other utopias. The real and the fantastically real are offered here and now.

Yet, the montage is ambiguous as ideology critique. On what voyage, if any, is its writer travelling? Is it just another people-moving tour, which does not get beyond the perimeter fence of the present utopia? Where stands this guide, the critic himself? Why is he wandering around Walt Disney World?

The montage is itself depopulated. Even the 'I' of the writer is absent. He does not reveal why he is spending his money along with the best of tourists. Just like Marin, the author of the montage (and, even now, further along the text, no 'I' appears) presents his writing as if it were reading signs which themselves have a real existence. So, too, does Baudrillard with his brief comments in *Simulations*. The text whispers between its words that the reading of the writer does not depend upon a particular 'I' – a 'himself' rather than a 'herself', or 'theirselves'. Anyone standing where the critic was standing – and equipped with sufficient critical irony – would read the signs in the same way. 'Trust me', whispers the prose, 'I am your guide, the real guide.' But the prose doesn't reveal where the guide was standing.

Benjamin wrote of the difficulty of critique in a world where distancing was not possible: 'Now things press too closely on human society' (1979: 89). The montage achieves a display of distance by a tone of irony. There is a coy use of 'we', as the critic-guide includes himself amongst the visitors. The coyness is not intended to deceive. This visitor is different, as the reader is urged to recognize by the voice of the text. And so the readers are flattered to think of themselves as different – a cut above the ordinary tourist. Perhaps, while other visitors experienced the sights directly and somatically, the writer was taking notes in the Carousel of Progress. The stance is ambiguous. Is this writer the post-tourist of other theorists? Are the readers being invited to imagine themselves as similarly sophisticated post-tourists? Or, perhaps, in an escalating game of chicness, the writer is the post-post-tourist.

The montage is depopulated, not merely because the author is presented as an absent figure. The other part of the 'we' – the author's fellow tourists – are also absent. No one is presented with any individuality. In this respect at least, the style resembles that of much contemporary cultural and ideological analysis (Billig, forthcoming). The cultural artifacts are portrayed, but not the lives of those who use, purchase and are affected by such artifacts (Miller, 1987). Barthes's *Mythologies* (1972) set the basic style. Marin's analysis likewise had the Disney visitors shuffling off-stage. No visitors are presented, so readers cannot judge whether the tourists' reactions are one-dimensionally thoughtless – perhaps even pre-post-tourists – as compared with the informed voice of the professional, critical post-tourist.

In short, the montage carries a smoke-trace of élitism, curling upwards between its paragraphs. The words claim the superior discernment of the critic. The absence of the others helps matters for no one else's inferior discernments are being insisted upon – at least noticeably. The author is not inviting the reader to mock directly the tastes of inferior individuals. Nevertheless, the smoke drifts lazily, barely perceptibly, across the landscape, without fiery reflection.

In the writings of Baudrillard, the same smoke of élitism billows, its fumes acrid. The masses are described as an undifferentiated, undifferentiating entity. The metaphors establish the contemptuous impression: the masses are magnetic flows, synaptic points in circuits of transmission, inert energy which absorbs – and so on (see Gane, 1991a). The texts struggle to separate themselves, and their writer, from the mass. Grim pleasure is conveyed at the thought of the masses resisting through 'hyperconformity', and destroying, the culture of their 'betters'. The masses flood into the Pompidou Centre (the Beaubourg), bringing it down on top of themselves (Baudrillard, 1982). The critic imagines the scene with cruelly grim pleasure.

Yet there is a crucial cost: ordinary lives are dismissed, theoretically sacrificed as the edifice of culture is pulled down. These lives do not matter – the text does not invite the reader to share their living, nor their dying.

Baudrillard makes the claim that new models of communication have taken over 'banal, everyday life' and that they haunt 'all the messages, all the signs of our societies' (1983b: 115). Yet, banal, everyday life is ignored, textually short-circuited, to be excluded from his pages. In one of his essays on the hyperreality of modern life, Baudrillard concedes that traditional domestic life might still be continuing. He adds in a footnote, 'how people actually live with their objects – at bottom, one knows no more about this than about the truth of primitive societies' (1985: 133n). The older patterns, even if they exist within the banal home, are beside the point: 'the stakes are no longer there' because 'another arrangement or life-style is virtually in place' (1985: 133n). This new life-style is known, inter alia, through the discourses of advertising.

Baudrillard's impatience with discovering the contours of banal, everyday life is part of an impatience with conventional sociology. He is not making the point that more sociological research needs to be conducted in order to discover how ordinary lives are being led. Quite the contrary, he suggests that the techniques of sociology, whose categories reproduce those of market researchers, will reproduce hyperreal descriptions, which themselves short-circuit the unknown banal life. The point can be crudely put: to understand how Disney is experienced, the last thing the critic should examine is the data from the questionnaire forms, dutifully returned by the customers to the Executive Vice President (Resorts). A sociology built upon such data would only reproduce hyperreal categories and the world of the researched 'is irremediably short-circuited and lost' (Baudrillard, 1983b: 130).

In order to avoid such short-circuiting, Baudrillard not only abandons conventional sociological methodology, but, just as crucially, he abandons the conventional sociological voice. His writing distances itself from the style of professional sociology by tone, form and vocabulary. As Gane argues, a new style of writing is essential for Baudrillard's project: 'His experiment is posed in such a way that the real has been withdrawn, and as a consequence, he is forced into fiction-theory' (1991b: 94). A new rhetoric – indeed a new poetic – is required for the age of the hyperreal. This rhetoric cannot claim the voice of empirical reality, for that reality no longer exists. The hyperreal is to be described by a 'hyper-rhetoric' (Harvey, 1989). The voice of this fiction-theory is that of detachment, and the result is a depopulation, which dismisses the banalities of everyday life.

Baudrillard's texts, which announce the end of ideology critique, seek to finish the tradition which began with Marx and Engels's declaration that 'we set out from real, active men' (1970: 47). The categories of 'real' and 'men' can no longer be naïvely reproduced by the critic. For the sake of argument, Baudrillard's point can be conceded: perhaps some sort of fiction-theory is needed to transcend the short-circuiting of sociology. However, this does not mean that Baudrillard's grandly depopulated style must be adopted. An alternative tactic can be proposed, which textually comes down to earth: this would be a repopulated fiction-theory of the banal.

The rhetoric of this fiction-theory would be not the hyper-statement, but the understatement. It would explore banal, rhetorical depths, and its form would be fiction (neither claiming nor disputing its own reality). It would not self-consciously use the latest forms of experimental fiction, for it is not seeking to catch the tones of the ultra-modern; instead, it seeks the voices which might indicate the possibility of a continuing common sense. But, of course, there is a paradox: traditional middle-brow forms of fiction, briefly inserted into conventional critique or into a professional bit of sociology, would themselves be experimental in a limited sort of way. If a hyper-rhetorical fiction-theory is a hyperreal response to the hyperreal, then an ironic fiction of common-sense discourse would be an under-stated response.

Regarding Disneyland, Baudrillard comments that 'you park outside, queue up inside, and are totally abandoned at the exit' (1983b: 23). In another sense, it is the social critic who totally abandons visitors. Disney's customers leave the park – they have done their brief job as anonymous extras in the narrative of the critic. But it doesn't have to be like this. An adjustment can be made: the fiction-theorist might eavesdrop a homeward-bound journey. A scene can be imagineered.

Mickey's Ears

At approximately the mid-point between Orlando and Gatwick, the flight attendants were collecting up the plastic trays. The film was still flickering on the screen. Something about golf. Vanessa couldn't concentrate; neither could she sleep. Her book lay open on her lap – face down, cover up. In the next seat, John was now snoring.

Vanessa turned her book the right way up. She glanced down, then immediately upwards. John's snoring was far too loud. Of course, he wasn't doing it on purpose, she had to tell herself. But he was still wearing the hat. That was on purpose. And the sweatshirt – despite the heat. That was on purpose, too.

Well, you've bought a Disney shirt, he had said. That was different, she'd replied. Of course it was. A discreet Mickey on the left pocket: the black and white stripes would have looked just as good without the Mickey. A huge Mickey on a luminously orange background – John was doing it on purpose. And then, the hat. He'd worn it all the time, Mickey ears wobbling high on top of his head. Just entering into the spirit of things, he'd said. Just spoiling things, she'd replied.

She looked at him now, sprawled, mouth open, oblivious, ridiculous Mickey ears. You couldn't always tell with John. He'd been the enthusiastic one, long after she was ready to flop. Oh, come on, the Universe of Motion, we're almost there. A quick look at Communicore. And so on. 'Do you know why they call it the EPCOT Center?', his intonation signalled unfunny joke on the way. 'Why do they call it the EPCOT Center?', she'd cooperated. 'Because Every Person Comes Out Tired.' Ha-ha. Certainly they'd been tired. Too tired, in their Disney Luxury Lodging, to do much. Well, she'd been too tired. The ears hadn't helped matters.

The golf on the screen had given way to men killing each other. Vanessa looked away. She let the sights and sounds from the last four days drift in and out. A montage of Disney memories, scene intercutting scene. And, oh dear, a pause at the Carousel of Progress.

It had been John's fault. In the dark, she had recognized the fatal signs. John trying not to giggle: shoulders heaving, head buried in hands, muffled snorts. Not the laugh, please, not the laugh, she had pleaded inwardly. Everyone else – all the rows of Americans – seemed to be taking it seriously, 'Now is the best time of your life, dah-dah.' On and on, it went. Keep a grip, she told herself, teeth biting lips, forcing chortles downwards into indigestion. It might have worked, had she then not noticed John stuffing the Mickey ears into his mouth. No power – certainly not that of inward prayer – could suppress her laugh any longer. John's soon followed, hooting its liberation to the ceiling.

The Disney attendants were advancing; at that moment, they were not having a nice day.

Even now, mid-way across the Atlantic at an uncertain time, Vanessa couldn't stop smiling.

The Mickey Vase was safe in the overhead compartment. You can't give that to your mother, John had said. She'll like it, Vanessa had replied firmly, just you see. Vanessa couldn't remember who'd said what next. But things were said – particularly about John's parents.

She glanced down at the book, reading the sentence which she had first tried a thousand miles ago. 'Fetishes, fetish objects, that have nothing to do with the world of the imagination, but everything to do with the material fiction of the image.'

What do you want to read that stuff for? John had asked in that needling way of his, as the last view of America had disappeared. Her reply had been a touch smug, a touch pompous: I want to understand what we've both just seen. That shut him up, for once.

She re-read the ungrammatical sentence. And again. Even more slowly. She still didn't understand it. John still snored. Why was he always so loud?

Sod Baudrillard! she snapped. Reaching down, she stuffed the awkward-shaped Frenchman back into her bag, and pulled out Fay

Weldon. 'Four blocks farther on, in her sorry basement home, Madeleine lies awake on her lumpy mattress . . .'

The noise of the engine, the murmurings of the passengers, John's snores – especially those – floated away, ' . . . and curses Jarvis, his second wife Lily and their son Jonathan . . .'

The second half of the Atlantic was infinitely shorter than the first.

John was wrong again. Vanessa's mother loved the Mickey Vase. She put it at the centre of her side-board.

The Carousel of Banality

A short guided tour of the Carousel of Banality is now available.

Visitors can note the gentler tones of this exhibit. 'We' readers are not invited to mock Vanessa and John from a position of superiority. Instead, a mood of sympathy – perhaps we could call it 'an imagineered identification – is on offer.

Certainly, Vanessa and John cannot be lightly sentenced to their death in a collapsing art gallery – there to be crushed, suffocated, by other screaming, desperate bodies. Afterwards, parents would have to bury their Vanessa and John in graves side by side. No joke, however fierce, should be stretched that far.

Note, too, the behaviour of 'our' characters. They display little acts of 'hyperconformity' and 'resistance'. They can laugh at the Disney culture and can mock serious social theorists. And, of course, 'we' (or, rather, 'you') are invited to do likewise. John snores while Vanessa reads her woman's novel. There is ambiguity in his Mickey Mouse ears. The conforming gesture is edged with resistance. Even Vanessa cannot tell where John's conformity ends and hyperconformity starts. And she's reading the book.

'We' and 'you' can enjoy the ambiguity of both being part of the banal (sod the élitists!) and above it: 'we' laugh, 'we' see ironies, whilst others passively accept the Disney sights.

A further point: the importance of purchased objects in our characters' displays. They position themselves, in relation to each other and to others, through their purchases. However much Vanessa and John display resistance, they continue purchasing products. The whole vacation, including air ticket, has been costly. In fact, the imperative to purchase shapes their displays of resistance. Even books, which express profound contempt for the consumer culture, can be useful markers of position. The opened Baudrillard puts Vanessa a notch above John, and several notches above the opened Jeffrey Archer on the row in front. But each move to position above invites a rhetorical resistance. 'What are you reading that stuff for?' is not an innocent question. Sod Baudrillard! Sod Fay Weldon! I'm watching the film. Sod the film! Sod the guided tour! I'm going to sleep.

Now, here is something visitors often fail to notice. Look closely at Vanessa and John. They are fogetting something. Do you notice what it is?

When John bought his Mickey Mouse ears, he glanced quickly, as is his habit, at the label: 'Made in Thailand.' The Mickey Vase was 'Made in Hong Kong'. John gave no thought to the labels – or rather to the miseries behind the labels. Nor do writer and reader give heed to the manufacture of the paper and printing machinery which enables their thoughtful activities to continue so thoughtlessly. The discontents of production are to be separated from the contents of consumption. There is a passage in Vanessa's book which she has not yet reached. The poor, in the world of the attained utopia, will be 'condemned to oblivion'. They will be dispatched from consciousness 'to die their second-class deaths' (1988: 111–12; see also Gane, 1991b: 187f). Such people are beyond the perimeter fence of utopia. They are not part of this guided tour.

One last point. The banal exchanges can be fun. A giggle. They be, as the old song goes, the best times of your life. These are not mournful, monotonous moments. Imagine a perfect world. You are not sitting passively, obediently, in a people-mover being taken to admire yet more sights. Or gazing upwards at a laser-filled heaven. You might be chatting, discussing, yes, even arguing, with friends.

In such moments, futures can be previsaged. These are not the futures of cosmic ecstasies, nor one person plugged into another in a sort of short-circuited communication. Instead, there are banal delights of disagreement, even misunderstanding, which at present, in our unenlightened times, [*micro-pause for heightened meaning*] cause so much trouble.

* * *

Cut to a suburban interior, Kingston upon Thames, south-west of London.

Vanessa's mother was chatting with her neighbour, Mrs Sterland, as they did every so often. They'd had their second cup of tea (just a quick one). Mrs Sterland really had to get going. Passing by the side-board, she just had to stop and ask.

'Oh that,' replied her neighbour, 'Vanessa and John brought it back from Disney World. They had a wonderful time.' Mrs Sterling hadn't moved to the door; she was expecting a bit more. So Vanessa's mother continued:

'Actually – and I wouldn't dare say this in front of Vanessa,' she was dropping her voice, as if her daughter were actually in the kitchen, 'I don't really like it. It's so – how can I put it? It's so, well, American, if you know what I mean.'

Mrs Sterland knew exactly. 'Just what I was thinking,' she said.

And, then, a moment, which surprised both women. Vanessa's mother reached for the large Disney Vase. 'Sod Mickey Mouse' she was saying out loud. Sod Vanessa, she was thinking.

The two friends were standing facing each other, laughing like children. All the more so when the vase slipped to the floor, scattering in bright fragments.

Finale

The students had copied the three headings from the overhead projector: Syntagm, Signifier, Metaphor. The lecturer was still speaking: 'Marx and Engels's use of Metaphor' (he points to the third projected word) 'is interesting – they descend from, um, heaven to earth – it is a downward motion – they are full of optimism – getting down to business, ha.' The lecturer produces a smile, which is reproduced by the student in the front row, but by no one else.

The lecturer continues: 'But in the other text, which we've been looking at, the downward motion, um, the vase falling to the floor, um, the downward motion is a *Metaphor* acting as a *Signifier* in the *Syntagm* for fractured hopes' (a trio of brisk raps on the screen).

As his outstretched hand beat the tattoo, he glimpsed his watch. 'Err, that'll be all for this week. Any questions?'

The students gathered up their things. They had their assignment – 'The Possibility of Ideology Critique' – to complete. A few, not necessarily the cleverest, would end up making a living by lecturing on this sort of thing. Others had already applied for managerial openings.

The lecturer would write up his notes. They had the makings of a journal article, he thought. The promotions committee of last year had advised him – indirectly, of course – that a few more publications would not be amiss. Things were more competitive nowadays, he was being told.

For now, he wasn't quite sure how his article would end – whether he would come out for the possibility or for the impossibility of ideology critique. Not that it matters. For both conclusions, there is the same small market.

References

Adorno, T.W. (1978) 'On the fetish character in music and the regression of listening', in A. Arato and E. Gebhardt (eds), *The Essential Frankfurt School Reader*. Oxford: Basil Blackwell. pp. 277–99.

Barthes, R. (1972) *Mythologies*. A. Lavers, trans. London: Jonathan Cape.

Barthes, R. (1977) *Roland Barthes by Roland Barthes*. R. Howard, trans. London: Macmillan.

Baudrillard, J. (1982) 'The Beaubourg effect: implosion and deterrence', *October*, 20: 3–13.

Baudrillard, J. (1983a) *In the Shadow of the Silent Minorities*. P. Foss, P. Patten and J. Johnston, trans. New York: Semiotext(e).

Baudrillard, J. (1983b) *Simulations*. P. Foss, P. Patten and J. Johnston, trans. New York: Semiotext(e).

Baudrillard, J. (1985) 'The ecstasy of communication', in H. Foster (ed.), *Postmodern Culture*. London: Pluto Press. pp. 124–36.

Baudrillard, J. (1988) *America*. C. Turner (Material Word), trans. London: Verso.

Baudrillard, J. (1990) *Fatal Strategies*. P. Beitchman and W.G.J. Nieslnchowski, trans. London: Semiotext(e)/Pluto Press.

Benjamin, W. (1979) *One-Way Street*. E. Jephcott and K. Shorter, trans. London: New Left Books.

Benmayor, R., Vazquez, B., Juarbe, A. and Alvarez, C. (1990) 'Stories to lie by: continuity and change in three generations of Puerto Rican women', in R. Samuel and P. Thompson (eds), *The Myths We Live By*. London: Routledge. pp. 184–200.

Billig, M. (1991) *Talking of the Royal Family*. London: Routledge.

Billig, M. (forthcoming) 'Repopulating the depopulated pages of social psychology', *Theory & Psychology*.

Bloch, E. (1990) *Heritage of Our Times*. N. Plaice and S. Plaice, trans. Cambridge: Polity Press.

DeLillo, D. (1990) *Americana*. Harmondsworth: Penguin.

Featherstone, M. (1991) *Consumer Culture and Postmodernism*. London: Sage.

Gane, M. (1991a) *Baudrillard: Critical and Fatal Theory*. London: Routledge.

Gane, M. (1991b) *Baudrillard's Bestiary: Baudrillard and Culture*. London: Routledge.

Gane, M. (ed.) (1993) *Baudrillard Live*. London: Routledge.

Harvey, D. (1989) *The Condition of Postmodernity*. Oxford: Basil Blackwell.

Hope, C. (1992) 'A fistful of francs', *The Guardian Weekend*, 3 October: 6–9.

Marcuse, H. (1968) *One Dimensional Man*. London: Sphere.

Marin, L. (1984) *Utopics: Spatial Play*. R.A. Vollrath, trans. London: Macmillan.

Marx, K. and Engels, F. (1970) *The German Ideology*. C.J. Arthur, trans. London: Lawrence & Wishart.

Miller, D. (1987) *Material Culture and Mass Consumption*. Oxford: Basil Blackwell.

Moskowitz, M., Levering, R. and Katz, M. (1990) *Everybody's Business*. New York: Doubleday Currency.

Smith, D.E. (1991) 'Writing women's experiences into social science', *Feminism and Psychology*, 1: 155–69.

Urry, J. (1988) 'Cultural change and contemporary holiday-making', *Theory, Culture & Society*, 5: 35–56.

8

The New Politics of the Workplace: Ideology and Other Unobtrusive Controls

Stanley Deetz

The modern private corporation is central to public decision-making today. In most modern societies, corporations make crucial decisions for the public regarding the use of resources, development of technologies, product availability and working relations among people. While state political processes are significant, the shaping of these central decisions through regulation and incentives is considerably less important than the central decision-making processes within corporations themselves. And, in addition, corporate officials are significant actors in state political processes through both direct action and the commercial domination of the mass media, the production of information, and information networks (Laumann and Knoke, 1987). Increasingly, political decision-making in state processes is replaced by economic decision-making organized in corporate practices (see Deetz, 1992a). Every contemporary political philosophy or investigation of societal decisions must consider the logic of market economy and the internal decision processes in corporations.

Such a situation has drawn the attention of numerous social theorists. Initially theories and studies from both the political right and left focused on macro-social issues. Conservative and old liberal factions tended to see this new political system in positive terms – proclaiming the 'end of ideology' and the rational and world interdependence possibilities in marketplace democracy (Bell, 1960; Parsons, 1956). The old left, in contrast, saw the decline of culture and the creation of false needs (e.g. Adorno and Horkheimer, 1972). They complained that the state had become a tool supporting world-wide capitalist domination, defining its role as applying bandages to social problems. Until recently, few authors of any persuasion have looked closely at how decisions made internal to corporate organizations have substituted for collective decisions in the public sphere. Changes in central theoretical understandings as well as more recent world political events leave these positions and this omission untenable.

The past twenty years have evidenced the growth of a new way of thinking about the political nature of internal corporate practices. The focus has turned to the practices at the 'point of production' – in the office and on the work floor – and away from the grander theories of society (Burawoy, 1979; Burrell, 1988; Deetz, 1992a, 1992b). Being rethought are both the traditional conservative interests in enhancing control in the workplace towards greater profit, and more radical change agent's interests in understanding the forms of domination that lead to exploitation. In this reconsideration, society, corporations, work roles and work practices are not simply seen as historical products or structures that control, constrain, direct or dominate. They have no life except as they are reproduced or re-enacted in concrete historical moments (Giddens, 1984; Weick, 1979). Rather than direct control or domination being the central issue, the focus has turned to reproduction systems that require active complicity of controlling/dominating and controlled/dominated groups.

Several recent authors have used concepts from critical theory to support studies of social arrangements and practices that are likely to foster wider and more open participation in the collective determination of the future (e.g. Alvesson, 1987a; Alvesson and Willmott, 1992; Forester, 1989). Much of this work has focused on power, ideology and symbolic/cultural practices (Alvesson, 1987b; Clegg, 1989; Mumby, 1988). In general these works have been useful in providing theoretical conceptions for discussing domination especially with regard to historical group distinctions such as class or gender. But these works have been less helpful in describing the concrete practices through which domination occurs or in providing specific alternative practices. Understanding the operant politics of the workplace requires descriptions of the relations among power, discursive practices and conflict suppression as they relate to the production of individual identities (such as class or gender) and the knowledge and experiences such individuals have.

Attempts to produce a more democratic workplace, one capable of making decisions for the general public, must consider the politics involved in the construction of the human subject and his/her experience. Traditional conceptions of both domination and democracy were useful in considering the manner and degree of the representation of different stake-holder interests. Most consideration of power and influence assumed that representation of pre-existing interests is the central question. But such conceptions tended to overlook or take for granted the social processes by which groups divisions were produced, individuals acquired identity by group membership, and different individuals as group members acquired specific experiences and interests. Traditional ideology critique, for example, could discuss how workers might misrecognize their own 'objective' interests, but rarely discussed the day-to-day reproduction of the historically arbitrary distinctions among 'workers', 'owners' and 'managers' and conflicting experiences within and between such groupings. Foucault's (1977, 1980) analysis of power as discipline has been an important addition since power is considered 'within' such arbitrary productions rather than power being a property of dominant groups and used to direct and control. Further, conceptions like Foucault's direct attention towards the everyday, practical manner in which this hidden power is deployed and potential workplace conflicts are suppressed in these identity productions.

In this chapter, I describe the uses and limitations of ideology critique, outline why ideological and other unobtrusive forms of power are of such interest in the workplace, and then demonstrate how a communication-based analysis focused on the construction of identity can be useful as a more expansive analysis than traditional ideology critique. Finally, I give a brief analysis of a worker's report to illustrate such an analysis. The purpose here is to consider alternative analytic frameworks for the analysis of ideology, power and control in the workplace. While references are made to general practices within corporations, no attempt is made here to analyse any particular corporate site. The described practices may be more or less present in any particular corporation. Rather than trying to represent specific practices, the point here is to illustrate the heuristic value of paying attention to relations of specific interpretive types wherever they may appear.

Traditional Ideology Critique of Corporate Practices

The earliest ideology critiques of the workplace were offered by Marx. In his analyses of the work process he focused primarily on practices of economic exploitation through direct coercion and structural differences in work relations between the owners of capital and the owners of their own labour. However, Marx also describes the manner in which the exploitative relation is disguised and made to appear legitimate. This is the origin of ideology critique. Economic conditions and class structure were still central to the analysis, whether this misrecognition of interests was a result of the domination of the ruling class's ideas (Marx and Engels, 1970) or of the dull compulsions of economic relations (Marx, 1977).

Clearly the themes of domination and exploitation by owners and later by managers has been central to ideology critique of the workplace in this century (see Czarniawska-Joerges, 1988; Deetz and Mumby, 1990). Attention by analysts from the left focused on ideology since workers often seemed to fail to recognize this exploitation and their class-based revolutionary potential in the industrial countries. Gradually these later analyses became less concerned with coercion and class and economic explanations as they began to focus on why coercion was so rarely necessary and on systemic processes that produced active consent (e.g. Althusser, 1971; Gramsci, 1971). Ideology produced in the workplace would stand alongside that present in the media and the growth of the consumer culture and welfare state as accounting for workers' failure to act in their own interests. This would fill out the tradition of ideology critique.

Four themes recur in the numerous and varied writings about organizations working from such a perspective: (1) concern with reification, or the way a socially/historically constructed world would be treated as necessary, natural and self-evident; (2) the suppression of conflicting interests and universalization of managerial interest; (3) the eclipse of reason and domination by instrumental reasoning processes; and (4) the evidence of hegemony, the way consent becomes orchestrated.

Reification

In reification a social formation is abstracted from the ongoing conflictual site of its origin and treated as a concrete, relatively fixed entity. As such the reification, rather than life processes, becomes the reality. This can be seen in most institutional formations. Berger and Luckmann (1967: 53) utilized this Marxian conception when they suggested that institutions can be thought of as the societal equivalent of personal habits. A habit is initially a set of choices for handling recurring practical problems and situations. Over time the practical reasons for the particular choices are forgotten and in place of choice the routine takes on a life of its own, both precluding options in thoughtlessness and building a set of secondary justifications for why it is done this way. Other habits at the personal level or institutions at the societal level spin off the initial one. Social arrangements and practices develop that depend on the initial habit and reproduce it. For example, a shy person may form relationships with others that speak for him or her and they may extend or enforce his or her shyness. Consequently, the continued habitualization and institutionalization are not carried by psychological investment but by the interrelated web of support and dependence that makes any single change difficult. In personal as well as in institutional arrangements we see less causality than structural interdependencies – hence powerful but not deterministic systems. The initial and subsequent institutional arrangements are no longer seen as choices but as natural and self-evident. Marx, like Berger and Luckmann, focused almost exclusively on the origin of reifications and the politics of their formation. In more recent works the concern has been with the structural interrelation of institutional forces, the processes by which they are sustained and changed, and the processes by which their arbitrary nature is concealed and hence closed to discourse. For later authors, the origin of institutional forms is less important than their continuation.

In short, in traditional ideology critique, organizations are reclaimed as social-historical constructions. They are formed, sustained and transformed by processes both internal and external to them (Giddens, 1979: 195; Lukács, 1971; Thompson, 1984). The illusion that they are 'natural' objects protects them from examination as produced under specific historical conditions (which are potentially passing) and out of specific power relations. Their arbitrary and power-laden character is denied. Ideology critique demonstrates their arbitrary nature and the power relations that result and sustain these forms for the sake of discovering the remaining places of possible choice.

Universalization of Managerial Interests

Lukács (1971), among many others (see, e.g. Giddens, 1979), has shown that particular sectional interests are often universalized and treated as if they were everyone's interests. In contemporary corporate practices, managerial groups are clearly privileged in decision-making. *The* interests of the corporation are frequently equated with management's interests. For example, worker, supplier or host community interests can be interpreted in terms of their effect on corporate – i.e. universalized managerial – interests. As such they are exercised only occasionally and usually reactively and are often represented as simply economic commodities or 'costs' – e.g. the price the 'corporation' must pay for labour, supplies or environmental clean-up. Central to the universalization of managerial interest is the reduction of the multiple claims of ownership to financial ownership. The investments made by other stake-holders are minimized while capital investment is made central. Management by virtue of its fiduciary responsibility becomes equated with the corporation. In such a move, since the *general* well-being of each group is conceptually and materially tied to the *financial* well-being of the corporation as understood by management, self-interest by non-managerial stake-holders is often ironically reinterpreted as accomplished by minimizing the accomplishment of their own self-interests (see Deetz, 1992a: Chaps 8 and 9). For example, since the corporation is conceptualized as having to make a profit to supply and pay for work, the worker may have to choose a pay cut to stay employed. The advantages given to management in such a conceptual and material arrangement are based on neither rational nor open consensual value foundations nor are they simply acquired through management's own (though often latent) strategic attempts. They can be seen as produced historically and actively reproduced through ideological discursive practices in society and in corporations themselves (Bullis and Tompkins, 1989; Deetz, 1992a; Deetz and Mumby, 1990).

The Primacy of Instrumental Reasoning

Habermas (1971, 1975, 1984, 1987) has traced the social/historical emergence of technical rationality over competing forms of reason. Habermas described *technical reasoning* as instrumental, tending to be governed by the theoretical and hypothetical, and focusing on control through the development of means–ends chains. The natural opposite to this Habermas conceptualizes as a *practical interest*. Practical reasoning focuses on the process of understanding and mutual determination of the ends to be sought rather than control and development of means of goal accomplishment (Apel, 1979; Stablein and Nord, 1985). Habermas described the practical interest as 'a constitutive interest in the preservation and expansion of the intersubjectivity of possible action-oriented mutual understandings. The understanding of meaning is directed in its very structure toward the attainment of possible consensus among actors in the framework of a self-understanding derived from tradition' (1971: 310). In a balanced system these two forms of reasoning become natural complements. But, in the contemporary social situation, the form and content of modern social science and the social constitution of expertise align with organizational structures to produce the domination of technical reasoning (Fischer, 1990). To the extent that technical reasoning dominates, it lays claim to the entire concept of rationality and alternative forms of reason appear irrational. To a large extent, studies of the 'human' side of organizations (climate, job enrichment, quality of work life, worker participation programmes and culture) have each been transformed from alternative ends into new means to be brought under technical control for extending the dominant group interests of the corporation (Alvesson, 1987a). The productive tension between the two becomes submerged beneath the efficient accomplishment of often unknown but surely 'rational' and 'legitimate' corporate goals.

Hegemony

Perhaps no work has been more important than Gramsci's (1971) in providing a powerful consideration of workplace ideology. While his own analysis and development of the concept 'hegemony' aimed at a general theory of society and social change with the workplace as one component, his conceptions have been widely used as a foundation for an examination of the workplace itself (e.g. Burawoy, 1979; Clegg, 1989). Gramsci conceives of hegemony as a complex web of conceptual and material arrangements producing the very fabric of everyday life. Hegemony in the workplace is supported by economic arrangements enforced by contracts and reward systems, cultural arrangements enforced by advocacy of specific values and visions, and command arrangements enforced by rules and policies. These are situated within the larger society with its supporting economic arrangements, civil society (including education/intellectuals/media) and governmental laws. The integration of these arrangements along the lines of those favouring dominant groups enables a mobilization and reproduction of the active consent of both dominant and dominated groups.

Compliance and stability in such systems are passively achieved since active systems of control would likely be resisted. A hegemonic system is maintained through four moves. (1) The system actively monitors and takes account of the needs and demands of different segments of the group. (2) Compromise on secondary issues is ongoing, hence lending support to inherently unstable political systems while not giving in on essential dominant group interests. (3) Support is organized for overarching goals which serve the long-term interest of the dominant group. (4) Moral, intellectual and political leadership are provided in order to form and reproduce a collective will or popular group outlook.

Such a system then pervades common sense and becomes part of the ordinary way of seeing the world, understanding one's self and experiencing needs (see Angus, 1992). Such a situation always makes possible a gap between that inscribed by the dominant order and that which a dominated group would have preferred. As Lukes argued, 'Man's wants themselves may be a product of a system which works against their interests, and in such cases, relates the latter to what they would want and prefer, were they able to make the choice' (1974: 34). The everyday person has some 'discursive penetration' (Giddens, 1979) and may be *able* to form a contrary worldview, hence ideology critique is useful and the possibility of a democratic project remains.

A Critique of Ideology Critique

Each of these four concerns raised in various ideology critiques has value. Yet, limitations of ideology critique have been demonstrated by many. Three criticisms appear most common. First, ideology critique appears ad hoc and reactive. It largely explains after the fact why something didn't happen. Second, it appears élitist. Concepts like false needs and false consciousness presume a basic weakness in insight and reasoning processes in the very same people it hopes to empower. The irony of an advocate of greater equality pronouncing what others should want is not lost on either dominant or dominated groups. And, third, the accounts from ideology critique appear far too simplistic. This point has perhaps been made best by Abercrombie et al.'s (1980) conception of the 'dominant ideology thesis'. The conception of the dominant group remains singular and intentional, as if an identifiable group worked out a system whereby domination through control of ideas could occur and its interest could be secured. Abercrombie et al. contend that the case can more easily be made that a dominant group's ideology is most deeply penetrated into the dominant group itself and very weakly in working-class or other group consciousness. It would appear that no dominant ideology is necessary for dominated groups to fulfil their existing roles in society. Further, the authors would argue that there is more pluralization of life-worlds than most have accounted for. The question remains whether the power of ideology critique can be maintained without falling to these criticisms.

Further, perhaps the very possibilities of reality and rationality that are retained in ideology critique from Marx to Habermas lack a sufficiently radical agenda. For it can be argued that it has not only been the left that has spent much of this century doing ideology critique; so have the conservative and liberal thinkers, though they have not done it by this name. Many of those advocating scientific management, having co-opted Weber's description of bureaucracy, have been pushing a case against ideology for the sake of rationalization of the workplace. Their work often differs from left studies of the same period only in terms of whose ideology and which ideologies are found oppressive and faulty. And they, too, hold out a hope for a 'real' world where ideology would not infringe on meeting human needs or where it could lead to a more fulfilling world. In many respects, Parsons can as easily be shown to be supporting a 'dominant ideology thesis' as can Gramsci (see Clegg, 1989: 164). But, of course, Parsons was looking for greater integration while Gramsci was looking to subvert it. But scientific management's and functionalists' own 'ideology critique' finally comes up short as the limits of rationality in the workplace are displayed. The contemporary interest in studying organizational cultures and programmes of creating and changing them is an admission of the end of the 'end of ideology' for management and conservatives. At the same time postmodern writings have shown many unexplored forms of local resistance.

Finally, the illusion of the centred agent-subject is as central to ideology critique as it is to dominant groups and the systems that advantage them. Both hold out the hope for a rational and reflective agent who is capable of acting autonomously. The modern corporation's legitimacy is based on both the assumption of the existence of such an individual and its ability to foster that individual's development. The very notions of free contract, social relations and agency, as well as personal identity as a manager, secretary or worker, are corporate productions and reproductions.

Laclau and Mouffe summarized the three positions central to the corporate individual: 'the view of the subject as an agent both rational and transparent to itself; the supposed unity and homogeneity of the ensemble of its positions; and the conception of the subject as origin and basis of social relations' (1985: 115). The first is necessary for the illusion of freedom which allows the subject to be conceptualized as freely subordinating him/herself in the social contract of the corporation and having choices based on self-interests there. The second sets out the hope of a well-integrated society where the work relations fit seamlessly into other institutions and coexist with the democratic processes and the basis for consensual decision-making and mutual understanding. And finally, the individual is conceptualized as the fundamental site of meaning production and chooser of relations with others, hence the personal itself is protected from the examination necessary if it were seen as an arbitrary historical social production resulting from certain social arrangements. Each of these conceptions is misleading and repro-ductive of forms of domination. Yet, it is often simply a better version of this agent that ideology critique hopes to foster.

The Interest in Ideological and Other Unobtrusive Controls

Despite the potential shortcomings of ideology critique within a general theory of social domination, the growing use of forms of ideological control within the modern workplace provides a context where the use of ideology critique, limited and extended by other types of analysis, can be so important. A brief reflection on the conditions giving rise to these new means of managerial control provides a basis for considering alternative forms of social analysis.

Control in the workplace can no longer be conceptualized in Weber's sense based on 'sovereign' rights, legitimate authority or simple reward/punishment systems (Alvesson, 1993). In response to the collapse of older control forms, managers initially sought national and regional cultures that externally provided corporate legitimation, work habits and/or greater responsiveness to reward/punishment systems. When this failed or was not possible, especially in economically developed countries with major techno-service corporations, corporate managers initiated new systems of control based on 'cultural management' and 'discipline'. The force of control in these organizations rests in processes of the social production of knowledge, individual identities and interests, rather than in the use of explicit control mechanisms. Because these are largely unobtrusive control processes, the possibility of massive systems of domination exists in corporations that appear open and participative (Czarniawska-Joerges, 1988; Kunda, 1992).

Social changes internal and external to the work process influenced the changes in the form of control. Less obstrusive control processes result from new expectations of participation and attitudes towards work that have developed over the past several years and from the growth of information technologies, service industries and new structural configurations. The following is a brief summary of the forces of change (see also Alvesson, 1987a, 1993).

1   Industrialized societies are experiencing a decline in the moral and ethical background necessary to sustain organizational practices in the absence of corporations' ability to justify themselves. Traditionally in the West, the work ethic provided an important extra-organizational motivational form. Basic standards of honesty, belief in quality and standards, and accurate reporting provided a voluntary conformity to social practices. Social change and trans-nationalism have undermined external systems. In response, most corporations have implemented explicit strategies of teaching values and loyalty. Since these are fragmented and do not provide the life-integration potential of traditional cultures, the modern employee is both more and less free.

2   Attitudes towards authority have changed. With the move of the 'backstage' of social relations into the 'social' arena (Donzelot, 1988), authority has lost its mystique and is more clearly seen as arbitrary and negotiated. In an age of the anti-hero and the loss of

traditional commanding myths, managerial authority has itself declined. The prerogative for control rests in produced symbols of superior ability, vision and the invisible good of efficiency for all, rather than in position. But because of this the manager cannot govern by authority permanently installed in the position; instead, command must be structurally and symbolically reproduced.

3   The centralization of power has created legitimation problems for corporations in democratic societies. Large centralized corporations have difficulty mimicking the characteristic of the family firm and thus achieving the loyalty and personal identification frequently attributed to the traditional workplace. The lack of personal and interpersonal contact places greater demands on reason-giving and explicit justifications, but these become increasingly abstract and hidden from view. Decentralization, thus, has become important of late, owing both to diseconomies of scale and to the desire to reclaim legitimacy.

4   Explicit systems of rewards and sanctions are difficult to administer in modern organizations. The supervisor frequently lacks the 'trade-relevant knowledge' necessary to assess the worker's effort. The complex processes of production and the nature of managerial work make it difficult to assign fault, or fault is shared at so many levels that 'scapegoating' is a common complaint. Monitoring the amount and quality of work in the service industries becomes increasingly difficult. And supervisors often lack the authority to reward meaningfully except in unusual cases.

5   Along with the difficulty of using sanctions comes the cost of member disruptions. Even sabotage becomes more likely in highly centralized and interdependent work settings. Employee exercises of control or unfocused resistance to the work environment and process have evoked great fear since management groups have generally relied on voluntary compliance to rules and internal regulations. While increased monitoring is likely in many corporations, surveillance is costly itself and often fosters an environment where increased disruption is likely (Alvesson, 1987a). Fostering employee self-surveillance is obviously preferred by most managerial groups.

6   Work itself has often become increasingly fragmented, monotonous and deskilled at the same time that the educational and expectation levels of new workers have increased. The managerial assumption that the problem is in education rather than work design is likely to lead to even more deskilling. Therefore, motivation must often be applied from the outside since the work experience is not intrinsically motivating. Job enrichment is only a beginning of the massive effort necessary to make products, production and coor-

dination meaningful. While new high-school and college graduates may be happy to have a job at all, the expectations of what will come with it do not disappear easily, especially with a consumer-advocating media pushing the good life.

7 High new worker expectations coupled with the slower economic growth and loss of competitiveness create a legitimacy problem in the heart of management. The system requires high pay increases, expanding markets and growth to meet its internally defined criteria of success (Peters, 1989). Initially periods of recession can be cast in positive Social Darwinian terms. Cleaning out the deadwood, trimming the fat and streamlining can help characterize individuals not making it as weak and add to the uniquely gifted perception of those who do make it, but events as they happen can be cast in alternative articulations that are not easy to suppress. Longer periods of slow growth start to suggest that no one can make it or that those at the top are denying opportunity.

Putting these changes together, it should come as little surprise that a number of changes in systems of control are occurring in the relations at the point of production. Behavioural control is difficult and costly and motivational techniques are complex and often ineffective. The management of the 'insides' of employees answers a lot of problems from a management's standpoint. The widespread appeal of a variety of 'cultural' management approaches has created a new industry and a new set of professional experts.

Teamwork, worker participation programmes and the management of culture become important modern means of control and conflict suppression. Clearly these are to be preferred over the more authoritarian forms of management, but modern management loses no control even if it fosters involvement. New managerial practices encourage a measure of dignity at lower levels of the organization, a reversal of some of the effects of deskilling, higher senses of self-worth in part because of higher quality products, and a site and routine whereby presently suppressed conflicts *could* be discussed (Lawler, 1986). But they also form, in the long run, more invisible and potentially more stultifying suppressions (Czarniawska-Joerges, 1988). If the enabling potential is to be realized, investigating the function and effects of these programmes is essential. Ideology critique aids in investigating such controls, but other forms of unobtrusive control require other forms of analysis.

Communication Analysis beyond Ideology Critique

Traditional ideology critique has come under considerable attack during the past decade or so. This is not because ideology is gone, but because the relations among language, experience, action and agency are articulated differently today, enabling and requiring a more sensitive and powerful form of critique. Ideology critique becomes a component of a larger project. Let me describe how we get to this larger project and then conclude with an example.

Control in the workplace today is clearly multifaceted. It includes material forms of coercion and authority analysable by classical Marxist conceptions and ideological meaning formations that are well analysed by traditional conceptions of ideology critique. But it also includes social processes by which the 'subject' is formed with particular identities and interests by what can be called social technologies of control that routinize and normalize the very movements and feelings of the body (Foucault, 1988). These processes produce an individual who is disciplined and actively engages in self-surveillance and correction. The development of social technologies of control replaces the passing authority in the managerial control process (Deetz, 1992a: 249ff.). With such a concept we no longer have to contend that the workplace is well integrated and hegemonic to demonstrate domination. Many corporations are filled with conflict, but only certain types of conflict are acknowledged and these hide potentially more important ones. People largely know a version of their own interests and act on them, but these interests are produced in standard codes along normalized and one-sided lines (see Deetz, 1994a and b). Surveillance is both internal and external to the individual, but understood as for the good of efficiency and all members. The new fear by many corporate employees is not a fear of an authoritarian manager, but that one's own self will not behave and conform. Trust is enacted in images, since the whole person, filled with emotions, urges and, importantly, wasteful conflicts, presumably cannot be trusted. The mind, body and will are transformed to *means* in a long instrumental chain towards some obscure end. But the individual's preoccupation with control of self as the means to personal ends leads him or her to overlook the way that this control serves as a means to self-denial and the accomplishment of unchosen ends for others. The individual thus constantly overlooks the disparate distribution of advantages, the marginalization of self and the arbitrary social identity control that continues to be produced as the critical outcome of many corporation practices (Deetz, 1994a).

In this fuller conception, managerial domination can be seen as taking place through economically based structures, ideological control *and* systems of discursive monopoly through which personal identity and group interests are formed. In most modern corporations, advantages, rather than being conceptualized as a right or as legitimate, are unproblematically reproduced in routines and discourses where rights and legitimacy never arise as concerns. As such, privilege is treated as natural and neutral and perhaps even necessary since the employee conceives of the self as lacking the information, expertise or self-control to decide on one's own behalf. This presumed neutrality of the organization makes understanding the political nature of organizations more difficult. Order, efficiency and effectiveness as values aid the reproduction of advantages already vested in an organizational form. Concepts of organizational effectiveness tend to hide possible discussion of whose goals should be sought and how much each goal should count (Cameron and Whetten, 1983). The goals of the self (about which every employee is an expert) are not discussed while the steering of the employee towards managerial organizational goals becomes the central interest and managerial expertise is accentuated (often to the detriment of products and services as well as the employee since management expertise is usually primarily in financial manipulation). Individuals may choose some degree of self-interested personal politics to get what they can from the system, but find it more difficult to participate in transforming the system to represent the diverse goals of all stake-holders (see Burawoy, 1979). And, ultimately, self-interested personal politics become co-opted into the systems so that the motivational drive involved in it is harnessed for the fulfilment of 'corporate' goals. To say that employees are passive and duped does not account well, or certainly not totally, for their active self-conscious activities here. More to the point, employees may be acting on the 'objective' condition of their existence, but systematic arrangements lead to constantly unknown and unexpected ends (see Bourdieu, 1990). Employees' ability to 'discursively penetrate' (Giddens, 1991) the system may be limited, but notions like 'false consciousness' or 'strategic apparatus' are not a helpful basis from which to approach the problem.

Critical theorists have shown that workers and the general society often have interests in work that are only partially and indirectly represented in corporate goals as implemented by management groups. These include the quality of the work experience and work environment, mental health and safety, the skill and intellectual development of the worker, the carry-over of thinking patterns and modes of action to social and political life, and the production of personal and social identity (Alvesson, 1987a). Organizational life could be an explicit site of political struggle as different groups try to realize their own interests but the conflicts there are often routinized, evoke standard mechanisms for resolution and reproduce presumed natural tensions (e.g. between workers and management). The essential politics in everyday interaction thus become invisible. Even more basically, the work site could be considered a polysemic environment where the production of the individual or group interests could itself be seen as an end-product (or temporary resting place) in a basic conflictual process defining personal and group identity and the development and articulation of interests (Deetz, 1994a). Such potential conflicts are even more completely suppressed in normalization of conception, identity formation and non-decisional practice than can be shown by critical theory's ideology critique. Focusing on the psychological understandings of individual or group consciousness or trying to reclaim a basis for objective interests misses what appears key here. The modes of representation of potential interests and the interactions that can take place among interest are faulty (Lazega, 1992). Systematically distorted communication (without Habermas's rational overtones) presents a one-sidedness in the production of people and interests (see Deetz, 1992a: 173ff.). It is not faulty in that it misrepresents what is present or real, but closed in that it arbitrarily reproduces a historical situation of advantage. The ambiguity and conflicting possibilities are lost. The future is colonized – it is not the known by some that is lost but the unknown by all.

Clearly ideology is still of interest. Subtle, ideologically based power differences often lead to inequitable interest representation. Different stake-holders are not always in a position to analyse their own interests owing to the lack of adequate undistorted information or insight into fundamental processes. Under such conditions what might be accepted as legitimate power differences are best represented as a system of domination since the empirical mani-festation is that of free consent yet structures are reproduced which work against competitive practices and fulfilment of the variety of interests. But beyond these ideological conditions, stock-holders and workers can be disadvantaged even more fully in constitutive, rather than representative, communicative practices. Particular ways of forming knowledge and information reproduce group advantages, standard accounting practices skew even the monetary code, and technologies for information distribution provide sensory as well as people domination (Deetz, 1992, 1994a). Further, the presence of ideology in the external social world or at the workplace, perpetuated through legitimation and socialization processes, can indicate the inability of certain or even all groups carefully to understand or assess the implicit values carried in their everyday practices, linguistic forms and perceptual experiences. However, even more basically, even if these implicit values could be assessed, the individual assessing the ideology is a product of a social situation. Any attempt to proclaim insight transcending this historical social situation reproduces some type of arbitrary privilege (Bourdieu, 1990). The best we can hope for is an open communicative context whereby more of what is possible is brought to experience and expression. This would move us toward a future which is more inclusive of the conflicts of social living. Ideology critique without the pretence of getting it right can be a step in reclaiming lost conflicts, and thus contribute to the communicative project.

Ideology critique alone is, thus, not sufficient to account for the full nature of modern domination. Ideological compliance and the inability to understand self-interest fail to account for situations where compliance and consent are a result of clear member understanding of the material conditions for their success. As Przeworski (1980) argued, the desire to live well provides a pressure towards active participation in the corporate system. In many workers' minds, corporations have delivered the goods and workers have received a necessary and even desired standard of living for their participation. Worker decisions in these circumstances lack an open democratic character not because the calculus or calculations are distorted, but because the human character and needs are specified in advance rather than responsive to the situational complexities. The lack of conflict in these self-referential systems precludes the discussion and open determination of the future (see Mingers, 1989). A non-contentious decision has already been made. These are the issues needing development in the move beyond ideology critique.

The Politics of Subject Formation and Reproduction: from Phenomenology to Communication

Any analysis of contemporary corporations must include an understanding of the social character of the human subject and his/her experience. Traditional ideology critique in this century grew out of a limited conception of the subject/object relation and of the nature of language in communication processes. Some of its historical strengths and its limitations grow out of the same conceptions. A dualistic conception of experience was present from the outset in Marx's works. Such a position allowed for a conception of objective conditions that could be separated from subjective understandings of them. While each was historically constructed there was no question of which was really real. Dualism could also allow a division of a real self from a lived self in which needs and the experience of them could be radically separated. In addition, language was clearly given an instrumental role which placed it on the side of the subject as a mode of self-expression. Experience was *in* the world but abstracted as being *of* the world. Ultimately this would leave those doing ideology critique to share with the rest of society a concept of experience as psychological and as such amenable to psychoanalytic interpretation. Through the concept of false consciousness, many of the studies in critical theory retain this perspective, which leads to élitism, a view of the person as easily fooled, and a need to control the interiority of people for the sake of reason. Ironically, as shown, this was not far from the assumptions managers were making about the organizational members they wished to control in the workplace.

Accepting a non-dualistic, phenomenological conception of experience enables the development of a communication-based analysis which can move beyond traditional ideology critique. Most of recent European social theory – from existentialism and hermeneutics to post-structuralism and critical theory – can be seen as an interpretation of Husserl's (1962) phenomenological description of the structure of experience. Whether 'existential project', 'body', 'language', 'habitus' or 'discursive formation', each conception tries to show the 'intending act' and hence experience itself as thoroughly social and historical. The human subject is neither singular nor a manifestation of the essential, but a motion which finds its subjectivity already inscribed as it takes its place in the already socially, historically structured world. It is precisely in that that the world appears given and objective and that the subject feels able to be separated. The illusion of the independent subject and world protects the constitutive activities from examination and obscures the understanding of social/historical construction. Since each of the modern and now postmodern philosophies is a different attempt to unpack this illusion, it is useful to review the shared views of these positions.

At root, all share an interest in the constitution of the structured world including the structure of both subjects and objects. The claiming of the subject as an identity and the world as filled with knowable objects takes place against the backdrop of the already structured world and competitive constitutive practices. All accept the structured world as holistic and potentially thematically organized, though all such unities are surrounded by a horizon of uncertainty and of that not yet unified, and held against other competing unities. All understand thematic unities as historical though often sedimented and taken for granted. Each of these issues is worked out in different and often competing manners. Even postmodern writings, with their emphasis on the unstable and fleeting character of historical unities, work with an understanding of phenomenological thematization as a backdrop.

The Phenomenological Critique of the Psychological Subject

As in Husserl's time, the primary problem today in understanding the construction of experience is the common treatment of it as subjective or psychological. It is partly for this reason that communication so often focuses on speakers' meanings rather than that which is spoken about. The historical emergence of such a position is not surprising. If, as commonly formulated, a structured objective world is 'out-there', its understanding and differences in understanding must arise 'in here'. The nineteenth-century preoccupation with the relation of the in-here to the out-there and culturally different experiences led to an early twentieth-century concern with language representation and procedures for an undistorted understanding of the out-there. Such a position allowed for individualism and privacy at the same time that it supported a collective truth, each separate and in its place. The phenomenological demonstration of the inadequacy of such a separation was important for the development of critical European thought.

Unfortunately, in the United States phenomenology was co-opted by humanistic psychologists who used only certain aspects of phenomenological thought to critique the presumed 'objectivity' of science without understanding the implications for their own position (e.g. Snygg and Coombs, 1949). The critical impact of phenomenology was, thus, lost. In Europe a similar development took place in the humanistic and existential writings of the 1950s and 1960s following Sartre (see Bourdieu, 1990: 42ff.). In these works unified experience in the here-and-now was privileged as authentic and assumed to be able to overcome the sedimented experience of the 'they'. This position held out for a singular unified self as the origin of experience against historical construction and the material conditions thereof. In Europe the structuralists would offer a decisive reconsideration, a move which would finally come to America in the 1970s.

Against such a background it is not surprising that the concept of the social construction of reality has been given such a shallow reading in the United States. In many analyses the idea of social construction is treated as individuals with independent experiences coming together to share them and reach a consensus. Such a conception of what is better called a 'negotiated order' overlooks the more fundamental issue that shared meaning arises out of a background set of constitutive practices (Deetz, 1994a).

The Social Subject

In phenomenology the 'subject' or intending act is not a 'real' person or psychological state, but rather is a structuring possibility which precedes the individual who takes it on as his/her own. Only on the basis of the structuring possibility can an individual have the experience at all. The structuring possibility is shared and thoroughly social before the individual actualizes it in a particular experience. Understanding the constitution of reality thus leads not to investigating the 'insides' of the individual but to the social possibilities which are neither inside nor outside alone, but which produce among other things the possibility of thinking about the inside and outside. Since thinking about the self with a particular identity is one of our possibilities, the self as an object can be abstracted. And, like any other object, it can be thematically drawn out of the flow of experience. But this identity is a constituted rather than constituting subject and its social origin is thus of interest. As a unity it can either be temporarily held as a point of view, sedimented to be reproduced, *or* returned to its temporary, process motion. Once constitutive acts are separated from the individual and psychological states a variety of analyses become available. The phenomenological subject thus is a position, or a positioning in a variety of integrated and conflicting institutional forms in which it appears to be an agent.

Institutional practices are historically produced and as such are imbued with and reproduce power differences and advantages. Everyday experience in that sense is thoroughly political. The politics is not in the competition of experiences but already *in* the experience at hand, the person and perception produced. Every building, every sidewalk, institutionalizes a point of view (a subject), a point of view sedimented out of the politics of the moment of production; individuals, as they find themselves instituted in this way, reproduce the view of the 'winner' of that decision process. It's not that the individual must do so, though sanctions and rewards may encourage it. It is in the habit, the routine and the thoughtlessness that it is reproduced. But this is not to say that it is neutral or innocent. The configuration of routines and other practices leaves it seemingly inevitable and necessary (Bourdieu, 1990: 58). And the thoughtlessness and routine are actively protected from thought and alternatives. Ideology critique is useful in disclosing the thoughtless and routine, but often fails to show the manner of the subject's active complicity in the reproduction of these configurations. Understanding how this works requires an understanding of power and how power both advantages and hides advantage.

The Linguistic Subject

Language is a, if not the, principal institution in modern society. Not only is it a major constitutive condition of experience itself but it serves as the medium through which other institutions are brought to conception, both in production and in understanding. As Berger and Luckmann argued, language is the 'depository of a large aggregate of collective sedimentation' which can be acquired as a whole 'without reconstructing their original process of formation' (1967: 69). In this sense linguistic discourse is deeply political, reproducing both an order and a disguise for that order. This politics is often missed as language is treated as representing experience rather than being intrinsic to its constitution. Language does not represent things that already exist. Language is a part of the production of the things that we treat as being self-evident and natural within the society. Words do not name colours, shapes and relations. Words recall and put into play the possibility of being interested in colour, texture, shape or relational acts. The historical nature of language is not such that a word stands in the place of an absent to-be-recalled object. Rather language holds forth the historically developed dimensions of interests, the lines along which things will be distinguished. Language holds the possible ways we will engage in the world and produces objects with particular characteristics. Thus when we consider language from a political point of view within organizations, the interest is not primarily how different groups use language to accomplish goals, or the rationality in language usage, or how the profit motive influences language use. Social groupings and their interests, types of rationality and the concept of profit are social linguistic productions. Each is produced as distinguished from something else. The questions are thus not whether these things exist, have power or explain organizational behaviour, but how they come to exist, co-exist and interrelate in the production and reproduction of corporate organizations.

From Language as Ideological Mediation to Discursive Practice

During the past three decades French authors such as Foucault, Derrida, Baudrillard, Bourdieu, Kristeva and Lyotard among others have added great depth to these analyses through their 'theories of the subject'. In general these works have moved from Marxist ideological criticism, to theories of language as ideological mediation, to the communication-based politics of representational practices as proposed here. Allow me to briefly trace the contours of this movement.

In Althusser's (1971) analysis, language is the most general ideological mediation. Building on Saussure, language to Althusser is not a system of signs that represent. Language appears as discourse, a material practice which is produced out of the same conditions which produce the objects of which it speaks. Language as an ideological practice mediates between individuals and the conditions of their existence. But this mediation is not between preformed individuals and objective conditions; it is the means by which the individual becomes a subject, a process called *interpellation*. Quoting Althusser: 'I shall then suggest that ideology "acts" or "functions" in such a way that it "recruits" subjects among individuals (it recruits them all), or "transforms" the individual into subjects (it transforms them all) by that very precise operation which I have called *interpellation* or hailing' (1971: 162–3). The specific relationship between subject in a particular world and the individual is *imaginary*. That is, the 'subject' is always an image or constructed self rather than an individual in a full set of relations to the world. A 'real' form of domination or control is unnecessary to the extent that the individual takes the imaginary construction as if it is real. The individual denies the important freedoms that exist in the situation. But these are not freedoms the subject could exercise if reflectively reconstituted. While Althusser equivocates on the point (see Woodiwiss, 1987), following such an analysis, the subject's sense of freedom and agency (only real in the imaginary world treated as real) is produced as part of the imaginary construction. The individual subject misses the mutual construction and treats both the self and experience as intuitively obvious. Thus, ironically, the individual misses the moment of constructive autonomy in proclaiming the already constructed self as autonomous.

It is of little surprise that the individual makes this mistake or 'misrecognition'; the processes through which it takes place are quite complex. Pêcheux (1982), following Althusser (1971), argued that ideology 'interpellates individuals into subjects' through many complex, 'forgotten' interdiscourses whereby each subject has a signified, self-evident reality which is 'perceived-accepted-submitted to'. As Thompson presented Pêcheux's analysis, the hidden-forgotten discursive formation

> creates the illusion that the subject precedes discourse and lies at the origin of meaning. Far from this being the case, it is the subject which is 'produced' or 'called forth' by the discursive sequence; or more precisely, the subject is 'always already produced' by that which is 'preconstructed' in the sequence (1984: 236).

But discursive sequences are never singular and closed. The issue of concern, however, is not that an illusion or image is produced, but that the politics preferring one type of image over others precludes the conflict and dialogue among them. There is no claim that there is some simple 'real' self. But only in the relation among conflicting images is the arbitrary character of each revealed and potentially open to renewed participation in construction. The presumed singularity is critical to the accepted realness of the imaginary. The conception of a relatively monolithic, coordinated production of the subject overlooks the diffused and everyday process of subject production. The ideological imaginary relation works primarily because it is hidden. As Weedon suggested,

> The crucial point . . . is that in taking on a subject position, the individual assumes that she is the author of the ideology or discourse which she is speaking. She speaks or thinks as if she were in control of meaning. She 'imagines' that she is the type of subject which humanism proposes – rational, unified, the source rather than the effect of language. It is the imaginary quality of the individual's identification with a subject position which gives it so much psychological and emotional force. (1987: 31)

The consideration of alternative meanings and alternative subjectivities thus poses a threat to the individual's claimed identity. The denial of the self-evidence through expressions that shows one's world as a construction with plausible alternatives is more often seen as political propaganda than the politically founded first meaning. The first is taken on as one's own and the alternative expressions are seen as attempts to control. The personal is forgotten as already political.

The subject is thus not fixed as mediated through language but is produced out of a set of discourses. There is no place out of the interplay of discourses to claim a simple, pre-existing, independent subject with knowable interests. The individual experiences a particular world, one which is the product of socially inscribed values and distinctions like the subject itself. Only on the basis of this does the individual claim personal beliefs or values or come to share them with others. The unitary (or at least tied together), one-sided perceptual experience is not so much merely a 'bounded rationality' or a false consciousness but a *delimited appropriation of discourse*' (Donzelot, 1988; Frow, 1985). The imaginary thus originates neither in the subject nor in a simple misrepresentation of the world, but in an arbitrary representational practice. In this analysis the possibility of studies based on ideology critique can be usefully supportive of the more detailed descriptive accounts of social technologies of control. Meaning is not a singularity claimed by an individual or intersection of texts. It is pluralistic and 'deferred' in the sense that there can be no final determination. Unitary meaning is temporary and only held in place by force before it drifts away in a never-ending web of other texts. Only on the basis of the appearance of plurality could ideology be identified at all or could the subject be claimed as an agent.

In brief, the notion of the psychological subject as an autonomous originator of meaning, which phenomenology first showed to be an abstraction, is now more precisely replaced by competing points of view arising in many simultaneous texts. People thus are not filled with independently existing thoughts, feelings, beliefs and plans which are brought to expression. As they move about the world, reading books, watching television or doing work they take on the subjects of these texts as their own. The self is not independent of texts but always finds itself in them. The power given to the self to define its own meaning is an unwarranted privilege, conceals the process of construction and leaves the subject unaware of multiple systems of control.

The primary effect of these moves is to suppress insight into the conflictual nature of experience and preclude careful discussion of and decision-making regarding the values implicit in experience, identity and representation. These are not themselves major value claims nor organized strategies. Rarely are they seen in regard to dominating ideologies or the politics of identity and experience. Rather, they are quiet, repetitive micro-practices done for innumerable reasons which function to maintain normalized, conflict-free experience and social relations. Examining alternative codes often demonstrates that 'free' and autonomous expression suppresses alternative representations and thus hides the monopoly of existing codes. The primary force of domination can no longer be seen as economic exploitation with false consciousness providing its alibi but can be conceptualized as the arbitrary, power-laden manners of world-, self- and other-constitution. With such a conceptual shift, analysis focuses on systems that develop each subject's active role in producing and reproducing domination. Organizations can be seen as sets of practices and routines which constitute identities and experiences and in so doing provide unproblematic asymmetries, privileged knowledge and expertise located in some and not others, thus instantiating inclusions and exclusions in decisional processes (Knights and Willmott, 1985). If discourse itself is understood as power-laden rather than neutral and transparent, we can better reveal the sites of power deployment and concealment beyond ideological controls.

Demonstrating Power-laden Identity Constructions

Allow me to close with a brief example of a power-laden identity construction and reproduction. Everyday descriptions show that workers provide their own accounts which can function to enable power configurations. This can be demonstrated by a re-analysis of an example from Huspek (1987). The story below is a worker's description of a meeting that he and the union shop steward had with a management group regarding a company policy of laying off workers irrespective of their seniority. They fail to win their case, and, more importantly, once in the setting they never effectively challenge the management group. As the worker told of his reticence:

> I would of jus' been lettin' off steam y'know. An' they already think I got a bad attitude down there. See they'll tell ya, sure he'd give up his wife to go with the company if the company asked that y'know. That's the kinna guy – well that's what he told me one time. He said if he had ta choose between the company and his wife he'd go with the company. Yeh, an' he's not talkin' money. He's talkin loyalty to the company. . . . An' like he told me I don't know what it's all about. I haven't had it hard. An' I definitely don't need anything yet. See it's all right to get a raise if ya say ya need it. But if ya want it, you'll never get it. An' I went in there askin' for a raise because I wanted it. I didn't need it. I wanted it. So I never got it. Ever since that day I've felt more pressure than I'd like ta have.

The worker clearly describes himself, his choices and the logic of the story in management terms. If he had challenged the management group, he already self-classifies the act as 'lettin' off steam' by one with a 'bad attitude', which is their classification he anticipatorily evokes without them having to. He suggests an inability to present a counter self-description or interpretation of his action. The potential managerial story of his behaviour becomes his story for the absence of it. The notice of potential alternative ways of approaching the task that wouldn't be just 'lettin' off steam' is never broached, managerial interpretive authority appears unquestioned. This is not to say that he made a poor choice, but rather he accepted being a loser in their game without consideration of a game of his own. Once this is set in motion the differences and conflicts are already established. Any challenge to company policy is read as disloyalty and the worker's loyalty cannot be compared with the manager's. Forgotten is the question of why it should be. While we can always conceptualize three possibilities in corporate opposition, *exit*, *loyalty* and *voice*, the worker can only conceptualize the first two (Hirschman, 1970). He feels he either needs to leave or be loyal. The right to define company policy by using 'voice' is not considered. He is a fixed entity with certain skills and ways of talking and management is also. The possibility of developing skills or transforming the context is considered unnatural. Existing representational practices are not contested.

Further, the discussion of money recalls a past meeting where a similar structure was present. The worker is not able to operate as a fellow man, wanting things, giving reasons for it, negotiating. Rather, he is rewarded for dependency and display of dependency. To gain any measure of self-determination, he must give up his adult status. Clearly he displays the discouragement of being caught in the contradiction, but he appears to accept the problem as one of him as an individual, not his group, and uses the contradiction as a reason for inaction. He is lost in a discursive trap where any request appears self-serving since he along with management defines the situation as 'he versus company group', rather than 'he for worker group' or 'he as company'. At the point he becomes self-serving in 'needing' the money, his loyalty is displayed as he re-enacts the hierarchy but not as just the right of management to determine pay but to determine his identity. The full tension of the contradiction is felt on the worker and he seeks only to not have a 'bad attitude' – to be silent and invisible. The evidence of systematically distorted communication is clear.

The worker is 'subjected' in a particular way in 'his' story – borrowed from management. But the full articulation and supportive power apparatus extends far beyond this. The worker does not just tell this story. Actual contracts, legal statutes, reward structures and places of talk are further reproductions of the same relations. Whether the management group intends it or not, this is a strategic exertion of power. The active complicity of the worker is only part of a larger system enabling fear, intimidation and active coercion to accomplish the same at other moments. But importantly, the conflict which would be displayed if those other means were used remains hidden and inoperative as a result of the worker's complicity.

References

Abercrombie, N., Hill, S. and Turner, B. (1980) *The Dominant Ideology Thesis.* London: Allen & Unwin.

Adorno, T.W. and Horkheimer, M. (1972) *Dialectic of Enlightenment.* J. Cumming, trans. New York: Herder & Herder.

Althusser, L. (1971) 'Ideology and ideological state apparatuses', in *Lenin and Philosophy and Other Essays.* Ben Brewster, trans. London: New Left Books.

Alvesson, M. (1987a) *Organizational Theory and Technocratic Consciousness: Rationality, Ideology and Quality of Work*. New York: Aldine de Gruyter.

Alvesson, M. (1987b) 'Organizations, culture and ideology', *International Studies of Management and Organizations*, 17: 4–18.

Alvesson, M. (1993) 'Cultural-ideological modes of management control', in S. Deetz (ed.), *Communication Yearbook 16*. Newbury Park, CA: Sage. pp. 3–42.

Alvesson, M. and Willmott, H. (eds) (1992) *Critical Management Studies*. Newbury Park, CA: Sage.

Angus, I. (1992) 'The politics of common sense: articulation theory and critical communication studies', in S. Deetz (ed.), *Communication Yearbook 15*. Newbury Park, CA: Sage. pp. 536–71.

Apel, K.O. (1979) *Towards a Transformation of Philosophy*. G. Adey and D. Frisby, trans. London: Routledge & Kegan Paul.

Bell, D. (1960) *The End of Ideology*. New York: Free Press.

Berger, P. and Luckmann, T. (1967) *The Social Contruction of Reality*. Garden City, NY: Doubleday.

Bourdieu, P. (1990) *The Logic of Practice*. R. Nice, trans. Stanford, CA: Stanford University Press.

Bullis, C. and Tompkins, P. (1989) 'The forest ranger revisited: a study in control practices and identification', *Communication Monographs*, 56: 287–306.

Burawoy, M. (1979) *Manufacturing Consent*. Berkeley: University of California Press.

Burrell, G. (1988) 'Modernism, postmodernism and organizational analysis 2: the contribution of Michel Foucault', *Organization Studies*. 9: 221–35.

Cameron, K. and Whetten, D. (eds) (1983) *Organizational Effectiveness: a Comparison of Multiple Models*. New York: Academic Press.

Clegg, S. (1989) *Frameworks of Power*. Newbury Park, CA: Sage.

Czarniawska-Joerges, B. (1988) *Ideological Control in Non-ideological Organizations*. New York: Praeger.

Deetz, S. (1992a) *Democracy in an Age of Corporate Colonization: Developments in Communication and the Politics of Everyday Life*. Albany: State University of New York Press.

Deetz, S. (1992b) 'Disciplinary power in the modern corporation: discursive practice and conflict suppression', in M. Alvesson and H. Willmott (eds), *Critical Management Studies*. London: Sage pp. 21–52.

Deetz, S. (1994a) *Transforming Communication, Transforming Business: Building Responsive and Responsible Workplaces*. Cresskill, New Jersey: Hampton Press.

Deetz, S. (1994b) 'Representative practices and the political analysis of the workplace: building a communicative perspective in organization studies', in B. Kovacic (ed.), *Organizational Communication: New Perspectives*. Albany: State University of New York Press. pp. 209–42.

Deetz, S. and Mumby, D. (1990) 'Power, discourse and the workplace: reclaiming the critical tradition', in J. Anderson (ed.), *Communication Yearbook 13*. Newbury Park, CA: Sage Publications. pp. 18–47.

Donzelot, J. (1988) 'The promotion of the social', *Economy and Society*, 17: 395–427.

Fischer, F. (1990) *Technology and the Politics of Expertise*. Newbury Park, CA: Sage.

Forester, J. (1989) *Planning in the Face of Power*. Berkeley: University of California Press.

Foucault, M. (1977) *Discipline and Punish*. A. Sheridan, trans. New York: Random House.

Foucault, M. (1980) *The History of Sexuality: Vol. 1. An Introduction*. R. Hurley, trans. New York: Vintage Books.

Foucault, M. (1988) *Technologies of the Self*. L. Martin, H. Gutman and P. Hutton (eds), Amherst: University of Massachusetts Press. pp. 16–49.

Frow, J. (1985) 'Discourse and power', *Economy and Society*, 14: 193–214.

Giddens, A. (1979) *Central Problems in Social Theory*. Berkeley: University of California Press.

Giddens, A. (1984) *The Constitution of Society*. Berkeley, CA: Campus.

Giddens, A. (1991) *Modernity and Self-identity: Self and Society in the Late Modern Age*. Stanford, CA: Stanford University Press.

Gramsci, A. (1971) *Selections from the Prison Notebooks*. Q. Hoare and G. Nowell Smith, ed. and trans. New York: International Publishers.

Habermas, J. (1971) *Knowledge and Human Interests*. J. Shapiro, trans. Boston, MA: Beacon Press.

Habermas, J. (1975) *Legitimation Crises*. T. McCarthy, trans. Boston, MA: Beacon Press.

Habermas, J. (1984) *The Theory of Communicative Action: Vol. 1. Reason and the Nationalization of Society*. T. McCarthy, trans. Boston, MA: Beacon Press.

Habermas, J. (1987) *The Theory of Communicative Action: Vol. 2. Lifeworld and System*. T. McCarthy, trans. Boston, MA: Beacon Press.

Hirschman, P. (1970) *Loyalty, Exit and Voice*. Cambridge, MA: Harvard University Press.

Huspek, M. (1987) 'A language of powerlessness: class, context, and competence among lumber industrial workers'. Unpublished doctoral dissertation, University of Washington.

Husserl, E. (1962) *Ideas: General Introduction to Pure Phenomenology*. W. Gibson, trans. London: Collier-Macmillan.

Knights, D. and Willmott, H. (1985) 'Power and identity in theory and practice', *The Sociological Review*, 33: 22–46.

Kunda, G. (1992) *Engineering Culture: Control and Commitment in a High-Tech Corporation*. Philadelphia, PA: Temple University Press.

Laclau, E. and Mouffe, C. (1985) *Hegemony and Socialist Strategy*. W. Moore and P. Cammack, trans. London: Verso.

Laumann, E. and Knoke, D. (1987) *The Organizational State: Social Choice in National Policy Domains*. Madison: University of Wisconsin Press.

Lawler, III, E. (1986) *High-Involvement Management: Participation Strategies for Improving Organizational Performance*. San Francisco, CA: Jossey-Bass.

Lazega, E. (1992) *The Micropolitics of Knowledge: Communication and Indirect Control in Workgroups*. New York: Aldine de Gruyter.

Lukács, G. (1971) *History and Class Consciousness*. R. Livingstone, trans. Cambridge, MA: MIT Press.

Lukes, S. (1974) *Power: a Radical View*. London: Macmillan.

Marx, K. (1977) *Capital*. B. Fowkes, trans. New York: Vintage Books.

Marx, K. and Engels, F. (1970) *The German Ideology*. New York: International Publishers.

Mingers, J. (1989) 'An introduction to autopoiesis – implications and applications', *Systems Practice*. 2: 159–80.

Mumby, D.K. (1988) *Communication and Power in Organizations: Discourse, Ideology and Domination*. Norwood, NJ: Ablex.

Parsons, T. (1956) *Economy and Society: a Study of the Integration of Economic and Social Theory*. Glencoe, IL: Free Press.

Pêcheux, M. (1982) *Language, Semantics and Ideology: Stating the Obvious*. H. Nagpal, trans. London: Macmillan.

Peters, T. (1989) *Thriving on Chaos: Handbook for a Managerial Revolution*. New York: Alfred Knopf.

Przeworski, A. (1980) 'Material bases of consent: economics and politics in a hegemonic system', *Political Power and Social Theory*, 1: 21–66.

Snygg, D. and Coombs, A. (1949) *Individual Behavior*. New York: Harper & Row.

Stablein, R. and Nord, W. (1985) 'Practical and emancipatory interest in organizational symbolism', *Journal of Management*, 11: 13–28.

Thompson, J. (1984) *Studies in the Theory of Ideology*. Berkeley: University of California Press.

Weedon, C. (1987) *Feminist Practice and Poststructuralist Theory*. Oxford: Basil Blackwell.

Weick, K. (1979) *The Social Psychology of Organizing*. 2nd edn. Reading, MA: Addison-Wesley.

Woodiwiss, A. (1987) 'The discourses of production (part 1): law, industrial relations, and the theory of ideology', *Economy and Society*, 16: 275–316.

9

For the Nation!
How Street Gangs Problematize Patriotism

Dwight Conquergood

[T]he nation is always conceived as a deep, horizontal comradeship. Ultimately it is this fraternity that makes it possible, over the past two centuries, for so many millions of people, not so much to kill, as willingly to die for such limited imaginings. (Anderson, 1983: 16)

He was at war, and two carloads of Folks [rival gang] came out on him so deep, came out on him with bats. He didn't have nothing. He wanted to fight them one-on-one single-handed like a brave man does, like a Latin King does it. See, but they came out on him with bats and guns. He was tough, he was going at it with them, and he was only one King against all those guys, and that showed how brave he was. He died for the crown, he died for his nation. He died still throwing up the crown – you know, he threw it up until the last minute of his breath. The poor guy got his head busted so many times and he still didn't give up, he was still fighting. . . . And all the other brothers who Rest in Peace and fought for the nation and died for it – we're always gonna remember them, and never forget them. That's just the way it goes. (Latino Boy, member of Chicago street gang)[1]

In Chicago, like many large urban areas, street gangs are a way of life and death, struggle and survival in the inner city. An intricate underground culture, gangs produce their identity through complex communication practices that are conflictually constituted and proliferated along fabricated borders, cleavages between Self and Other. Turf tensions and boundary vigilance both emplot and energize the signifying practices of gang culture. The trespass of borders and the desecration of symbols, in short, transgressions of the space of the Other – both physically and figuratively – are the performative moments of gang identity.

Street-fighting both contests and clarifies boundaries, and becomes the rhetorical grist for self-defining and culture-celebrating narratives. War is the master narrative that mobilizes and uplifts local incidents and particular actors on to a sacred plane of meaning, memory and motivation. The idea of war enables street youth to name and make sense of the violence within which they are enmeshed and complicit: 'It's a war. It's us against them. That's all that is.' Likewise, the mainstream press and media draw on the vocabularly of war to heighten the violence of the inner city, as the following headline illustrates: 'Welcome to the War Zone: 15-year-old shot in front of church by rival gang member' (*Chicago News Star*, Tuesday, 25 July, 1989: 1). The rhetorical practices of street gangs hang nakedly on what Kenneth Burke has called 'Order, the Secret, and the Kill' (1969: 260).

For more than three years I have studied, in situ, the cultural practices of street gangs in a multicultural Chicago neighbourhood as part of a larger ethnographic research project co-sponsored by the Center for Urban Affairs and Policy Research, Northwestern University, and the Ford Foundation.[2] I began the study by moving into Big Red, a huge dilapidated tenement, where I daily passed by ten death murals – stylized 'Rest in Peace' graffiti memorials for slain gang brothers – displayed on the walls of my stairwell between the lobby front door and the door to my second-floor apartment (see Conquergood, 1992). Since no one knew or cared what an 'ethnographer' was, initially I was simply the stranger, the outsider who had entered a densely woven web of symbols and meanings pulled together all the more tightly against an outside world that was emphatically Other, and threatening. Even though I was in the middle of everything, I remained on the edge, outside of the cultural system of meaning. Secrecy is a powerful constituent of the communication practices of street gangs, and other marginal cultures: 'Secrecy is the creation of centers in peripheries deprived of stable anchorages' (Feldman, 1991: 11). Although most of the surfaces of Big Red were inscribed with graffiti displays of gang identity, territoriality, taunt, challenge, as well as meticulously coded histories of gang warfare fought in and around the tenement, and stylized eulogies for the dead, these walls, redolent with meaning, were opaque to me. During the early months of fieldwork, as I shopped in the neighbourhood stores, washed my clothes in the laundromats, ate at the greasy spoon diners and walked the streets, much of the intensely meaningful action, both verbal and non-verbal, was either invisible or inscrutable to me.

As the weeks and months unfolded, however, I became more and more connected with the people in my building, and then by extension the neighbourhood. Because I was living in a place where strangers are suspect, and not easily tolerated, the people got rid of the stranger in their midst by transforming me first into an acquaintance, then a neighbour, eventually a friend, and, in some special cases, a 'bro' (short for 'brother', a tight friend). Once I was 'placed', through talk, as part of the local scene, I was gradually but guardedly granted access to the 'local knowledge' that discursively transforms this contested area into a distinctively familar lifeworld, an intimate space (see Certeau, 1984: Geertz, 1983). Partly through experience and inference, partly through explicit tutoring from friendly gang members, I developed (and am still developing) 'street sense', the local cultural currency through which communication is transacted and survival enabled.

As my access to and understanding of gang culture deepened, some of the practices that seemed most alien and Other, such as the killings, became, in multiple destabilizing ways, familiar. Familiar not because of repetition, because one never gets accustomed to the shock and heart-breaking grief that follow the murder of a neighbour and friend. Actually, this part of the fieldwork becomes more acute, because the longer you live in the field, the more attached and involved you get with the people in the community. I am using 'familiar' in the sense of recognition, having heard this before. As I learned to listen to the rhetorical address and narratives that surrounded violence and death and endowed them with meaning, I heard familiar appeals to patriotism, pride of nation, bravery. At the wakes, funerals and grave-sites of neighbours and friends who had been murdered brutally, I heard this violence rhetorically transmuted into sacrifice (see Girard, 1977). Much of the rhetoric of gang culture echoed or mimicked the patriotic appeals of mainstream culture to nation, flag, colours, honour, noble sacrifice, for example 'he died for his nation', 'he died for the crown', 'flying the colors', 'cross-flagging', 'bring peace to our departed brothers and sisters who died for our cause', 'pledge devotion to the Almighty Latin King Nation'. The death murals that inscribe the name of the slain hero over RIP are embellished with all the honorific insignia befitting an official war memorial. The local term for these commemorations is 'making a wall', or 'putting up a wall', a term that recalls the Vietnam Veterans' Memorial, a national monument that draws on the affective power of a wall inscribed with the names of fallen comrades (see Haines, 1986).

The Otherness and remoteness of gang members and their culture began to slip as I listened to their rhetorical appeals and self-defining narratives. Their stories unsettled the boundary – so carefully policed in official discourse – between disreputable gang member and respectable citizen, and created openings between Self and Other. Michel de Certeau noted this border-crossing, subversive potential of story: 'What the map cuts up, the story cuts across. In Greek, narration is called "diegesis" it establishes an itinerary (it "guides") and it passes through (it "transgresses")' (1984: 129). Particularly when working with subordinate groups, the critical ethnographer seeks to locate these liminal intersections between the official and the underground, the legitimate and the transgressive, the privileged and the suppressed.

If ethnography is to do something other than reinscribe domination through collapsing or fetishizing difference, it needs to juxtapose cultures and dialogize voices in such a way that the investigator's culture is defamiliarized in the encounter with the Other. George Marcus and Michael Fischer (1986) call for this 'critical strategy of defamiliarization' (p. 137) that struggles to hold in productive tension 'the open-ended nature of similarities and differences' (p. 161). They contend: 'The challenge of serious cultural criticism is to bring the insights gained on the periphery back to the center to raise havoc with our settled ways of thinking and conceptualization' (p. 138). In the same vein, James Clifford excavates 'the surrealist moment in ethnography' and promotes more explicit use of the techniques of collage and juxtaposition in order to 'mock and remix institutional definitions' and received categories (1988: 146, 147). Clifford hopes to recuperate a 'critical cultural politics': 'Ethnography, the science of cultural jeopardy, presupposes a constant willingness to be surprised, to unmake interpretive syntheses, and to value – when it comes – the unclassified, unsought other' (p. 147).

I want to focus on the slippage between gang subculture and mainstream culture that reverberates in the rhetoric of nationalism and war deployed by both groups, the mighty and the marginal. By juxtaposing street gangs with the ruling powers, and listening for the resonances across their rhetorical practices, we aim towards the critical goal of deconstructing 'the bases on which we normally differentiate ourselves (in the center) from others (on the periphery)' (Marcus and Fischer, 1986: 138; see also Conquergood, 1991). Through jarring juxtapositions and wrenching realignments, we strive to achieve that special decentring insight that Kenneth Burke calls 'perspective by incongruity' (1984: 308).

Of Gangs and Nations and Other Constructions

> What kind of a cultural space is the nation with its transgressive
> boundaries and its 'interruptive' interiority? (Bhabha, 1990: 5)

Gangs in Chicago are organized primarily around turf, bounded space, not race or ethnicity. They are street gangs, sometimes taking their name from the local street, such as the Kenmore Boys in Uptown, or the 2–6 Boys around 26th Street on the South Side of

Chicago. Large gangs that have spread in patchwork fashion through several neighbourhoods, such as the Latin Kings, break down into local chapters – called 'branches' – named after the major intersection where they hang out, for example the Lawrence and Kedzie Kings, the Montrose and Paulina Kings, the Beech and Spaulding Kings. Each branch has its own leaders, the prez or chief, vice-presidents and assorted lieutenants, who are responsible for 'holding down the hood', taking care of the neighbourhood. Each branch identifies with and draws on the symbols of the larger gang, but functions more or less autonomously in its everyday activities. There is an intense loyalty to the local branch, the homeboys with whom one shares and defends the graffiti-marked turf. The attachments to the homeboys are projected in spatial terms of protective intimacy, what Gaston Bachelard calls 'eulogized space' or 'topophilia': 'the human value of the sorts of space that may be grasped, that may be defended against adverse forces, the space we love' (1964: xxxi).

Temporary departures and returns to the 'hood' are verbally punctuated passages across inside/outside boundaries. These border-crossing remarks mediate temporary displacement and return to the centre. Particularly the release of tension that comes from return to the hood – being back 'in place' – is expressed in remarks that range from the pointed and heartfelt, 'Now we're back in *our* hood', to the following encomium (expressed by a Latin King after returning by car from a four-hour trip with me across enemy gang turf to other neighbourhoods in the city): 'Now we're in our neighborhood. Now you're in the land of plenty. The land of thrones and diamonds and pearls – diamonds and pearls – and rubies!' Gangs possess and poeticize space, imbuing it with emotional intensity, aesthetic and moral power.

There are hundreds of street gangs in Chicago, but all of them align with one of two Nations: People or Folks (see Table 9.1). In my neighbourhood, Kimball Street – three blocks west of Big Red – is the dividing line between People and Folks. To the west of Kimball Street are the gangs of the Folks Nation: Maniac Latin Disciples, Insane Spanish Cobras, Simon City Royals, Imperial Gangsters, Latin Eagles and others. To the east of Kimball Street are the gangs of the People Nation: Latin Kings, Future Puerto Rican Stones, Assyrian Eagles, Vicelords and others. Because turf, territory, overrides race or ethnicity as the primary organizer of gang affiliation, one cannot read ethnic membership from the name of a gang. Many of these street gangs originated during the 1960s and 1970s when much of Chicago was residentially segregated. The Latin Kings, the dominant gang in my neighbourhood (the

Table 9.1 *Chicago street gangs according to Nation*

People Nation	Folks Nation
Latin Kings	Black Gangster Disciples
Vicelords	Simon City Royals
Future Puerto Rican Stones	Maniac Latin Disciples
Gaylords	Insane Spanish Cobras
Warlords	Insane Popes
Insane Unknowns	Imperial Gangsters
Bishops	2–6 Boys
Jet Black Stones	Latin Lovers
Latin Lords	Latin Jivers
Jousters	Harrison Gents
Ghetto Boy Organization	Ambro's
Assyrian Eagles	Latin Eagles

Note: This list is selective, not comprehensive. The four largest street gangs in Chicago are Black Gangster Disciples, Latin Kings, Vicelords and Simon City Royals.

Lawrence and Kedzie Kings), originated in a section of the city farther south that was almost exclusively Puerto Rican, and therefore signalled a Latin identity in their self-naming. As soon as neighbourhoods became integrated, however, the local turf gangs likewise became culturally diverse, even though they retained their ethnically-specific name. For example, my neighbourhood, a port of entry for new immigrants, refugees and internally displaced migrants, is one of the most ethnically diverse in urban America: more than fifty languages and dialects are spoken at the local high school (see Conquergood et al., 1990). Correspondingly, the Latin Kings among whom I live are Mexican, Assyrian, African-American, Appalachian, Lebanese, Filipino, Palestinian, Guatemalan, Greek, Panamanian, Salvadoran, Laotian, Korean, Vietnamese and others – in addition to Puerto Rican. One of the vice-presidents of the Latin Kings was born in Iraq, and another one is a blond-haired freckled youth from Appalachia. The *Latin King Manifesto* acknowledges the heterodox diversity encompassed by the idea of the nation: 'We, the Almighty Latin King and Queen Nation, are entrusted with a divine mission, one that transcends personal gains and recognition. . . . For, though we are of different Nationalities, we all share the same cultures of our ancient ancestors whose every word is law throughout the world.'[3] They construe 'nation' as an acronym – *N*atal *A*llies *T*ogether *I*n *O*ne *N*ucleus – invoking the 'natural' and the 'divine' to legitimate pre-eminently *cultural* constructions.

Sometimes individual Latin Kings will take a 'tag' (street name) that signifies race or ethnicity. A Latin King I know who is white goes by the street name of 'Blanco' (Spanish for white), another Latin King who is African-American goes by the street name of 'Blackie', and a Vicelord (historically an all-black gang originating on Chicago's racially segregated West Side) who is Cambodian goes by the street name of 'Yellow Boy'. But even individual 'tags' subvert and play with racial and ethnic categories. Negro (Spanish for Black), the 16-year-old youth who was beaten to death with baseball bats and eulogized by Latino Boy in the epigraph at the beginning of this chapter, was actually Guatemalan.

The 'colour line' in gang culture has been transposed from racial categories and radically resymbolized as an important element in the theatricality of signifying practices. All street gangs in Chicago are associated with a distinguishing colour, but one that has nothing to do with the colour of their skin. They adopt colours to fabricate an emblematic identity in the same way that sports teams, and nations, deploy totemic colours in their flags and insignia. Street gangs proclaim their identity by 'flying the colours' and 'flagging', that is, wearing colour-coded clothing, painting graffiti acronyms and icons in the appropriate colours. In Chicago, the totemic colour usually does not achieve semiotic force unless it is articulated with black. Here are some examples of the signifying colours of Chicago street gangs: Latin Kings, black and gold; Future Puerto Rican Stones, black and orange; Insane Spanish Cobras, black and green; Maniac Latin Disciples, black and light blue; Simon City Royals, black and royal blue; Harrison Gents, black and purple; Vicelords, black and red; Gaylords, black and gray; Imperial Gangsters, black and pink. Each gang will stake the symbolism of their colours in mimetic and ennobling referents. For example, the Latin Kings say that black stands for the strong dominant colour of the earth, and gold stands for the shining, glowing radiance of the sun: 'It is the Sun glowing in the essence of our being, the brightness in our eyes that cast reflections of its rays spitting fire in all directions . . . all our powers and all our desires thrown into the mission of human service and united into one Single Gold Sun.'[4]

But there are more gangs in Chicago than there are colours to go around. The Mexican Braziers, members of the Folks Nation, use black and red, the same colours as their mortal enemies the Vicelords, members of the People Nation; likewise, black and pink are used by two enemy gangs, the Assyrian Eagles, who are People, and the Imperial Gangsters, who are Folks. Colour, therefore, is a necessary but insufficient signifier of gang identity and must be read against other discriminations. The colour apartheid among street gangs – for all its surface theatricality – is deadly serious and eerily mirrors and mocks the violence in South Africa. During my first year of fieldwork, an Ecuadoran immigrant youth wearing a dark navy blue and gold soccer outfit was murdered one block north of Big Red by attacking gang members of the Folks Nation who in the darkness thought he was wearing black and gold colours and mistook him for a Latin King. Urban narratives of similar incidents in which people are killed, often mistakenly, over colour abound on the streets.

I must emphasize that the division between the two Nations, People and Folks, is absolutely arbitrary and constructed, and does not rest on race or ethnicity: it is *inscribed*, not *ascribed*. Gang affiliation cuts across and subsumes racial and ethnic differences. Intergang rivalry and violence absorb ethnic and racial tensions and reconstruct difference along the fabricated borders between the People and Folks Nations. The Latin Kings belong to the People Nation, but they are mortal enemies of the Latin Disciples, Latin Eagles, Latin Jivers, Latin Lovers and Spanish Cobras, all members of the Folks Nation. Further, one must remember that an ethnically marked name of a gang, for example, Latin Kings, does not signify an ethnically homogeneous membership. Further, the two largest gangs that historically have been rooted in segregated African-American neighbourhoods, the Black Gangster Disciples from Chicago's South Side and the Vicelords from the West Side, are members of rival Nations: the Black Gangster Disciples are Folks and the Vicelords are People. Likewise, two of the large gangs that historically arose from white ethnic neighbourhoods, the Gaylords and the Simon City Royals, are on opposite sides of the division of Nations: Gaylords are People and Simon City Royals are Folks.

The cultural power of gangs to subsume multiple ethnicities and races, and refract and re-articulate difference through the construction of the People–Folks binary opposition, is a remarkable feat of remapping the discourse of identity. This redrawing and redistribution of the lines of difference according to performatively produced poles of identity are poignantly revealed in case studies of the killings. For example, the first killing I experienced in the field was the April 1988 murder of Goofy, a Future Puerto Rican Stone who was actually a white youth, gunned down allegedly by Stretch, a Latin Disciple who was an African-American youth. Throughout all the street talk and commemorative graffiti surrounding the crisis of Goofy's murder, no one noted the race of the victim, white, or the alleged killer, African-American. Without the cultural reframing of gang discourse, the killing of Goofy could have become racially charged. However, all the talk and anger on the streets – Goofy was shot just two blocks from Big Red – pivoted on the fact that a Latin Disciple, member of the Folks Nation, killed a Puerto Rican Stone, member of the People Nation. Moreover, to avenge the killing of Goofy, the Puerto Rican Stones crossed Kimball Street late one night and killed a Latin Disciple, who turned out to be a white youth. From the perspective of the streets, Goofy had been appropriately avenged; any Latin Disciple could serve as scapegoat for the murder of a Puerto Rican Stone. It did not matter that the scapegoat Disciple was also white, or that the Disciple who allegedly killed Goofy was African-American.

The most recent killing was the April 1991 murder of Lucian, another Puerto Rican Stone who was a 16-year-old Romanian refugee. Lucian was shot allegedly by a Spanish Cobra who was a Vietnamese youth. Again, neither the nationality of the victim, Romanian, nor that of the alleged killer, Vietnamese, figured into the street fight that escalated to murder. The dispute was grounded in the enmity between the Nation of People, represented by Lucian, and the Nation of Folks, represented by the Spanish Cobra who was Vietnamese. There is a surrealist quality to the discourse of gang identity in the way it deconstructs the received categories of race, ethnicity and nationality. These categories, as Werner Sollors argues, are themselves rhetorical inventions.

The awful tragedy of intergang warfare – all the killings committed 'for the nation' – is that the People Nation and Folks Nation are interchangeable, mirror images of one another. Indeed, some of the Latin Kings – one of the largest and most powerful gangs of the People Nation – in my neighbourhood have older brothers who were members of Folk Nation gangs. Poor families have to move frequently, and thus older brothers will sometimes come to the age of gang recruitment (early teens) when the family is residing in Folks turf, and then a younger set of siblings will reach their teenage years after the family has moved to People territory. Moreover, I currently know more than one Latin King who has confided to me that he was formerly a member of the Folks Nation (this, of course, is a dangerous, closely guarded secret, and I am honoured by the trust of those who take me as a confidant). One young fellow told me of his dilemma when his family moved from Folks turf to a building near Big Red, the heart of Latin King territory. In preparation for the move, he painted in a public place the street name he used as member of a Folks Nation gang over RIP, thus symbolically killing himself through the making of his own death mural. Shortly after the move to my neighbourhood, he was reborn (resymbolized) as a Latin King, with a new street name. He is now one of the most dedicated and valorous of the Latin Kings in my neighbourhood, with the intelligence and charisma to emerge as one of the leaders in the near future. However, on the night he shared perhaps his deepest secret with me, he pulled down his jeans just a bit to reveal his red underwear and explain that red (with black) was the colour of the Folks Nation gang to which he formerly belonged. Although now he is a 'straight up' Latin King, 'flying the colours' of black and gold, he is a walking palimpsest of the oppositional struggles, and cultural contradictions, of gang Nations that inform his personal history. The boundary slippages, ambivalences and ambiguities of identity are layered on his body.

Because gang Nations are cultural constructions, invented affiliations of spectacularly plural and mobile constituencies, they have developed an intricate network of representational practices through which they 'rep' (short for 'represent', 'representation') that is, signify their Nation and gang allegiance, and read the identities of others. Because most of the time all the gangs aligned with one or the other of the Nations will 'ride' together, the most fundamental and important discrimination to make is that between People or Folks. Using the body as a site of signification, gangs of the People Nation represent to the left, while gangs of the Folks Nation rep to the right. Reppin' to the left encompasses an array of signifying practices: wearing the bill of one's baseball cap cocked to the left, wearing an earring in the left ear, sporting a colour-coded bandana scarf in the left hip pocket, wearing the belt buckle slightly left of centre, dangling a coloured feather or iconographic ornament or sunglasses from the belt just left of the buckle, tearing jeans on the left leg, tattooing on the left arm or thigh, wearing bib overalls with only the left strap up (leaving the right strap unbuckled and dangling), carrying a jacket or sweater over the left shoulder, standing 'in position' with left foot turned out, leaning against a wall in 'low-rider' pose with left knee bent, placing one's right hand over the left upper arm, or standing with the left wrist gripped by the right hand. The last two gestures are called specifically 'crossing up' and are among the most common ways of reppin' on the streets. Folks rep to the right in all the same ways except the earring. An earring in the right ear is read as gay, therefore Folks pierce their left ear but wear a special kind of earring. Recently, however, I have noticed some Folks wearing earrings in their right ear. They explained that since some gays are adopting the practice of wearing earrings in both ears, they now feel secure about reclaiming the right ear for their own semiotic use.

The significant number for the People Nation is five, for the Folks Nation six. These numbers are sacralized as mnemonic enumerators of key virtues. The five sacred virtues of the Latin Kings are Love, Honour, Obedience, Sacrifice and Righteousness. The six sacred virtues of the Folk Nation are Love, Wisdom, Strength, Sincerity,

Knowledge and Understanding, but, typical of oral traditions, there is some variation across sources. People Nation gangs rep with five-point stars, and Folks with six-point stars. The major icon of the Latin Kings is a crown, specifically a five-point crown. There is a Folks Nation gang, the Imperial Gangsters, that also reps with a crown as its icon, but it is a six-point crown. Sometimes just the number five, or six, is inscribed straightforwardly in graffiti displays: '5 Alive – 6 Must Die!'

Numerology informs signifying practices in more subtle but significant ways, for example, lacing five or six eyelets of one's tennis shoes, co-articulated with the colour and thickness of laces, is a common way of reppin' gang identity (neither Folks nor People tie a bow, but push the laces inside the shoe under or behind the heel). The Latin Kings have a ceremonial rallying cry: 'King Love! Yesterday, Today, Tomorrow, Always, and Forever.' It is significant that the temporal conjunctions are expressed in five units. People Nation gangs digitally rep by holding up a hand with five fingers spread; Folks do the same but add the index finger of the other hand.

More common than the simple, straightforward reppin' of identity is the representational strategy of affirmation by negation. The performer condenses and recapitulates the binary coded grid upon which the entire system is based with a single representational act that simultaneously affirms the Self by negating the Other. There are three semiotic moves that negate the symbols of the Other: reversals, inversions and fractures. In my neighbourhood, the heart of the Latin King turf, one seldom sees a graffiti depiction of a five-point crown that is not astride an upside-down pitchfolk (the pitchfolk is an important icon of the Disciples, a Folks gang). Likewise, when Latin Kings 'throw up the crown' with their stylized hand signals – right hand digitally reppin' over the left side of upper body – they simultaneously make a Folks Nation hand signal with their left hand pointed downwards, and crossed over the right side of the lower body, and held below the waist. Many of the Rest in Peace death murals will invert and reverse the letter 'R' as a way of defiling the Simon City Royals, a Folks Nation gang responsible for some of the killings in the hood. Because the heart with wings is a major icon of the Maniac Latin Disciples, a Folks gang, on walls, doors and park benches throughout my neighbourhood one sees drawings of inverted, cloven hearts, or sometimes just a grotesque heart ripped in half with a jagged fracture line. This was the emotionally resonant symbol that inspired the title for the documentary based on my fieldwork (see Siegel and Conquergood, 1990).

During the first year of my fieldwork, the turf two blocks east of Big Red belonged to the Insane Popes, a Folks Nation gang (since then, the Latin Kings successfully raided and routed the Insane Popes and extended Latin King turf eastward by a few blocks). While that area still belonged to the Folks there was a large graffito on the border that simply spelled the word 'FOLKS' but the letters 'LK' were printed backwards (as if the writer were dyslexic) to debunk the Latin Kings (LK, of course, is their acronym), and standing in for the letter 'O' was a six-point star. Just across from the graffito on the Latin King side, there was a drawing of a large six-point star, fractured top to bottom and pulled apart so that the number '5' was breaking it in the middle. The Latin Kings prefer to wear Converse tennis shoes because the Converse logo is a five-point star. Folks gangs, however, also will wear Converse high tops, but fold down the flaps, thus breaking the five-point star in the crease and thereby putting down the People Nation. In the alley behind Big Red, the Kings painted a large 'Die-sciples', with the capital 'D' reversed and the 'i' dotted with a five-point star. This represents a symbolically complex way of killing the Other through the desecration of his or her name – a symbolic kill achieved through making a hit on the linguistic signifier. Space does not permit a more comprehensive catalogue of all the manifold and highly nuanced ways of reppin' that pivot on affirmation by negation, but the examples above may suggest the variety, creativity and complexity of this cultural practice.

On Rhetoric, Representation and Textual Violence

> What links writing to violence? (Derrida 1976: 101)

This 'production of identity through negation' is the practice that links, rather than separates, gang culture with mainstream culture. Richard Weaver, speaking for and from the centre, not the barbarous margins, concludes: 'we need the enemy in order to define ourselves' (1953: 222). Peter Stallybrass and Allon White analyse the historical construction of the bourgeois public sphere in terms that are resoundingly apt for street gangs:

> it is, like any form of identity, created through negations, it produces a new domain by taking into itself as *negative introjections*, the very domains which surround and threaten it. It thus produces and reproduces itself through the process of denial and defiance. (1986: 89)

Killing is the ultimate performance of negation for purificatory and generative purposes. Killing – for the nation! – is a profound act of both boundary clarification and mediation, division and merger. It simultaneously retrenches 'identity' and expands the space and intensity of 'identification' through 'the solemnizing spirit' of sacrifice. 'We cannot deny', argues Kenneth Burke, 'that consubstantiality *is* established by common involvement in a killing' (1969: 265). This communion of the kill is achieved through symbolic action – to 'slay the enemy in effigy' (Burke, 1969: 5) – or through actual violence. Allen Feldman, however, collapses the distance between the effigy and the corpse in his brilliant analysis of the transcription of the slain body into an ideological text: 'The body marked by violence encapsulates certain political purposes, mediations, and transformations. . . . Subsequent to this transcription the stiff [murdered corpse] circulates as a political sign' (1991: 70).

Benedict Anderson's seminal study of 'the nation' as an 'imagined community', a compelling fiction, extends our understanding of the semiotic encompassment and meaning-making priority of sacrificial killing: 'from the start, the nation was conceived in language, not in blood' (1983: 133). It is not rhetoric that inspires patriots to shed their own and others' blood for the nation; instead, it is the sacrificial blood that underwrites the rhetoric through which the nation is imagined and performatively constituted, 'the nation as a symbolic force', and 'the nation's "coming into being" as a system of cultural signification' (Bhabha, 1990: 1; see also McGee, 1975).

Ensemble killing in the theatre of war is a powerful medium for performing and producing the text of national solidarity. Eric Hobsbawm provides a vivid example of what Kenneth Burke (1969: 22) calls war as 'a disease of cooperation', a 'perversion of communion'.

> Above all, where ideologies are in conflict, the appeal to the imagined community of the nation appears to have defeated all challengers. What else but the solidarity of an imaginary 'us' against a symbolic 'them' would have launched Argentina and Britain into a crazy war for some South Atlantic bog and rough pasture. (Hobsbawm, 1990: 163)

The gang wars between the People and Folks Nations in Chicago demonstrate the remarkable symbolic fecundity of the idea of the 'nation': 'the "nation" proved an invention on which it was impossible to secure a patent. It became available for pirating by widely different, and sometimes unexpected, hands' (Anderson, 1983: 66). Gang wars are fought primarily to stabilize and consolidate 'the ambivalent margin of the nation-space' (Bhabha, 1990: 4). The space of the Other is attacked in order to clarify identity and clear more space for self-representation. The struggles over turf, geographical space, are the wellspring for renewal of rhetorical invention and topoi, the space of representation (see Harvey, 1989).

Although the generative reciprocities between violence and representation are seen most clearly perhaps in the symbolic agency of the nation, Feldman goes so far as to affirm that 'violence still remains the founding language of social representation' (1991: 260). Robert Scholes roots violence in the fundamental nature of language: 'culture comes to us like a language, already organized in terms of certain powerful binarisms' (1989: 31). Binary opposition, difference, dualism, dichotomy, Us against Them polarities, either–or exclusions and Self–Other discriminations are staked in the nominative nature of language. This constitutive, classificatory act of naming reality is often celebrated as an Adamic rite of world-making, but it is also a divide-and-conquer tactic. Scholes reminds us that 'language differentiates by an act of violence' and that 'violence and alienation are aspects of the price we pay for the textual power of language' (1985: 112). Texts do not spring forth from vacuums but emerge, sometimes painfully, from contexts of struggle, and they displace other texts. Every text positions itself against other texts, and thereby acquires both its meaningfulness and ethical force: 'We sense the presence of things through this resistance' (Scholes, 1985: 112; see also Armstrong and Tennenhouse, 1989; Shapiro, 1988).

Far from seeing violence as a psychopathology erupting from some demonized, disorderly Other, Scholes soberly situates violence at the heart of all human symbolizing practices and calls for a new rhetorical criticism that would deconstruct the link between this textual 'will to power' and violence:

> Starting from this position we can examine all our uses of language from a new point of view . . . to ask the question 'What violence is being done here?' The most basic and most violent acts of differentiation are those that divide a field into two opposed units. This sort of 'binary opposition' . . . is fundamental to the phonemic nature of speech and is deeply embedded in all Western thought. (1985: 112)

Scholes's position encourages self-reflection and self-criticism by bringing the problem of violence home to the centre of order-creating processes, instead of pitting violence against order and deploying it as cause for exile from the moral community. The representational practices and 'reading protocols' of street gangs demonstrate vividly how power, order and violence are enmeshed in texts.

Further, the underground and transgressive text-making practices of street gangs can help us defamiliarize mainstream texts and unveil their violent dynamics. The violence in the rhetoric surrounding Desert Shield and Desert Storm that authorized the collective killing of Other people in the name of 'the nation' and 'a new world order' is so close to the surface that explication is scarcely necessary. The rhetorical demonizing and polluting of Saddam Hussein was so massive that his contagion spread to the civilian population in a way that enabled the killing of tens of thousands of women and children.

More subtle, perhaps, and closer to home are the turf wars fought by academics in sharply contested and binary coded battles over discursive space. A recent issue of *The Quarterly Journal of Speech* provides an exemplar of an academic street fight: 'The Forum: Writing Ethnographies' (Carbaugh, 1991; Fiske, 1991; Philipsen, 1991). Gerry Philipsen (1991) introduces the combatants, 'the objectivist ethnographer, such as [Donal] Carbaugh is', against John Fiske, someone who takes 'a particular political and theoretical stance', and stakes out their discursive terrain of conflict: 'description' vs 'critique'; 'find and report' vs 'expose and condemn'; 'investigation' vs 'assumption'; 'consensus' vs 'conflict'; 'the ideal of objectivity' vs 'a personally prejudiced account'; 'Carbaugh's empirical approach' vs 'such hunches as Fiske proposes'; the 'cohering of disparate voices' vs the respect for 'social differences'; 'a sense of coherence, the bases for coordinated action, a capacity for aesthetic appreciation' vs 'discourses of power'. Ostensibly a non-combatant, Philipsen, 'as an admittedly interested party', strategically reps his own position with the following sentence: 'For ethnography to perform only a liberating, and not a conserving, function, is to reduce its scope and power by theoretical fiat' (p. 329).

Although Philipsen situates himself as referee, of sorts, it is actually Carbaugh who structurally occupies the mediating position. Within this academic triptych, Carbaugh is the wounded figure in the middle who mediates the ideological (couched as 'methodological' and 'theoretical') positions of his mentor (Philipsen) on the right, and tormentor (Fiske) on the left. It is across his scholarly corpus (body) – specifically, his book *Talking American* (Carbaugh, 1988) – that the oppositional stances represented by Philipsen and Fiske get articulated and sharpened.

Although masked in the genteel language of liberal tolerance – 'Contribution to a Dialogue' (Fiske, 1991: 330) – this Forum is the academic counterpart of what people in my neighbourhood call 'throwing down' and 'going heads up'. It is a follow-up fight to Fiske's earlier review of Carbaugh's book *Talking American* when he drew blood by calling Carbaugh's text 'politically reactionary'

(Fiske, 1990: 451). More than anything else, those were the fighting words that incited this counter-attack. Philipsen (1991: 327) frames the dispute by citing Fiske's 'politically reactionary' charge in his opening paragraph, and Carbaugh (1991: 340) tellingly cites it twice in a single paragraph. Much of the ensuing discourse has to do with finely calibrated tiltings of one's hat to the right or to the left.

In order to extend this 'perspective by incongruity' (Burke, 1984: 308), we can compare Fiske's review of Carbaugh's book, and the Forum response, in street culture terms to 'splashing a wall', the defacing of the graffiti texts of turf rivals by spraypainting over their work with oppositional colours, crossing it out, or writing over it with one's own inscriptions. Such splashing intensifies along the territorial borders, the potentially contaminating points of contact and zones of contestation that are more fluid and volatile. Both Fiske and Carbaugh have staked a claim in the disciplinary space between ethnography and communication, cultural studies and televisual discourse. Their sites of potential interface lead understandably to the reciprocal defacings that function as boundary clarifications for both of them. In street culture, each gang rewrites the graffiti texts on the other side of the boundary as a reterritorializing act of eviction, erasure and displacement, an occupation of the representational space of the Other. Further, the splashed text becomes a dramatic *mise-en-scène* for staging one's own identity as a powerful occupier of the Other's space of representation. Few gangs (and, for that matter, scholars) will countenance this attack on their texts. One splash leads to a counter-splash – and sometimes more serious consequences. (My neighbour, Negro, was killed the night he was caught splashing Folks' walls just to the west of Kimball Street, the Folks–People boundary running through my neighbourhood.)

Beyond the initial 'politically reactionary' salvo, not much blood is drawn in the boundary struggle between Fiske and Carbaugh. Both sides are extraordinarily civil and devote most of their space simply to reppin' their own programmatic alignments. Actually, this Forum reminds me of a certain kind of street fight that is really more about saving face for both sides than defacing the Other. Under certain circumstances rival gangs will agree that although some taunt or breach of street politesse requires a fight, it is not worth 'going down' (getting killed) for. They frame these fights as redressive, rather than murderous, by shouting 'No weapons, blood!' to ensure that the participants will fight only with fists, not guns or knives.

Academics are not always as polite as Fiske and Carbaugh. In a remarkably candid essay, 'Fighting Words: Unlearning to Write the

Critical Essay', Jane Tompkins confronts the textual violence that pervades and animates scholarship:

> Violence takes place in the conference rooms at scholarly meetings and in the pages of professional journals; and although it's not the same thing to savage a person's book as it is to kill them with a machine gun, I suspect that the nature of the feelings that motivate both acts is qualitatively the same. This bloodless kind of violence that takes place in our profession is not committed by other people; it's practiced at some time or other by virtually everyone. (1988:589)

Her incisive discussion of a defining, generative moment in the academy, 'the moment of murderousness' (p. 590), grounded in a rhetorical analysis of 'an academic conference, where a woman is giving a paper', merits quoting at length:

> It is an attack on another woman's recent book; the entire paper is devoted to demolishing it, and the speaker is doing a superb job. The audience has begun to catch the spirit of the paper, which is witty, elegant, pellucid, and razor sharp; they appreciate the deftness, the brilliance, the grace, with which the assassination is being conducted; the speaker's intelligence flatters their intelligence, her taste becomes their taste, her principles their principles. They start to laugh at the jokes. They are inside the paper now, pulling with the speaker, seeing her victim in the same way she does, as the enemy, as someone whose example should be held up to scorn because her work is pernicious and damaging to the cause. . . . By the time the paper was over, I felt as if I had been present at a ritual execution of some sort, something halfway between a bullfight, where the crowd admires the skill of the matador and enjoys his triumph over the bull, and a public burning, where the crowd witnesses the just punishment of a criminal. For the academic experience combined the elements of admiration, bloodlust, and moral self-congratulation. (pp. 587–8)

This textually enacted violence is terribly seductive for academics because it is 'an experience of tremendous empowerment' (p. 590).

Tompkins is objecting to an endogenous form of textual violence, academics hitting on other academics. I am even more concerned about the textual violence perpetrated by academics against subordinate groups outside the academy. Edward Said in *Orientalism* brilliantly analyses the 'intellectual imperialism' of academic disciplines producing knowledge about other people that is complicit with administrative structures of oppression (1979, 285; see also Said, 1985; Said and Hitchens, 1988). I am particularly sensitive to the massive textual violence wreaked against inner-city youth in the name of social science research on 'gangs'. The term 'gang' has become one of the ultimate devil terms of contemporary society, deployed to gloss and condense enormous diversity and complexity of experience into one fetishized image of mindless mayhem and evil. The 'gang' powerfully cathects and projects middle-class fears and anxieties about social disorder, disintegration and chaos that are made palpable in these demonized figures of inscrutable, unproductive, predatory, pathological, alien Others lurking in urban shadows and margins. Before inner-city youth tattoo themselves with the empowering insignia of street gangs, they are branded by journalists who are backed up by academic 'researchers', as transgressive Others, outside the moral community of decent people (see Becker, 1963).

Lewis Yablonsky's *The Violent Gang* epitomizes this genre of cathartic textual violence thinly veiled as scholarly research. Through redundant and incantatory proclamations not far removed from 'Ds die, Cobras cry, IGs say why!',[5] Yablonsky sets out to dehumanize, demonize and discursively destroy gangs:

> Today's delinquent is a displaced person – suspicious, fearful, and not willing or able to established a concrete human relationship [*sic*]. . . . Violent-gang organization is ideally suited to the defective personality and limited social ability of these disturbed youths. . . . The gang is a convenient and malleable structure quickly adaptable to the needs of emotionally disturbed youths who are unable to fulfill the demands required for participation in more normal groups. The gang boy . . . makes lying, assault, thievery, and unprovoked violence – especially violence – the major activity or dream of his life. (1962: 3–4)

He concludes: 'Today's gangs are, in action, hysterical, moblike cliques that kill and maim for no logical purpose' (p. 5). I am shocked by the coarseness of Yablonsky's analysis and the meanness of his labels. Although I have experienced first-hand some of the violence of which gang culture is capable, I do not see violence as the totalizing essence of gangs, or as more constitutive and emblematic of gangs than of mainstream culture. I stand against Yablonsky's psychopathological generalizations because instead of 'the defective personality' and 'disturbed youths' I have encountered face-to-face the human complexities of a Juan, Rogelio, Chiquito, Alfas, Aurelio, Issam, David, Jody, Tony and many others. For three and a half years I have observed details of their everyday life, that include helping their mothers fold clothes in the laundromat, taking pains to communicate with and 'look out for' the deaf-mute Filipino boy who roams the streets of our neighbourhood, tenderly playing with baby sisters and nieces, and raising money to help pay for someone's rent, jail bond or funeral expenses. I have learned how to listen for their articulate, conscious expressions of lived experience, often fraught with ambivalence, awareness of paradox, and self-critique. I have mourned with them at funerals of loved ones.

I challenge, therefore, the ethnographic quality of any research that finds that gang members are 'not willing or able to establish a concrete human relationship' (Yablonsky, 1962: 3). Whatever else one might say about gangs, one cannot say that they are not based on a remarkable capacity to bond with others in deeply meaningful relationships: 'We're like a family,' Latino Boy says, 'that's what it's all about.' The keyword of gang culture is 'bro' (brother), an expressive term of endearment as well as a shibboleth that signals entrance and intimacy within an otherwise secret society. Regarding race and ethnicity, gangs do much better with integration and cultural diversity than legitimate organizations such as business corporations or universities. And, after some initial testing, they have even integrated me into their world, who, no doubt from their perspective, surely must be the strangest one of all. Not so much now, because time is a great naturalizer of difference, but during the first year of my fieldwork they frequently commented self-reflexively on our relationship: 'We never had a friend like you before. You're kinda like a probation officer, and kinda like a lawyer, but not really. At least you live in the hood.'

The fundamental problem with Yablonsky's research is the presupposition of *absence* (abnormality) in the Other that rendered him blind and deaf to their human *presence*. I can read the same extended quotations of gang members in his book and reach conclusions sharply different from Yablonsky's. His theoretical stance predisposed him to approach the Other as mute specimen to be labelled and explained, instead of interlocutor to be engaged, and listened to. Indeed, he assumes their inarticulateness and then casts himself in the role of ventriloquist, speaking for them: 'Because the average gang youth's ability to conceptualize his own condition is limited, I assumed this task' (p. xii). The gang youths, however, resisted being cast in the role of passive wooden dummies, as is apparent from Yablonsky's parenthetical notation in the preface of 'those who wanted to throw me in the Hudson River, blow up my office, or "burn me" for being a "stoolie" to the "nabs"' (p. xii). (Here, I am aware that I am 'throwing down' with Yablonsky, 'splashing' his text. The challenge is how to resist 'the moment of murderousness' [Tompkins, 1988: 590] in my own writing, and still dislodge Yablonsky's classic text that continues to be cited as an authority on gang culture by academics and journalists.)

Instead of merely an object to be explained, gang culture needs to be juxtaposed with mainstream culture and engaged dialogically

(Bakhtin) for the mutual deepening of insight that leads to compassion and humility, and the self-understanding that leads to critique, social responsibility and ethical action. Instead of grist for moral self-congratulation, as if *we* were violence-pure, and *they* were violence-prone, we need to recognize street gangs as magnifying mirrors in which we can see starkly the violence, territoriality and militarism within ourselves. We have much to learn about the human condition from encounters with street gangs, and other marginalized groups. The greatest lesson perhaps is to recall Scholes's question when approaching any text: 'What violence is being done here?' (1989: 112).

Notes

This chapter was first published by the Speech Communication Association in R. Troester and C. Kelley (eds), *Peacemaking Through Communication*, 1991, pp.7–18. Used by permission of the Speech Communication Association.

1. All quotes from gang members are from my fieldnotes and recordings. This particular speech is from a transcript of a video-recording of Latino Boy standing on the roof of a three-storey building in front of a large Rest in Peace death mural eulogizing Negro, a 16-year-old Guatemalan youth, who had been beaten to death with baseball bats two months earlier.

2. The research for this essay is part of a larger ethnographic study of new immigrants and refugees in Chicago's multicultural Albany Park neighbourhood. The Chicago project is one of six field sites that comprise a national research project sponsored by the Ford Foundation: 'Changing Relations: New Immigrants and Established Residents'. I am grateful to the Ford Foundation, Northwestern University's Center for Urban Affairs and Policy Research and the Illinois Humanities Council for financial support of my work.

3. The *Latin King Manifesto* is a very closely guarded, underground typescript document that is circulated only among the upper echelon of gang members. It is an extraordinary manuscript, a collection of treatises, maxims, prayers, acronyms, symbols, ritual texts and exegetical materials. It is referred to as 'the laws', 'the constitution' or 'the book'. Much of the material collected in this document circulates in oral tradition and performance practice. But the secret manuscript collection of this material is charged with a sacred aura. I was not shown a complete manuscript until my third year in the field. I first became aware of 'the book' at the beginning of my second year of fieldwork when two Latin Kings ushered me far down a remote alley and into an enclosed gangway where they showed me a single page from this manuscript that they had hidden underneath their clothes. They themselves recently had been given this one leaf from the manuscript as part of their initiation into the deeper mysteries and high status within the gang, and they couldn't resist sharing their excitement.

4. This passage is quoted from the *Latin King Manifesto*.

5. Fully spelled out this is 'Disciples die, Cobras cry, Imperial Gangsters say Why?' This taunt is performed by People Nation gangs to put down three prominent gangs of the Folks Nation.

References

Anderson, B. (1983) *Imagined Communities: Reflections on the Origin and Spread of Nationalism*. New York: Verso.

Armstrong, N. and Tennenhouse, L. (eds) (1989) *The Violence of Representation*. New York: Routledge.

Bachelard, G. (1964) *The Poetics of Space*. Maria Jolas, trans. New York: Orion.

Becker, H.S. (1963) *Outsiders: Studies in the Sociology of Deviance*. New York: Free Press.

Bhabha, H.K. (ed.) (1990) 'Introduction' to *Nation and Narration*. New York: Routledge.

Burke, K. (1969) *A Rhetoric of Motives*. Berkeley: University of California Press.

Burke, K. (1984) *Attitudes toward History*. 3rd edn. Berkeley: University of California Press.

Carbaugh, D. (1988) *Talking American: Cultural Discourses on Donahue*. Norwood, NJ: Ablex.

Carbaugh, D. (1991) 'Communication and cultural interpretation', *Quarterly Journal of Speech*, 77: 336–42.

Certeau, M. de (1984) *The Practice of Everyday Life*. Steven Rendall, trans. Berkeley: University of California Press.

Clifford, J. (1988) *The Predicament of Culture: Twentieth-Century Ethnography, Literature, and Art*. Cambridge, MA: Harvard University Press.

Conquergood, D. (1991) 'Rethinking ethnography: towards a critical cultural politics', *Communication Monographs*, 58: 179–94.

Conquergood, D. (1992) 'Life in Big Red: struggles and accommodations in a Chicago polyethnic tenement', in L. Lamphere (ed.), *Structuring Diversity: Ethnographic Perspectives on New Immigrants in Six US Cities*. Chicago, IL: University of Chicago Press. pp. 95–144.

Conquergood, D., Friesema, P., Hunter, A. and Mansbridge, J. (1990) *Dispersed Ethnicity and Community Integration: Newcomers and Established Residents in the Albany Park Area of Chicago*. Evanston, IL: Center for Urban Affairs and Policy Research, Northwestern University.

Derrida, J. (1976) 'The violence of the letters', in *Of Grammatology*. G.C. Spivak, trans. Baltimore, MD: Johns Hopkins University Press. pp. 101–40.

Feldman, A. (1991) *Formations of Violence: the Narrative of the Body and Political Terror in Northern Ireland*. Chicago, IL: University of Chicago Press.

Fiske, J. (1990) 'Review of Donal Carbaugh, *Talking American: Cultural Discourses on Donahue*', *Quarterly Journal of Speech*, 76: 450–1.

Fiske, J. (1991) 'Writing ethnographies: contribution to a dialogue', *Quarterly Journal of Speech*, 77: 330–35.

Geertz, C. (1983) *Local Knowledge: Further Essays in Interpretive Anthropology*. New York: Basic Books.

Girard, R. (1977) *Violence and the Sacred*. Patrick Gregory, trans. Baltimore, MD: Johns Hopkins University Press.

Haines, H.W. (1986) ' "What kind of war?" an analysis of the Vietnam Veterans' Memorial', *Critical Studies in Mass Communication*, 3: 1–20.

Harvey, D. (1989) *The Urban Experience*. Baltimore, MD: Johns Hopkins University Press.

Hobsbawm, E. (1990) *Nations and Nationalism since 1780: Programme, Myth, Reality*. Cambridge: Cambridge University Press.

Marcus, G. and Fischer, M.M.J. (1986) *Anthropology as Cultural Critique: an Experimental Moment in the Human Sciences.* Chicago, IL: University of Chicago Press.

McGee, M.C. (1975) 'In search of "The People": a rhetorical alternative', *Quarterly Journal of Speech*, 61: 235–49.

Philipsen, G. (1991) 'Two issues in the evaluation of ethnographic studies of communicative practices', *Quarterly Journal of Speech*, 77: 327–9.

Said, E. (1979) *Orientalism.* New York: Vintage.

Said, E. (1983) *The World, the Text, and the Critic.* Cambridge, MA: Harvard University Press.

Said, E. and Hitchens, C. (eds) (1988) *Blaming the Victims: Spurious Scholarship and the Palestinian Question.* New York: Verso.

Scholes, R. (1985) *Textual Power.* New Haven, CT: Yale University Press.

Scholes, R. (1989) *Protocols of Reading.* New Haven, CT: Yale University Press.

Shapiro, M.J. (1988) *The Politics of Representation.* Madison: University of Wisconsin Press.

Siegel, T. and Conquergood, D. (producers) (1990) *The Heart Broken in Half.* Video documentary (58 mins). Chicago, IL: Siegel Productions.

Sollors, W. (ed.) (1989) *The Invention of Ethnicity.* New York: Oxford University Press.

Stallybrass, P. and White, A. (1986) *The Politics and Poetics of Transgression.* Ithaca, NY: Cornell University Press.

Tompkins, J. (1988) 'Fighting words: unlearning to write the critical essay', *Georgia Review*, 42: 585–90.

Weaver, R. (1953) *The Ethics of Rhetoric.* South Bend: Regnery/Gateway.

Yablonsky, L. (1962) *The Violent Gang.* New York: Macmillan.

10

'Socialism of the Mind': the New Age of Post-Marxism

Dana L. Cloud

A sort of bazaar socialism, bizarre socialism, a hedonist socialism: an eat, drink, and be merry socialism because tomorrow we can drink and be merry again . . . a socialism for disillusioned marxist intellectuals who waited around too long for the revolution – a socialism that holds up everything that is ephemeral and evanescent and passing as vital and worthwhile, everything that melts into air as solid, and proclaims that every shard of the self is a social movement.

(Sivanandan [1989: 23] defining post-Marxist theory)

A socialist criticism is not primarily concerned with the consumers' revolution. Its task is to take over the means of production.

(Eagleton, 1986: 184)

A cluster of discourses and practices – ranging from lifestyle workshops such as erhardt seminars training (est), meditation and Eastern mysticism to vegetarian evangelism and New Age businesses, from anti-nukes to environmentalism and crystal worship – New Age philosophy centres on the care of the self in an oppressive society. The aim of this essay is to posit and elaborate an analogy between a New Age politics and the post-Marxism represented by Ernesto Laclau and Chantal Mouffe (1985). Through this analogy I hope to reveal the hidden political and social context of otherwise seemingly diverse ideologies.

Most New Age texts argue for personal responses to social, economic and political practices.[1] At first glance, the rhetoric of the New Age would seem to have little to do with post-Marxist social theory. Nevertheless, this chapter will foreground what New Age and post-Marxist politics have in common, and critique *both* theoretical systems as idealist, relativist and individualist discourses. The generation of idealist (spiritual or discursive) explanations for material (economic or physical) problems is a therapeutic rhetorical strategy[2] often couched in the language of sickness and healing to code social 'ills'. This therapeutic approach, which demands not activism but self-transformation, not collective work but individual consumerism, is appealing to upper-middle-class intellectual élites, a perception confirmed by demographic evidence (Wilson, 1988).[3]

An illustrative case can be found in the resistance of New Agers to a 1992 labour protest against Berkeley's Whole Foods Market, a 'politically correct' grocery store that offered its (mostly black and Latino) workers lower wages and fewer health benefits than other stores in the Berkeley area. When the workers attempted to unionize and went on strike, both management and shoppers (ostensibly members of the left counter-culture) criticized them for interfering in the process of transformative consumption. *Nation* reporter L.A. Kauffman describes the event as 'a parable of the fate of countercultural politics: a tale of *what happens when the personal overwhelms the political*' (1992: 74; my emphasis). Kauffman argues that the shift in left politics to an emphasis on life-style and consumption reflects

> a larger shift in advanced capitalist countries from a politics centered on the point of production (the workplace) or the point of distribution (the state) to a politics oriented toward the decentered sites of consumption and daily life. (p. 75)

The anti-labour stance and personalization of politics of the New Age movement bears directly on the analogy I hope to establish in this chapter between the New Age movement and the politics of post-Marxism. Like the New Age, post-Marxism represents a shift to a politics of consumption, identity and everyday life. Both the New Age movement and the new (post-Marxist) left have refused participation in the struggles of the working class (defined simply as those people who must work for a wage in order to survive, without whose labour the capitalist system of production could not move forward) in favour of 'a politics oriented toward the decentered sites of consumption and daily life'. Far from being grounded in the struggle of the exploited and oppressed for liberation, the New Age movement encourages upper-middle-class professionals to consume politically and environmentally correct products as the panacea for social change.

But in some senses, the New Age is typical of social movements in the United States since the upheavals of the 1960s and 1970s, and can be said to represent the hegemonic boundaries of political engagement in late capitalist America:

> The New Age Movement is a genuine *movement* – it has no central headquarters, and its adherents hold to widely varying opinions concerning its exact nature and goals. . . . The movement is, however loosely, held together by its very real transformative vision of a new world. (Melton, 1988: 35–6)

By this definition, the New Age meets Ernesto Laclau and Chantal Mouffe's (1985) post-Marxist criteria for a popular political struggle on ideological terrain. But is New Age really a movement (by definition a collective, organized popular uprising) – or just a retreat into narcissism and inaction? By implication, is post-Marxism an unwitting collaborator with the capitalist system it claims to challenge?

As represented by Mark Satin's (1978) movement-encompassing treatise *New Age Politics*, the New Age movement is plural in its expressions of antagonism towards relations of subordination in the United States. It calls for a new revolutionary strategy appropriate to our time, and focuses its efforts on the discursive plane, at the level of consciousness. Its goal is a radical plural democracy, although it lacks specific criteria for the ideal world or ideal political work. And it rejects, explicitly, the working class as the primary agent of change, emphasizing instead plural struggles from diverse standpoints.

This chapter argues that the New Age does not represent an adequate political response to the conditions of late capitalism. Rather, it is a hegemonic discourse dislocating political movements of the late 1960s into a track of personal life-style work and conspicuous consumption. Alex Callinicos (1990) has argued that postmodernist, post-Marxist political theories (which I will define in detail below), likewise, constitute an ideological justification for the withdrawal of a new intellectual middle class from politics altogether since 1968. It is my purpose here to construct an analogy between the discourses of New Age and of post-Marxism to show that both are ideological rhetorics generated to console activists after the failure of post-1968 revolutionary movements and to legitimate participation in liberal politics (or the adoption of an explicit anti-political stance).[4]

The goal of an argument made by analogy, as Kenneth Burke (1954: 97–124) argues, is to provide 'perspective by incongruity', to reveal hitherto obscured features of one thing by drawing out what it has in common, unexpectedly, with another. Such a demonstration can have the effect of calling into question our 'pieties', or blind intellectual commitments to projects with latent ideological dimensions. While the New Age movement and post-Marxist social theory may seem at first glance to be completely incongruous, it is possible to reveal quite extensive similarities in commitment between them. This comparison is not meant as a complete dismissal of the complex contributions post-Marxist and poststructuralist theory offer political activists today.[5]

The New Age movement as a political theory suffers from

idealism (or 'textualism' – the assumption that the revolution will happen at the level of discourse and consciousness rather than economics; Callinicos, 1990: 63, 70, 73–80), humanism (the belief in the sovereignty and boundedness of the individual as agent that emerged with liberal capitalism),[6] and ethical and political relativism. This chapter attempts to reveal that – despite claims to radical, oppositional, anti-humanist and revolutionary import – poststructuralism's contributions to political theory and practice are undergirded by the same idealist/textualist, liberal humanist and relativist assumptions – with significant debilitating consequences for left politics. These assumptions represent the 'retreat from class' (Wood, 1986) as the foundation of oppositional politics.

To the extent that the New Age movement is obviously an ideologically conservative, pro-capitalist and therapeutic discourse, we are forced to examine the ideological weight of the theoretical discourses of post-Marxism. This examination leads to scepticism about post-Marxist definitions of the state and criteria for struggle around three central questions. First, what is at stake in locating revolutionary agency in the working class? Even if one resists class essentialism, don't some standpoints or nodal points in the discursive order give certain groups more of a stake in change? Second, is it possible to win radical political democracy before achieving economic democracy (socialism)? Finally, what are appropriate criteria to judge the value of an adequate left political practice? If socialism is not our yardstick, how do we evaluate the fidelity and efficacy of various strategies?

The argument proceeds as follows. First, I summarize the central suppositions of post-Marxism, placing this tendency in the context of Eurocommunism's rejection of the class struggle as the centre of left politics. I summarize the major critiques to date of this tendency. Then I explore a central political text of the New Age movement, Mark Satin's (1978) synthesis *New Age Politics*, outlining its idealist, individualist and relativist elements. By analogy, the critiques of the New Age movement apply to post-Marxism, and I conclude the chapter by asking whether the failure to base left opposition in the struggles of the working class and the exhortation to work within the liberal imaginary locate post-Marxism as an unwitting collaborator with the hegemonic liberal capitalism of the 1990s.

Post-Marxist Theories of Discourse and Politics

The work of Gramsci (1971) and Althusser (1984) marked a turn in Marxist theory towards the ideological or discursive levels of the state (see Clegg, 1991), initiating a still-evolving theoretical discussion in left circles as to the relationship between base and superstructure, between the material relations of production and the cultural or ideological expressions that win social consent to those relations. As Wood (1986: 18–19) explains, Althusser inaugurated an academicist obsession with the structures of language and consciousness within Marxist theory, and rejected any notion of the subject as political agent within a class. With the postmodernists (Baudrillard, 1975; Foucault, 1980; Lyotard, 1984) this turn is taken to its logical conclusion, in arguments that reject the economic and political realms as sites of struggle. Now the theoretical focus shifts to discourse (the symbolic articulation of the social relationships) as both the source and the site of contradictions and political struggle.[7] Baudrillard (1975) takes this position to its extreme, arguing that people can be 'oppressed by the code' that establishes relations of consumption, which he views as more foundational to late capitalism than the relations of production. Since 1929, Baudrillard argues, capitalism has exerted its control on the level of consumption, on which subjects are positioned in ways that subordinate them to the code, whether or not they happen to be workers. Thus social control happens through discourse, ideology: 'prolonged education, . . . endless personal development. . . . All the institutions of "advanced democracy"' (1975: 132).

Likewise, Mouffe (1988a) argues for recognition of social antagonisms that are the product not centrally of class relations but rather of relations of subordination at the level of consumption, resistances to bureaucracy, mass culture, sexism, racism and homophobia, to name a few. She argues that the proliferation of new antagonisms is something to be accommodated by the left. She does not consider that the dissolution of class politics into myriad fragmented movements (in 'postmodern' social space) opposed in vague ways to 'the system' may actually collude with the system in some ways. As with the New Age phenomenon, other new social movements may represent capitalism's recuperation of radical political challenges.

But for Laclau and Mouffe (1985) as for Baudrillard, revolutionary agency is located not in the working class as a discrete entity, but rather in other groups subordinated within the complex and shifting discursive formation. In *Hegemony and Socialist Strategy* (1985) and 'Post-Marxism Without Apologies' (1987) Laclau and Mouffe offer a definition of political struggle with five basic components: the discursive nature of the state and its autonomy from the economic base; the subject as site of overdetermined contradictions, out of which agency arises; the rejection of the working class as agent of change in late capitalism; the concept of resistance defined as discursively articulated antagonism to the system; and, finally, a definition of revolution as the establishment of a new hegemony within the democractic imaginary.[8]

Overall, they see the social as the site of struggle because social relations, including those of class, are discursively constituted in a system of differences and equivalencies. There are regularities in this system that make the concept of opposition and struggle meaningful, in that social space is more or less seamlessly structured, and clear positions of subordination and oppression exist. It is out of contradictions in social space that struggle emerges, but struggle is not antagonism (the systematic expression and coordination of collective opposition) until some identity among struggling forces is rhetorically established, dividing social space into two camps.

Below I argue that the post-Marxist conflation of the discursive and the real results in an idealist and relativist political model analogous to the therapeutic consolations of the New Age movement. However, in the second half of their book, Laclau and Mouffe (1985) do posit a political programme based on the rhetorical articulation of the interests of the subordinated. As Eagleton (1991) suggests, implicit here is a theory of oppression of certain categorically defined groups – workers, women, racial minorities, etc – even if the categories involved are discursively constituted. It is at this point that Laclau and Mouffe's two projects – one deconstructive of the Marxist political tradition, and one reconstructive of a political programme – become unhinged, suggesting that the authors actually do acknowledge the relative stability of a social formation whose discourses, while not entirely sutured, are still constitutive of dominated and dominating groups. Like Laclau and Mouffe, I acknowledge the importance of the rhetorical constitution of oppositional consciousness, and I recognize that Laclau and Mouffe themselves do not promote self-absorption and life-style politics as emancipatory.

It is unfortunate, however, that their emphasis on discourse as the only site of struggle (indeed, as all there is) leads to an abandonment of the working class as the agent of historical change, and prevents them from linking their rhetorical perspective to the project of formulating collective consciousness among the working class. According to Laclau and Mouffe, 'society', or the political-ideological component of the state, does not consist of material and discursive levels, but is rather purely discursive (although discourse here is defined broadly to include any symbolic utterance, action or relation). In this work, culture becomes theoretically detached from material reality. Therefore, political struggle is now something that takes place not at the site of production but rather through the unevenly progressive expressions of oppositional cultural identity. In discourse, ideological elements are discursively linked to other elements and to subject positions, forming a complex, dispersed, but relatively stable totality (Laclau and Mouffe, 1985: 105).

It is in the provisional order of this totality that relationships of domination and subordination are constituted:

> The practice of articulation, therefore, consists in the construction of nodal points which partially fix meaning; and the partial character of this fixation proceeds from the openness of the social, a result, in its turn, of the constant overflowing of every discourse by the infinitude of the field of discursivity. (Laclau and Mouffe, 1985: 113)

Thus the state is a constellation of discursive nodal points, around which subjects are positioned in the process of articulating and re-articulating social identities and relations. For example, 'woman' and 'nature' are by themselves floating elements of discursive space until they are articulated together, so that historically womanhood has been identified as close to nature. Such moments are relatively permanent, and yet open to challenge when contradictions arise that point out the constructedness of this articulation (e.g. when women's association with beauty, achieved through artifice, runs up against the definition of woman as 'natural'). More to the point is Laclau and Mouffe's (1985: 115–17) example of the nodal point 'human being', defined as having inalienable rights, in contradiction with the fact that certain people are deprived of those rights.

According to this analysis, the state is discursive; because contradictions can occur around nodal points independent of class conflict, the state is completely autonomous from the economic base. For this reason, the working class is no longer the privileged site of disruption and conflict. The authors write, 'Hence, there are a variety of possible antagonisms in the social, many of them in opposition to each other' (Laclau and Mouffe, 1985: 131). And later they add,

> Today it is not only as a seller of labour-power that the individual is subordinated to capital, but also through his or her incorporation into a multitude of other social relations: culture, free time, illness, education, sex and even death. There is practically no domain of individual or collective life which escapes capitalist relations. (p. 161)

Struggle is displaced from class relations on to other social relations, namely those involving people as consumers of culture, leisure activity, medical care, etc. But it is important to note here that although the working class is no longer the sole agent of change, the enemy to be fought is still capitalism for Laclau and Mouffe. However, because of the autonomy of the state from the relations of production, any struggle against any subordination, *whether or not it is perceived to be subordination to capitalism*, is a legitimate struggle. This openness about what constitutes a legitimate political practice has its pitfalls, as I will explain below.

Struggles against subordination become antagonisms when they are articulated together to present a unified front, and when these articulations divide social space into a clear 'us' and 'them'. These divisions are not given a priori by the economic structure of society, but are constructed in discourse, and involve alliances that go beyond boundaries of economic classes. Laclau and Mouffe write that antagonisms emerge from 'equivalential displacement between distinct subject positions' (1985: 159). I take this to mean that where there are unequal relations of power between subject positions constructed in a relationship of difference to each other (e.g. woman–man), there is potential for antagonism. Further, in a discourse that unifies various subordinate positions (i.e. expresses commonality in the suffering of various oppressed groups) there is hegemonic power.

Hegemony, for Laclau and Mouffe then, involves more than the engineering of consent of the dominated by the dominators. It is the establishment of a social order based on the ability to articulate together a variety of subject positions, unified in their antagonism to a discursively identified enemy or evil (1985: 189). In their own phraseology, 'A situation of hegemony would be one in which the management of the positivity of the social and the articulation of the diverse democratic demands had achieved a maximum of integration' (1985: 189). It is not enough to be simply anti-system; one must take the pieces of the social order and put them together in a new vision. This process can take place on the left – as the 'attempt to establish different nodal points from which a process of . . . reconstruction of the social fabric could be instituted' (1985: 189) – or on the right, in the maintenance of the nodal points that already are fixed in place.

Because hegemony is a process of positivity, of not only antagonism and deconstruction but also social reconstruction, the left must work within the 'democratic imaginary' (the dominant liberal ideology, with its core values of individual liberty, equality and responsibility) of the liberal state in order to achieve its goals. Laclau and Mouffe suggest using the primary nodal points of this imaginary – the rights of liberty, equality and the human being itself – as elements that can be re-articulated in the interests of those struggling against the current limiting and oppressive understanding of those terms:

> In the face of the project for the reconstruction of a hierarchic society, the alternative of the Left should consist of locating itself fully in the field of the democratic revolution and expanding the chainings of equivalents between the different struggles against oppression. *The task of the Left therefore cannot be to renounce liberal-democratic ideology, but on the contrary, to deepen and expand it in the direction of a radical and plural democracy.* . . . The *meaning* of liberal discourse on individual rights is not definitively fixed; and, just as this unfixity permits their articulation with elements of conservative discourse, it also permits different forms of articulation and redefinition which accentuate the democratic moment. (Laclau and Mouffe, 1985: 176, original emphasis)

This new formulation of the left's task is not unique to Laclau and Mouffe, but rather is characteristic of all of Western Marxisms after 1968 (Anderson, 1983), including post-structuralist discourse theory and especially the Eurocommunism of the British journals *Marxism Today* (the journal of the Communist Party, ironically abandoning Marxism), *Rethinking Marxism* (1988) and *Strategies* (see Hall, 1989, 1991).

Clearly, post-structuralism and Eurocommunism are explicit reactions against a Marxist practice based on class politics. This tendency includes the post-Fordism/'New Times' hypothesis, which argues that postmodernity represents a break with organized capitalism and mandates new forms of dispersed, local and non-working class organizing (Rustin, 1989). 'New Times' refers to the argument that global capitalism has entered a new period of disorganization and dispersion, instead of remaining concentrated and consolidated in discrete sites of production. Ostensibly, according to 'New Times' advocates, this dispersion will result in a proliferation of local struggles (not necessarily articulated as a class struggle) against the system, which capitalists will be unable to control. This model of struggle was posited as a left populist response to the long hegemony of the right in Britain and the United States.[9]

Wood (1986: 3–6) summarizes the major propositions of this approach, which she argues resembles the 'true' (utopian) socialism of Marx's day. (1) The working class has failed to make revolution. (2) There is no necessary correspondence between economics and politics. (3) The left does not need the working class to enact a political transformation. (4) Politics can be isolated to ideological and political (discursive/textual) planes. (5) Everyone, regardless of class, has an interest in making a socialist society, therefore (6) instead of a unified class movement, radical socialist democracy can be achieved through a plurality of liberal movements. Socialism is an extension of liberal democracy. Finally, (7) intellectual élites should be at the forefront of these movements because of their ability to recognize and articulate the universal interest in socialism, in contrast to the baser interests of the masses.

Hall (1991: 58–60) also provides a definition and summary of this theoretical development, endorsing a view of our times as representing a 'post-industrial', 'post-Fordist' epoch in capitalism. This epoch is ostensibly characterized by flexible, decentralized forms of labour; the preponderance of 'soft', 'information age' technologies; the dispersal of industries into hives of segmented work activity; the rise of multinational corporations and a new corresponding division of labour; an elaboration of a consumer culture targeted towards groups according to life-style and taste rather than class; and multiplicitous subject forms inhabiting a complex social world (see Graham, 1991, for a contrasting viewpoint).

Paramount in the shift to 'New Times', argues Hall, is the *return of the subjective* in left political theory – in other words, a focus on the elaboration of the self through consumption and discursive expression rather than on transformative politics. Interestingly, it is that shift to and exclusive focus on the subjective that also marks New Age thinking.

New Age *Politics*?

Mark Satin's *New Age Politics* (1978) is, like *Hegemony and Socialist Strategy* (Laclau and Mouffe, 1985), a concentrated version of a diffuse set of ideas. It is a 1970s polemical vision of and strategy for New Age society which resonates strongly with Laclau and Mouffe on several points, including the acknowledgement of a need for a new political model appropriate to the current conjuncture, the idea of politics as articulation of many interests together across classes, the focus on the discursive sphere and consciousness as sites of struggle, and the ultimate goal of a radical plural democracy, achieved through working with already-established democratic ideals. Particularly, both political visions are characterized by idealism, individualist humanism and relativism. After treating each of these tendencies in both discourses, I will turn to the ways in which a critique of New Age as represented by Satin – specifically regarding the problems of idealism/textualism, individualist humanism and political relativism – reflects back on to post-Marxist prescriptions for revolutionary strategy.

Like Laclau and Mouffe, Satin labels himself a post-Marxist. Having abandoned socialism after becoming a draft resister during the Vietnam conflict, he sought a new approach to politics. He argues, like Laclau and Mouffe, that the situation in the United States since the 1970s is so different from the context of much Marxist theorizing that 'a whole new way of looking at the world' becomes necessary, 'one that comes out of our own experience' (1978: 7). Like Laclau and Mouffe, he finds this new perspective in the diverse 'fringe movements' of his time:

> It dawned on me that the ideas and energies from the various 'fringe' movements – feminist, ecological, spiritual, human potential, and the rest – were beginning to come together in a new way . . . in a way that was beginning to generate a coherent new politics. (Satin, 1978: 1)

In that Satin's expressed project in this book is to bring together all of the 'bits and pieces' of the new politics and to articulate them together in a new way, he is attempting to establish a hegemonic antagonism that represents a dissatisfied people.

The Idealism of the New Age

This attempt takes place in discourse, against a state that is purely discursive in form. Like Laclau and Mouffe, Satin wants to get beyond a Marxism that sees the problems of the world in 'simple' economic terms: 'Our problems are only superficially economic, and . . . they have much more to do with culture: with who we are and what we want from life' (1978: 17). Satin's concern with subjectivity and culture resonates with the post-Marxist idea that subjects are struggling against subordination at the level of the code, identity and consumption. The goal of analysing and reconfiguring identities ('who we are') is a therapeutic one, a practice that offers psychological insight as a consolation for the impossibility of structural transformation. Throughout his book, Satin argues that because our problems inhere not in our institutions but in our consciousness and belief systems, we must struggle to rework our beliefs before meaningful change can happen.

It is our current belief system, according to Satin, that is our biggest obstacle to founding a new society. Satin calls this belief system the Prison. The Prison has six components or walls: patriarchal attitudes, egocentricity, scientific single vision, the bureaucratic mentality, nationalism, and the big city outlook (p. 23). None of these is the product of capitalism, which is not in itself an obstacle to freedom. Similarly, racism is a result not of capitalist relations, but is rather a symptom of the Prison itself. According to Satin, the Prison leads to what he calls 'monolithic institutions', or institutions with totalizing, controlling power: transportation, medicine, schooling, religion, the nuclear family, nuclear power, the defence system, the monolithic state, the governing élite and so on. Again, these institutions are enabled not by the capitalist mode of production, but by our negative belief systems.

Satin writes,

> Basically the Prison is a way of *seeing* the world, a *mental construct, or an illusion* [my emphasis] . . . that we create every day anew. And because we create it in our minds, we can undo it in our minds. *We can change our consciousness* [my emphasis] individually and collectively so that we're not Prison-bound.
>
> And if enough of us do this . . . then *and only then* [emphasis in original] would the institutions, goods, and services that are set up to meet the needs of Prison-bound people lose the Prison-bound aspects of their appeal. (p. 24)

Clearly, then, Satin is calling for therapeutic, self-oriented work within the democratic imaginary, a reworking of individual consciousness in place of public struggle. Notice how similar his definition of the Prison-bound mentality ('a way of *seeing* the world, a construct, or an illusion') is to an Althusserian definition of ideology, and to Laclau and Mouffe's 'discourse', although they would reject the idea of calling discourse an illusion. Satin does not call his enemy capitalism – but by Laclau and Mouffe's definitions of struggle as antagonism from any relationship of subordination and of hegemony as the joint articulation of many antagonisms, he is engaged in hegemonic struggles against the state.

Another aspect of hegemony, according to Laclau and Mouffe, is the articulation of a new social order, a radical, plural democracy based on the ideals of liberty (autonomy or difference) and equality (sameness and collectivity). In this regard, Satin offers his readers a satisfying utopian vision of a New Age world, a globally connected, yet locally focused set of communities of androgynous, peaceful, spiritual people who depend on 'biolithic' (*sic*) ('grounded in life?') or life-centred institutions for their well-being. All of these institutions would encourage diversity and autonomy in balance with community needs. And this again resonates with Laclau and Mouffe's (1985: 167) vision of a radical democracy, radical in its lack of a hierarchy of meaning and rules for conformity, yet democratic in that each element or member of this plural democracy is equally valued. Laclau and Mouffe might well agree with Satin's statement, 'Autonomy and community: Marxism stresses community at the expense of autonomy, and liberalism does just the reverse' (Satin, 1978: 106). Both Satin and Laclau and Mouffe are concerned with 'deepening the democratic imaginary' to include both terms.

The Relativism of the New Age

In such an open plurality, however, there can be no criteria for a 'correct' strategy or society, and the result is political relativism. Satin writes, 'New Age people aren't interested in creating a "perfect" or "utopian" America run according to the "correct" political principles. Instead, *diversity* would be treasured' (1978: 106). Similarly, Laclau and Mouffe (1985: 179) argue that one cannot tell a person where and how to struggle, because such discourse would be totalizing and suturing, that is, inherently undemocratic. They write,

> The first condition of a radically democratic society is to accept the contingent and radically open character of all its values – and in that sense, to abandon the aspiration to a single foundation. (Laclau and Mouffe, 1987: 101)

To me it seems that it would be difficult to generate a true antagonism out of such open plurality. How does one create an 'us' and a 'them' (a directed antagonism based on the ability to locate blame for the problem or an enemy) if there is no basis on which to evaluate a political practice? On this view, any collective expression of dissatisfaction from the Klan to Earth First! (although perhaps not, ironically, a workers' struggle) would represent an appropriate antagonism. In order to enact a transformative politics, one must identify correctly the source of the problem – but from a relativist perspective, there can be no such thing as a correct analysis.

Satin does not provide a much-needed set of guidelines in his discussion of political strategy. Action loosely involves cultural change, 'group-work' and political and institutional change, but Satin holds these impulses in check, citing the 'emerging consensus among many New Age people that would avoid all talk of stages and . . . all advice to others about what they "should" do next' (1978: 211). So instead of a programme he advances the concept of 'critical mass':

> If enough of us, a 'critical mass', share the New Age ethics and political values and are active in the areas that are most accessible to us or that 'feel right' to us when we've begun to meet our needs of love and esteem and self-actualization and self-transcendence – then society will begin to move in a New Age direction. (p. 211)

In the language of humanist psychology, this passage equates the therapeutic goals of love, esteem, self-actualization, 'feeling' right, with a political programme. While Laclau and Mouffe do not describe the process of hegemony-building in terms of feeling and self-actualization, they put forward a conception of hegemony in which subjects struggle locally and in discourse until the democratic imaginary takes on new shape. In its idealism, this vision resembles Satin's assurance that, given enough work on consciousness, the real structures of power will transform themselves.[10] Michael Rossman explains the process in New Age terms:

> Our social reality is a construct also, a coherent but arbitrary web of relations which could well be other than it is. . . . We can imagine yet other arrangements. At certain transcendent moments of history, political or spiritual, we become aware of the power we have to change the rules we play by – not piecemeal but throughout all the dimensions of life, creating a changed and integral conspiracy of social reality. (1979: 67)

A 'conspiracy of social reality' – a synonym for cultural hegemony? Like Rossman, Laclau and Mouffe express faith in the power of human beings to transform society through shifts in consciousness and cultural expression.

So far we have seen that with regard to the goals and strategies of politics, the New Age movement as represented by Mark Satin fits a post-Marxist model. However, New Age falls short of radical antagonism in many ways, all of which hinge on the problem of individualist, voluntarist humanism.

The Humanism of the New Age

Like Laclau and Mouffe, Satin explicitly rejects the working class as the privileged agent of social change. Satin devotes an entire chapter to this question, in which he divides the world into life-seekers and death-seekers instead of into capitalists and workers. He writes,

> According to Marx, socialism would be fought for by the proletariat, by the working class, by all those whose basic needs were frustrated by predatory capitalism. In the United States, most members of the working class weren't willing to fight for socialism. But they did change capitalism enough so that they could meet their material needs, their physiological and security needs.
> The working class finds it incredibly hard to meet its non-material needs, but so do the rest of us. We're all in the same boat when it comes to these needs, when it comes to the Prison and its institutions.
> But we can't expect all the classes to join together and work for New Age society. In fact, we can be almost certain that none of them will. For every social and economic class, *as a class* . . . , has a substantial stake in monolithic society. . . .
> No, New Age society won't be brought about by any particular class acting in its interests as a class. But it may be brought about by all those *individuals* who are able to see that Prison society is making it impossible for them to meet their needs as individual human beings. (Satin, 1978: 82; emphasis in original)

Satin's concept of non-material needs is reminiscent of Baudrillard, who argues that needs are a construct of a society that worships labour and consumption. In other words, to posit a set of non-economic needs is to posit a set of non-economic relations of subordination, and thus to allow for agents of change other than those who are victims of economic subordination. This position is not far off from that of Laclau and Mouffe's idea that no one has an 'objective' or material stake in change, but we all have constructed interests on many levels of society.

For Laclau and Mouffe, contradictions in social space locate people in overdetermined subject positions, enabling them to act strategically as agents despite the provisional and discursive nature of the positions they take up. Laclau and Mouffe renounce the liberal 'category of subject as unitary, transparent and sutured entity' (1985: 166), yet they argue for a kind of strategic humanism to resolve the paralysis that results when conceiving of a completely dispersed and fragmented social subject (p.117).

Although recognizing that subjects are not the origin of social relations, Laclau and Mouffe argue that when people located in overdetermined subject positions engage in antagonistic relations in the democratic imaginary (their left-lingo euphemism for the liberal ideology), those relationships are necessarily embodied in humanist subjects. For the left, they advise taking advantage of the rhetoric of rights and freedoms associated with the humanist subject, working to articulate those rights with the needs and interests of subordinated groups (1985: p.116). They write,

> Insofar as of the two great themes of the democratic imaginary – equality and liberty – it was that of equality which was traditionally predominant, the demands for autonomy bestow an increasingly central role upon liberty. For this reason many of these forms of resistance are made manifest not in the form of collective struggles, but through an increasingly affirmed individualism. (The Left, of course, is ill prepared to take into account these struggles, which even today it tends to dismiss as 'liberal'. Hence the danger that they may be articulated by a discourse of the Right, of the defence of privileges.) (1985: 164–5)

This passage is a critique of the left's unwillingness to use the rhetorical tools or elements provided by the democratic imaginary for assuming antagonistic positions (although in fact, Marxist organizations do join with reform struggles). This critique has its merits. However, the affirmation of individualism is a risky undertaking for any movement seeking economic justice in terms of collective interests. Any left struggle that attempts to articulate its demands in the terms of individual rights risks co-optation.[11] It is the translation of socio-economic problems and responses to them into an individualist framework that most centrally characterizes therapeutic discourse. Indeed, I would suggest that post-Marxism's rhetoric of the individual resembles Marxism less than it resembles liberalism; it is a dressed-up concession to the stability of liberal capitalism.

In the New Age movement, the consequences of articulating an almost-oppositional vision in the terms of liberal individualism become quite clear. According to this analysis, individuals *choose* workaholism or leisure, success or poverty, in much the same way as one chooses between organic and non-organic produce. Liberation is equated with the transformation of selves presumed to possess the economic and cultural means of self-articulation and enlightened consumption. Collective struggle or public work is ruled out in the refusal to develop a coherent programme for suprapersonal change. The values of liberal individualism embed the movement in the upwardly mobile middle class, whose interests do not lie with fundamental economic transformation of society.

While Laclau and Mouffe are aware of the dangers of strategic individualism, their analysis of non-working-class agency gives us no grounds on which to critique the New Age's conception of agency. For Satin, clearly, agency resides within the individual. He believes that social change inevitably follows self-change, as reflected in the 'critical mass' hypothesis above. And self-change is possible because of what Satin calls the 'trans-material world view' (1978: 91–101). We escape the Prison through encounters with our spiritual or religious selves, through meditation, religious ritual or therapy. Through such practices we find (or, as I see it, are hailed by the illusion of) power in ourselves and transcend the material level of reality and the Prison. Here the agent is the individual isolated humanist subject, imagining a new world in isolation, substituting the project of self-transformation and imagination of new worlds for actual political struggle.

There are two problems with this conception of the human agent. First, its spiritual idealism leads to a definition of action as withdrawal and isolation. Instead of taking the power discovered through consciousness-raising practice (whether it be individual or group) and organizing a confrontation with the state or corporation, on this argument one simply waits for everyone to come to the same realization, and automatically the world will be a better place. In this way, the possibility of a collective, public struggle is subverted.

The second problem is that the notion of isolated individual human agent is inextricably linked with liberal capitalism's investment in a certain notion of individual privacy. As Wood (1986: 150) explains, capitalist hegemony rests on the separation of the political and economic, and in the political sphere people are defined as individual sovereigns without reference to their economic position or interests.[12] The consequences of this separation are the preclusion of radical change occurring on the plane of the political, and the mystification of the collective and structural foundations for power. Both the New Age and the post-Marxists accept this separation between political activity and economic interests.

To translate the radical project of structural economic and political transformation into the language of individual agency and individual freedom is to self-destruct. The ideology of liberal individualism subverts the analysis of economic exploitation and oppression that characterizes a radical, as opposed to a simply liberal, political programme. Satin's discourse exemplifies this problem. In fact, Satin (1978: 166) cites the historically embedded connection between capitalism and individual freedom as a significant reason behind his choice to defend capitalism in his book.

This defence is based on the following assumptions. First, capitalism supposedly disperses power away from the centre of the state (also a central argument of post-Marxism; see Callinicos, 1990: 132–44). Second, capitalism is not the problem in modern society – once we are free of the Prison mindset, capitalists will not exploit people any more (Satin, 1978: 166). Finally, economic oppression is not serious. Satin fallaciously argues that United States society has overcome the problem of material deprivation and what we are really hungering for is 'strokes', or affirmations of our self-esteem. For these reasons, Satin celebrates entrepreneurship and worker-managed (but, of course, not worker-owned) enterprises. At one point he celebrates a General Foods plant for its work-team approach that gave workers control over their production. The result was a marked increase in efficiency and cost-effectiveness. Of course, the workers did not receive a corresponding control over the profits of their supposedly self-actualized labour.

Critiques of the New Age
Predictably, the New Age movement has been soundly taken to task by left critics in the popular press for its celebration of capitalism, its élitism, its retreat into individualism, and its lack of real political action. Richard Blow writes,

> The New Age way is not to deny differences between people, but to deny that they matter. It's an attempt to create an egalitarian society based not on equal distribution of wealth or property, but on spiritual equality – a sort of *socialism of the mind*. It's an illusion. But for New Agers, even an illusion can become real if you believe in it long enough. (1988: 27)

Here one problem for Blow is that the New Age denies the importance of material differences among people. The same critique might be levelled against Laclau and Mouffe, since they argue that all interests are discursively constructed and that no one has more of a stake in social change – or more of a say in the form that change should take – than anyone else. Both the New Age and post-Marxism represent a 'socialism of the mind' – an idealist project without grounding in material interests or working-class political strategy.

Blow accurately and succinctly expresses a second flaw in New Age thinking: the merging of 'liberal political views with the ability to earn a profit':

> New Age language sounds suspiciously like Republican social policy. Economic growth leads to personal growth, and that is always worthwhile. Even better, the pursuit of profit will also take care of social concerns, like poverty, hunger, and war. In the New Age lexicon, there is no mention of sacrifice, duty, or responsibility. Those concepts are regressive, unprofitable in any sense. (1988:26)[13]

While the New Age has a politics that is generally left of centre – 'anti-war, pro-environment, anti-nuke, pro-feminist' (Blow, 1988: 26) – its individualism keeps it from articulating a truly radical agenda that addresses the need for the redistribution of wealth as a necessary precondition for true democracy. As the *New Age Journal*'s fifteenth anniversary retrospective ('Where We've Been', 1990: 39) put it, the left counter-culture went from 'Abbie and Jerry to Ben and Jerry's' – from political activism to profit-making ice cream chains.

Blow criticizes New Agers for their therapeutic responses to political problems, including their unwillingness to confront problems in a way that would involve challenging another person or group ('They never tackle issues; they hug them' [1988: 27]) and the inefficacy of the 'critical mass' strategy ('No one really seems to know what happens when an idea becomes unstoppable' [p. 27]). The therapeutic discourse of the New Age provides an idealist, individualist framing for some people's dissatisfaction with their material lives – discontent which, given access to alternative and truly political social analyses, might fuel public political activity.

If the New Age movement (along with its more mainstream therapeutic variations) is the popular political expression of our time, what does that say about the state of left politics? And what does it say about left theories that celebrate popular, discursive politics? For me the New Age, as represented by Satin, reveals the risks of therapeutic hegemonic politics in late capitalism. It is clearly not antagonistic to the state, although it does articulate diverse antagonisms. It demonstrates the ease with which a radical pluralism can be recuperated by the dominant ideology when one preaches inclusiveness where judgements are necessary. Its thera-peutic notion of the subject, one firmly embedded in the democratic imaginary, leads to withdrawal from political life and an endorse-ment of capitalism. And finally, the New Age, by focusing so intently upon consciousness, turns what should be a political struggle into a moral one involving a battle between 'the forces of life and the forces of death'.

The 'New Age' of Post-Marxism

Like New Age-ism, post-Marxism has been subjected to extended critique in left publications.[14] Norman Geras (1987, 1988) argues, albeit stridently, that Laclau and Mouffe set up and dismiss a straw version of Marxist arguments about class, discourse and the state. One does not, as Geras points out, have to be a doctrinaire determinist to embrace notions of relatively stable cultural forma-tions in which some groups are systematically subordinated to others. Geras's (1987: 77) strongest point, I think, is that Laclau and Mouffe themselves are forced to adopt some version of a theory of fixed, stable class relations that require subverting.

Terry Eagleton (1991) has added his voice to the fray, critiquing the 'inflation of discourse' represented by Laclau and Mouffe and other post-Marxist theorists. He, along with Alex Callinicos (1990), argues convincingly that the theoretical conflation of discourse and material conditions undercuts the critique of ideology (Eagleton, 1991: 219). In addition, he notices that the anti-capitalist political vision of Laclau and Mouffe is at odds with their relativist and idealist philosophical commitments, since a politics of liberation must assume the real existence of exploitation and oppression (Eagleton, 1991: 216–17).

When one leaves behind class interests and agency, one makes it easy to imagine that the problems of society, all the relations of subordination that the discursive formation of the state produces, are not inherent in any real structure of power. Without a notion of class interest, moreover, it is not necessary to struggle for socialism, because it is possible to envision a democracy that does not meet the needs of the economically exploited. Finally, a radical pluralism does not provide adequate criteria by which to judge political strategies and goals.

In short, I disagree with Laclau and Mouffe on the following point: The process of democratic revolution, they write, does not pass through a direct attack upon the State apparatuses but involves the consolidation and democratic reform of the liberal State. The ensemble of its constitutive principles – division of powers, universal suffrage, multi-party systems, civil rights, etc – must be defended and consolidated. It is within the framework of these basic principles of the political community that it is possible to advance the full range of present-day democratic demands. (1987: 105)

In my view, articulation of the elements of the democratic imaginary will necessarily be recuperated in favour of the dominant order unless it also involves the articulation of a subordinated class or group's interests in conjunction with the democratic ideals. As I have shown with regard to New Age politics, the centrepiece of the democratic imaginary – the humanist subject – is incompatible with the Marxist goal of working-class emancipation, leading so often into pro-individualist and anti-collectivist positions.

Let me make it clear that I am not arguing for a reductive notion of class interests, one that interprets them as structurally pre-given and absolute.[15] I claim only that simply because relations of domination and subordination are discursively articulated and discursively challenged does not make them or the material inequalities they generate any less real. Nor is there an issue with Laclau and Mouffe's idea that struggle is the discursive articulation of antagonistic subject positions in an attempt to establish hegemony. Politics is a discursive and rhetorical phenomenon, on some level, after all. Finally, this hegemonic articulation can, as Laclau and Mouffe suggest, embrace a wide range of struggles from a variety of subject positions.

If political organizing and rhetoric on the left is to get beyond the indiscriminate celebration of self-expression and co-opted social movements, it is important to retain a notion of collective 'interests'. Laclau and Mouffe reject the idea of a priori class interests as an outmoded, totalizing realist formulation. But it is absurd to argue for an emancipatory politics without presuming that some *real* group or groups of people need emancipating, and thus have a material stake in the project of change. Laclau and Mouffe themselves affirm that the discursive totality of the state is relatively fixed around certain nodal points (i.e. that domination of certain social groups is systematic and real). On the other hand, they reject any 'essentialism' or 'reductionism' (or, any privileging of any social category as unit of analysis or as historical agent). Mouffe writes,

A person's subjectivity is not constructed only on the basis of his or her position in the relations of production. . . . There is no reason to privilege, a priori, a 'class' position as the origin of the articulation of subjectivity. Consequently, a critique of the notion of 'fundamental

interests' is required. . . . Interests never exist prior to the discourses in
which they are articulated. (1988a: 90)

A classical Marxist perspective, to the contrary, argues that while a
person's *subjectivity* is not a simple matter of class determination,
his or her *oppression* and *exploitation* are directly connected to
his/her economic status and position in the relations of production.
Marxists believe there is more to liberation than the articulation of
alternative subjectivities; an end to poverty, hunger, exploitation
and abuse are more central, and require a notion of class position,
agency and interests. From this perspective there are two good
reasons for privileging working-class struggles. First, the working
class has the power to stop production and bring the profit-making
system down. Second, the working class,[16] the group of men and
women of all races and sexual orientations whose labour produces
profits for the few, has an objective (Mouffe would say 'fundamental') interest in overthrowing capitalism, whereas some
members of many cross-class, non-socialist groups organized
around other antagonisms (women's rights, environmental issues)
have vested interests in maintaining the profit system.

Some relations of subordination and domination are fairly stable
and constant, especially those around nodal points of race, class and
gender. There is a reality to oppression outside its discursive
construction, a reality on which we can base political analysis and
strategy. For this reason, the standpoint of an oppressed or
exploited person should be used to ground political theory and
practice epistemologically (Hartsock, 1983). In other words,
oppressed and exploited people have access to a clear interpretation
of social reality by virtue of their subordination. This concept is a
feminist reformulation of the materialist idea that social contradictions between the dominant ideological constructions of freedom,
equality, etc. and the conditions of life in the working class, or as a
woman or minority, will generate critical insight among the
exploited and oppressed at some point. Hartsock writes,

> Because the understanding of the oppressed is an engaged vision, the
> adoption of a standpoint exposes the real relations among human beings
> as inhuman, points beyond the present, and carries a historical and
> liberatory role. (1983: 118)

The central significance of this concept is that it acknowledges that
some people have more of an interest or stake in fundamental social
change than others.

The working class – again, broadly defined as those whose labour
generates profit for capitalists and whose rebellion could put an end

to the profit system – is the group with the greatest objective interest and stake in revolutionary change. Race and gender oppressions can be viewed as symbolically complex (as well as partially autonomous) cultural modalities of class oppression. By this I mean that skin colour and sexual characteristics are markers of difference that become linked with other discursive elements to justify economic exploitation and oppression; that is, they place members of these marked groups into a position of class subordination. For example, women's sexual difference has been historically linked to arguments that women should stay in the domestic role, and this difference is thus used to keep women's wages low in the workplace. Thus there is a tendency for class oppression to be co-extensive with gender and race oppression. While the stand-points of people oppressed around gender or race are legitimate in and of themselves, a unified politics regarding their struggles must take into account class interests as well.

Furthermore, to enable the constitution of a truly radical democracy, everyone's material needs must be met, despite Satin's outright assertions that consciousness change precedes social change and that no one is really suffering from material needs anymore. It follows from the preceding points that any revolution-ary project that attempts to overcome oppression for all people should be faithful to these groups, and this means articulating an anti-capitalist, collectivist position that acknowledges the different degrees to which various groups have a stake in social change. The final implication of these observations is that in order to wage an adequate struggle on behalf of subordinated groups, one must, to the extent that one must avoid individualism and its hegemonic effects, challenge the democratic imaginary.

To a certain extent, Laclau and Mouffe would agree with this critique of the New Age project, and yet their politics of discursive antagonism bears some resemblance to the New Age in its idealist, individualist and relativist foundations. We are witnessing a trend in the study of discourse that includes post-Marxism, interpretivism and post-structuralist theorists of power (see McRobbie, 1992, for an overview of post-Marxist influences on cultural studies). Charac-teristics of this formation are a retheorization of power and a move away from structuralist explanations of society and discourse. Raymie McKerrow's (1989) 'critical rhetoric' and Michael McGee's (1990) theory of cultural fragments (in addition to the recent interpretivist turn in cultural studies), both of which argue for a discursive politics of critique, are typical of this episteme. These articles reveal an eagerness to adopt an understanding of the social as fragmented, unfixed and open to appropriation by resistant readers who are said to be the agents of textual construction. Like Laclau and Mouffe, these theorists hail the alleged unfixity of the social as a source of cultural power and new articulations that will somehow liberate us from capitalism. Both post-Marxist political theory and post-structuralist critical theory rest on foundations of relativism and idealism. I mean for this essay to re-assert the importance of materialist assumptions (of objective class interests and material conditions of exploitation and oppression) for both critical and political practice.

Post-Marxism as Therapeutic Consolation

In an early essay on populism, Laclau (1977) argues that democratic ideals can be linked with the interests either of capitalists (as in entrepreneurial individualism) or of workers (as in socialism). In the hegemonic struggle, class contradictions, which are not essential but are the result of discursive formations, are primary. So instead of conceiving political practice as the rearticulation of elements contained within the democratic imaginary, here Laclau maintains that the democratic imaginary is itself merely an element that needs to be connected with a class in political discourse, preferably the working class.

With the early Laclau, I maintain that the 'full development' of the democratic imaginary depends on the articulation of 'the people' with the interests of the working class on behalf of socialism. A successful socialist strategy, however rhetorically subtle its aspirations, must acknowledge the interests of the working class as the central organizing principle of a radical democratic struggle. Laclau and Mouffe do have in mind such a confrontation when they argue for the articulation of a new hegemonic bloc based on a coalition of a collection of radical social movements. Perhaps the post-Marxist embrace of the student, gay rights and environmental movements – all cross-class struggles of consciousness and identity rather than projects of revolutionary transformation – offers a palatable radicalism that might move some readers to the left.

But I think it is more likely that the availability and hegemony of the postmodern, post-Marxist view in the academy is attractive to intellectuals as a way to justify continued lack of engagement in non-academic radical politics. Post-Marxism tells academics that they do not have to struggle with issues of class. It is all right to attend instead to the trendy new movements and to the development of one's own oppositional life-style and identity. When post-Marxism (and post-feminism and post-structuralism generally) is the dominant critical theory in the academy and the Marxist insistence on class politics is derided as passé, these new theories might not move people to the left but rather offer readers a cloak with which to dress up/conceal their ossified liberalism.

As my analysis of the New Age movement demonstrates, the articulation of progressive antagonisms at the level of discourse or consumption will not be likely to result in a society free from exploitation and oppression. At best, such a coalition can build support for legislative reforms such as those won by the civil rights and women's movements. At worst, the messages of individual freedom in the context of radical democracy are appropriated by the New Right and reframed in terms of consumer choices within capitalism, self-fulfilment, property ownership and right-wing libertarianism.

We have seen this description and warning – of a 'bazaar socialism' for the disillusioned – hold true in the case of the New Age movement, and, for my part, I find Laclau's earlier formulation of left political strategy to be more satisfying than the approach developed in *Hegemony and Socialist Strategy* (1985). Laclau (1977) succeeds in resisting simplistic economism while acknowledging the importance of class-based articulations in struggle. Using his conception of discursively constructed class interests and Hartsock's notion of standpoint, we can keep Laclau and Mouffe's insights into rhetoric and politics, while retaining the ability to judge a left political struggle on one major criterion: that it represent working-class interests in the struggle for democratic reforms and ultimately for socialism.

As Alex Callinicos (1990: 162–3) argues, post-Marxism, post-structuralist, 'post-Fordist', 'post-industrial' theories are (like the New Age movement) ideological buttresses of an upwardly-mobile intellectual élite, disillusioned over the failure of revolutionary politics since 1968 and distant from the revolutionary project. The late capitalist epoch is characterized by a 'process of personalization' (Callinicos, 1990: 153; also noted by Giddens, 1991) that is not liberating for the individual, but rather complicit with the ideology of liberal individualism that obscures structural oppression and the need for collective struggle against it. Callinicos writes,

'Personalization' involves an intense investment of *private* life and the reduction of the public sphere to the merest shell. And the limits to the participation on offer are plain enough. The classical democratic tradition from Machiavelli to Rousseau and Marx had something more extensive in mind when they spoke of freedom rather than the ability . . . to choose between various items of consumption offered by competing multinational corporations. (1990: 153)

Callinicos goes on to say that alienation 'seems as good a term as any to sum up this society of privatized activity and public apathy' (1990: 153). Callinicos's critique could apply equally well to the New Age movement as it does to his immediate object, the personalized politics endorsed by post-Marxist theorists.

The motives behind post-Marxist theories include the therapeutic solace offered in the retreat from class after 1968. Perry Anderson (1976, 1983) has argued that the story of Western Marxism in general has been a tale of decline and betrayal of revolutionary political principles in the context of material abundance, upward mobility for intellectuals, and the entrenchment of academic Marxism. Callinicos (1990: 166) notes the therapeutic dimension of this decline, when, after summarizing the political upheavals of 1968, he suggests that the narcissistic individualism identified by Lasch, Sennett and others grew out of disillusionment with and betrayal of a left politics rooted in the working class. He goes on,

> What could be more reassuring for a generation, drawn first towards and then away from marxism by the political ups and downs of the past two decades, than to be told . . . that there is nothing that they can do to change the world? 'Resistance' is reduced to the knowing consumption of cultural products. (p. 170)

Like post-Marxism, the New Age movement offers a definition of resistance as consumption and self-therapy. The New Age clearly fits the model of struggle within the democratic imaginary posited by Laclau and Mouffe and other post-Marxists. I have attempted to set the New Age movement, as represented by Mark Satin, and the radical democratic politics espoused by Laclau and Mouffe against each other to support the idea that there is a fundamental incompatibility between certain aspects of the democratic imaginary and radical political and critical goals. To embrace post-structuralism's or post-Marxism's vision of a fluid and unsutured democratic social space is in my view both inaccurate and disabling to the left.

The ordering of society into relations of domination and subordination is no less real for being the product of discursive articulations. Capitalism may be global and flexible (as Harvey, 1989, argues), but it is still founded on the expropriation of the labour of workers for the profit of capitalists. Capitalism's flexibility around the world should be taken not as a sign of the system's immediate dissolution but as a sign of its profound stability and reach. Rejecting the post-Marxist postulation of 'New Times', Lazarus writes,

> It seems to me, on the contrary, that the New World Order – an

imperialist and capitalist world system – is from an internationalist or postcolonial perspective disturbingly reminiscent of the old world order. Against current conceptualizations of postmodernity, I believe that it is necessary to insist . . . upon the sustained globality of capitalism. (1991: 95)

In the face of such a system, a project like the New Age movement is revealed to be a pacifier, a discourse of therapeutic consolation over deeply felt effects of the system. The goal of radical democracy-socialism is something to be achieved through real-world struggle against capitalist relations of power, not 'articulated' into being out of a collection of social movements – 'shards of the self' – without structural power to overthrow the system. Without a foundation in the working class, radical democracy will be, like the New Age, a 'socialism of the mind'.

Notes

1. I refer the reader to a 1990 retrospective of *New Age Journal* ('Where We've Been', 1990) that includes excerpts and letters from the past fifteen years of the New Age movement as a representative sample. It is noteworthy that several readers (including Abbie Hoffman) in the selection criticize the journal and the movement for encouraging self-centred responses to political problems. See also Ferguson (1980) as a representative New Age text. Ferguson argues that a leaderless loving conspiracy is silently putting into place a new human agenda based on spiritual values of love and harmony, without a programme, an organization or a manifesto. Individuals working on their own consciousnesses are unconsciously in rapport with others engaged in the simultaneous quest for personal change. Her vision is strongly similar to that of Satin (1978), explicated at length below.

2. This essay is part of a larger project analysing cultural texts that deploy the themes and motifs of therapy – illness, healing, coping and consolation – in political contexts. I argue that therapeutic discourse, as a hegemonic strategy of liberal capitalism in the United States, dislocates social and political conflicts on to individuals, privatizes both the experience of oppression and possible modes of resistance to it, and translates political questions into moral issues to be resolved through personal, spiritual or psychological change.

3. Wilson notes that 'Affluent baby boomers are the group most likely to embrace the so-called New Age movement. . . . New Agers tend to be educated, affluent, and successful people. They are hungry for something that mainstream society hasn't given them. And they are willing to pay for it' (1988: 34). Ninety-one percent of New Agers are college-educated. Most make more than $40,000 a year and are in their thirties. They are three times as likely to travel internationally for business or pleasure than working-class people. They are concerned with 'ethical investing, organic food, holistic health, and mind/body awareness' (1988: 36).

4. The wholesale collapse of Stalinist so-called communist states since 1989 has reinforced the disillusionment of the left and added fuel to the argument that the current historical period calls for a politics not of working-class revolution but of reforms within liberal market capitalism (see Bauman, 1990; Norris, 1990; Wallerstein, 1992). However, if one views bureaucratic state 'socialism' as the

betrayal rather than the consequence of 'socialist' revolution, it is not necessary to interpret its demise as a vindication of liberal capitalism.

5. In particular, post-Marxist political theory is attractive to scholars of discourse and power because it focuses so extensively on how the hegemony of any power bloc is rhetorically constituted and maintained. As Rustin (1989: 55) puts it, post-Fordist Marxism is concerned more with 'the reproduction of the social relations of capitalism' than with the system of production itself. Insofar as the social relations of race and gender are discursively constructed and maintained in late capitalism, it is important to have a rhetorical understanding of how discourse functions in the service of power. However, if the social relations of capitalism are themselves generated in the interest of capitalists, revolutionary workers' struggle is necessary to end those relations – they cannot be eliminated through the production of alternative rhetorical constructions. This is an explicitly idealist proposition.

6. By humanism I mean the illusion of agency as inhering in the individual alone, the dominant ideological individualism that serves to obscure our position in structures of class, race and gender in capitalism. By critiquing the humanism of post-Marxist politics I do not mean to endorse the radical anti-humanism of Foucault or Althusser, whose theoretical erasure of the agent has been so complete as to render political activity for change theoretically impossible. As Clegg puts it, any political theory should accept that to some degree 'human beings engage in conscious political activity and can transform social relations' (1991: 71).

7. For other contributors to this shift see 'Beyond the Modern' (1988), Docherty (1990), Hindess (1987), Hindess and Hirst (1975), 'Marxism Now' (1990), Mouffe (1988a; 1988b), Poster (1989), Ross (1988).

Laclau and Mouffe (1985) are at the centre of my analysis because their text *Hegemony and Socialist Strategy* is the most-cited and most 'beautifully paradigmatic' (Wood, 1986: 47). See Dallmayr (1988) for a favourable reading of Laclau and Mouffe.

8. Chantal Mouffe (1988a, 1988b, 1990) makes a condensed version of this argument.

9. Clarke writes, 'The loosely integrated threads of New Times are an attempt to diagnose and cure this crisis by delineating the new social terrain on which the left must fight if it is not to be politically marginalized . . . The dominant signifier in the New Times analyses is *post-*: post-Fordist, postmodernist, post-labourist, and, rather more ambiguously, post-Marxist' (1991: 155). 'New Times' is also characterized by a determined optimism about the possibility of new social subjects being able to achieve emancipation through the articulation of self within popular culture, prescribing a cultural/identity-based politics rather than a politics of militant struggle for material justice and equality.

10. Post-Marxism is linked theoretically with the (unsubstantiated) hypothesis that capitalism itself has become disorganized in the transformation from national to international capital organization (see Urry, 1988). Therefore political responses to the oppressions generated in capitalism must remain disorganized, plural and local in order to be effective. Implicit in much of this argument is the idea that capitalism will eventually undo itself without the organized self-activity of the working class, an idea which has much resonance with the New Age 'critical mass' formulation. For a summary and critique of this position, see Callinicos (1990: 121–71).

11. To her credit, Mouffe argues that the post-Marxist project of a radical democracy differs in principle from the assumptions of liberal democracy – separation of power and politics, the presumption of individual responsibility and

agency, etc. 'To value the institutions which embody political liberalism's principles does not require us to endorse either economic liberalism or individualism' (1990: 58). The problem with this statement is that economic liberalism (the free market and the separation of the market from the sphere designated as politics) and individualism are foundational to political liberalism, which cannot be randomly disconnected from its economic and ideological counterparts.

12. This is not, of course, to reject entirely the humanist discourse of rights, liberty, equality, justice and so on that emerged with liberal capitalism. Marxism itself begins with the assumption of human rights, but argues that real human liberty, equality and justice cannot be achieved so long as rights are conceived in political but not in economic terms.

13. In a similar warning, Sivanandan calls post-Marxism 'Thatcherism in drag' (1989: 1).

14. In particular, see the *New Left Review* exchange: Geras (1987, 1988) Laclau and Mouffe (1987), Mouzelis (1988). See also Anderson (1983), Callinicos (1990), Clarke (1991), Eagleton (1991), Norris (1990), Wood (1986).

15. I like the following lines from Eagleton: 'That social interests do not lie around the place like slabs of concrete waiting to be stumbled over may be cheerfully conceded. There is no reason to suppose . . . that the mere occupancy of some place within society will automatically supply you with an appropriate set of political beliefs and desires' (1991: 206).

16. I am not arguing that workers, by virtue of their labour alone and in the absence of constitutive discourse (such as that provided by a revolutionary party), possess consciousness of their collective interests as workers.

References

Althusser, L. (1984) 'Ideology and ideological state apparatuses', in *Essays on Ideology*. B. Brewster, trans. London: Verso. pp. 1–60. (Work originally published 1960.)

Anderson, P. (1976) *Considerations on Western Marxism*. London: Verso.

Anderson, P. (1983) *In the Tracks of Historical Materialism*. London: Verso.

Baudrillard, J. (1975) *The Mirror of Production*. M. Poster, trans. St Louis, MO: Telos Press.

Bauman, Z. (1990) 'From pillars to post', *Marxism Today*, February: 20–5.

'Beyond the Modern' (1988) *Strategies* [special issue], 1.

Blow, R. (1988) 'Moronic convergence', *The New Republic*, 138 (25 January): 24–7.

Burke, K. (1954) *Permanence and Change: An Anatomy of Purpose* 3rd edn. Berkeley: University of California Press.

Callinicos, A. (1990) *Against Postmodernism: a Marxist Critique*. New York: St Martin's Press.

Clarke, J. (1991) *New Times and Old Enemies*. London: Harper Collins.

Clegg, S. (1991) 'The remains of Louis Althusser', *International Socialism*, 53 (Winter): 57–78.

Dallmayr, F.R. (1988) 'Hegemony and democracy: on Laclau and Mouffe', *Strategies*, 1: 29–49.

Docherty, T. (1990) *After Theory*. London and New York: Routledge.

Eagleton, T. (1986) *Against the Grain*. London: Verso.

Eagleton, T. (1991) *Ideology: an Introduction*. London: Verso.

Ferguson, M. (1980) *The Aquarian Conspiracy*. Los Angeles: J.P. Tarcher.

Foucault, M. (1980). *History of Sexuality: Vol. 1. An Introduction*. R. Hurley, trans. New York: Vintage Books.

Geras, N. (1987) 'Post-*Marxism?*', *New Left Review*, 163: 40–82.

Geras, N. (1988) 'Ex-Marxism without substance', *New Left Review*, 169: 34–62.

Giddens, A. (1991) *Modernity and Self-identity: Self and Society in the Late Modern Age*. Stanford, CA: Stanford University Press.

Graham, J. (1991) 'Fordism/post-Fordism, Marxism/post-Marxism: the second cultural divide?', *Rethinking Marxism*, 4 (1): 39–58.

Gramsci, A. (1971) *Selections from the Prison Notebooks*. Q. Hoare and G.N. Smith, eds and trans. New York: International Publishers.

Hall, S. (1991) 'Brave new world', *Socialist Review*, 21(1): 57–64. (Originally published in *Marxism Today*, October 1988: 24–9.)

Hall, S. (1989) *New Times: The Changing Face of Politics in the 90s*. London and New York: Verso.

Hartsock, N. (1983) *Money, Sex and Power: toward a Feminist Historical Materialism*. Boston, MA: Northeastern University Press.

Harvey, D. (1989) *The Condition of Postmodernity*. Oxford: Basil Blackwell.

Hindess, B. (1987) *Politics and Class Analysis*. Oxford: Basil Blackwell.

Hindess, B. and Hirst, P. (1975) *Pre-capitalist Modes of Production*. London: Verso.

Kauffman, L.A. (1992) 'Tofu politics', *Utne Reader*, March/April: 72–5.

Laclau, E. (1977) 'Toward a theory of populism', in *Politics and Ideology in Marxist Theory*. London: Verso. pp. 143–99.

Laclau, E. and Mouffe, C. (1985) *Hegemony and Socialist Strategy*. W. Moore and P. Cammack, trans. London: Verso.

Laclau, E. and Mouffe, C. (1987) 'Post-Marxism without apologies', *New Left Review*, 166: 79–106.

Lazarus, N. (1991). Doubting the new world order: Marxism, realism, and the claims of postmodernist social theory. *Differences, 3.5*, 94–138.

Lyotard, J. (1984) *The Postmodern Conditions*. G. Bennington and B. Massumi, trans. Minneapolis: University of Minneapolis Press.

McGee, M.C. (1990) 'Text, context, and the fragmentation of contemporary culture', *Western Journal of Speech Communication*, 54: 274–89.

McKerrow, R.E. (1989) 'Critical rhetoric: theory and praxis', *Communication Monographs*, 56: 91–111.

McRobbie, A. (1992) 'Post-Marxism and cultural studies', in L. Grossberg, C. Nelson and P.A. Treichler (eds), *Cultural Studies*. New York and London: Routledge. pp. 719–30.

'Marxism Now: Traditions and Difference' (1990) *Rethinking Marxism* [special issue], 3 (3–4).

Melton, G. (1988) 'A history of the New Age movement', in R. Basil (ed.), *Not Necessarily the New Age: Critical Essays*. Buffalo, NY: Prometheus. pp. 35–53.

Mouffe, C. (1988a) 'Hegemony and new political subjects: toward a new concept of democracy', in C. Nelson and L. Grossberg (eds), *Marxism and the Interpretation of Culture*. Urban and Chicago: University of Illinois Press. pp. 89–104.

Mouffe, C. (1988b) 'Radical democracy: modern or postmodern?', in A. Ross (ed.), *Universal Abandon? The Politics of Postmodernism*. Minneapolis: University of Minnesota Press. pp. 31–45.

Mouffe, C. (1990) 'Radical democracy or liberal democracy?', *Socialist Review*, 20 (2): 57–66.

Mouzelis, N. (1988) 'Marxism or post-Marxism?', *New Left Review*, 167: 107–23.

Norris, C. (1990) *What's Wrong with Postmodernism?* New York: Harvester.

Poster, M. (1989) *Critical Theory and Poststructuralism*. Ithaca, NY: Cornell University Press.

Rethinking Marxism (1988) 'Introduction', *Rethinking Marxism*, 1 (1): 5–13.

Ross, A. (ed.) (1988) *Universal Abandon? The Politics of Postmodernism*. Minneapolis: University of Minnesota Press.

Rossman, M. (1979) *New Age Blues: On the Politics of Consciousness*. New York: Dutton.

Rustin, M. (1989) 'The politics of post-Fordism: or, the trouble with 'New Times', *New Left Review*, 175: 54–77.

Satin, M. (1978) *New Age Politics*. New York: Dell.

Sivanandan, A. (1989) 'All that melts into air is solid: the hokum of New Times', *Race and Class*, 31 (3): 1–30.

Urry, J. (1988) 'Disorganized capitalism', *Marxism Today*, October: 30–3.

Wallerstein, I. (1992) 'Remarx: post-America and the collapse of Leninism, *Rethinking Marxism*, 5 (1): 93–100.

'Where We've Been and Where We're Going' (1990) *New Age Journal* [special anniversary issue], January/February: 39–62.

Wilson, L. (1988) 'The aging of Aquarius', *American Demographics*, 10 (September): 34–7, 60–1.

Wood, E.M. (1986) *The Retreat from Class*. London: Verso.

Index